# It Could Be a Little Gold Mine

## Tales by Mr A, A Country Innkeeper

### David Allingham

Johnson Publishing

Published by Johnson Publishing
email: johnson.publishing@virgin.net

First published 2005

ISBN 0-95425-746-4

Text © David Allingham
Illustrations © Bill Tidy

A CIP catalogue record for this book is available from the
British Library

Printed and bound in China, through Albion Asia Publishing
email: albionasia@hongkong.com

# Contents

This book is dedicated to Jeanne, my wife of 42 years, who has put up with me.

# CHAPTER ONE

# From Profession to Vocation

It is a truth universally recognised that any café, restaurant, pub, inn, hotel, or corner shop for that matter, could be 'a little gold mine'. Most owners of family-run small businesses tire of overhearing their customers trot out this hackneyed aphorism. With seemingly unlimited finance and unconstrained imagination, they tell each other how they would develop this underdeveloped opportunity. It is a well-established English custom. I have done it myself, I am sure you have too. Napoleon had it right; the English are a nation of shopkeepers or at the very least, would-be shopkeepers.

In a somewhat jaundiced remark at the beginning of his book *An Innkeeper's Diary*, first published by Chatto and Windus in 1931, the author, John Fothergill, records the phrase 'a little gold mine'. He gives it as an expression used by the brokers, solicitors, and valuers during the lurid changeover proceedings on the day when he first bought an inn. In his well-received book, he selected from amongst his 'tired notes' some of the things that happened to him during his time as innkeeper of the Spread Eagle at Thame. Fothergill's diary, lying deep in my subconscious, as well as at my bedside, has prompted me to write, not tired notes, but true tales about some of the fun and fiascos that actually happened when my wife Jeanne and I bought the Bentley Brook Hotel, determined to change it into our 'little gold mine'.

# It Could Be a Little Gold Mine

I was born in Halifax, in 1936, by right a Yorkshireman, the third and last child of my father Bill Allingham and my mother, his beloved wife Winnie. Father was a policeman, and although mother was ten years his junior, she could not work. No, there was nothing wrong with her, but in those not far off days, the Watch Committee did not allow policemen's wives to work. Growing up with my elder brother and sister, I had a supremely happy childhood. Being the runt of the family, my father and mother, aunts, uncles, doctors, nurses and teachers spoilt me rotten. At last, aged sixteen, finally reared, I left school to work as an apprentice in a foundry. By study at technical college on day release from work and by attending an additional two or three nights study each week, aided by some clever question spotting, I passed all necessary exams required for my eventual election to the status of Chartered Mechanical Engineer.

Deferred by my apprenticeship, I did not start my two years' national service until I was twenty-one. After a false start, I was commissioned into the 26th Field Regiment Royal Artillery. Because my mess bill was always greater than my salary, I fell into the habit of living on an overdraft, a condition from which I have never recovered, although I did learn a great deal about food and wine.

Having had their way with me, the army allowed me to go home. I then had the best of luck because the once great English Electric Company, led by Lord Nelson, Baron of Stafford, took me on. During that time, I had the good fortune to meet and marry Jeanne Edwards who was a high-flyer, already working as a nursing sister, a post she was promoted to when just twenty-one.

In 1965, the English Electric decided that a spell overseas

would be good for my career development and packed me off to Hong Kong, with Jeanne to look after me. We arrived just in time to experience the Kowloon motorbus riots, and two years later, the more serious Red Guard riots during Mao's, Cultural Revolution.

For twelve years, we enjoyed living and working in Hong Kong. The English Electric Company had planned for me to stay for two years, to learn how to build power stations, but once the project was complete, their customer HongKong Electric took me on to their staff to help them build more power stations, at less cost. I also worked, in honorary capacity, with some splendid colleagues, to create The Hong Kong Institution of Engineers. In 1975, the members of the new Institution elected me their president. During the same year Jeanne found time to be founder chairwoman of the Ladies Circle in Hong Kong, the distaff side of the Round Table.

While I was playing power stations and professional engineer, Jeanne got on with the more important job of bearing and rearing our three sons. The first was Christopher John Robert, followed by Edward William David and finally William Charles Baden. In addition to entertaining friends and business colleagues on quite a grand scale at home, Jeanne also worked for the Cathedral charities, cooking hundreds of pounds of fudge, marmalade and Christmas puddings for sale at the annual Michaelmas Fair. My contribution to the fair was to run a makeshift fish and chip stall, my first venture into commercial catering for the public.

In Hong Kong, we had worked hard but lived very well. The company provided a large comfortable house with garden and swimming pool. I had a good salary, free electricity, company car and driver, school fees looked after and long

# It Could Be a Little Gold Mine

holidays that took us around the world, with all fares paid. Then things changed. Early in 1976, my forty-first year, the company Chief Executive handed me the biggest parallel promotion since Nixon lost the White House. It directed that I should work in the City of London as 'Technical Director for Europe'. The job was a sinecure of which I wanted no part. Cut by corporate calumny, I was unwilling to continue my professional career. We therefore faced a different and challenging future. We had children to feed, clothe and educate. We also had a need to re-establish a good quality of life for ourselves. It was this change in circumstance which led us to search for 'a little gold mine'.

We had not chosen the best of times to return to cold climate Britain. It was in fact the worst of times. The beginning of the year had brought the need for Britain to take on the burden of a huge loan from the International Monetary Fund to bail out its failing economy. The IRA detonated bombs in London, Birmingham, Bristol and other cities. Harold Wilson was no longer Prime Minister but the Labour Government, led by Jim Callaghan, was still in power. Labour unrest spread from the Grunwick dispute to the winter of discontent, with rubbish uncollected, the dead unburied. Worst of all, for a new business venture, interest rates were rising.

There were a few good things happening. The Queen and Country celebrated her Silver Jubilee, Red Rum won the Grand National for a third time, Geoff Boycott scored his hundredth century in first-class cricket, and Freddie Laker got Skytrain off the ground to provide, for the first time, cheap air fares across the Atlantic. Despite the ominous portent of national recession I was damned if I was going to work again for a wage or salary. Jeanne and I agreed that it was of

# From Profession to Vocation

prime importance to protect what capital we had. The knowledge that no member of either of our families had ever had money sufficient to count as capital greatly influenced our decision. Secure in our home in Halifax, we sat down and discussed what we could do, and then, what we would do.

We decided that any business we would undertake must meet certain criteria, with an understanding that none should take precedence. The criteria we agreed, and there were no others, we wrote down on a piece of card that we kept to remind us of our resolve.

1) We would be equal partners.
2) We would not live over the shop.
3) We would not work overseas.
4) Whatever we bought, we must buy without any loan.
5) The freehold property value must be sufficient to cover immediate needs should the business fail.
6) It must generate sufficient profit to pay the school fees.
7) It must be people oriented.
8) It must provide work for the boys, if they wished.
9) It must be unrelated to my previous career as an engineer.
10) It must be north of the River Trent.

The last was a late addition. Good friends had convinced me that my blunt Yorkshire manner would not go down too well in the South. These simple guidelines led us to a firm decision to capitalise on our strengths by purchasing the freehold of a hotel, inn, restaurant or pub located in the north country. This we would run as a family business, founded on Jeanne's natural flair as hostess, and her skill and love of cooking. I was confident that during my travels I had learned the basic truths about food. Exotic holidays had taken us twice around the world. My company sent me to more than sixty countries where I could, and did, indulge my passion for good food, always asking, "How was that made?" This twenty-year study was better than any catering college could hope to provide and was far more useful than a degree in food technology.

The first that Jeanne and I heard or saw of the Bentley Brook was an advertisement in the trade magazine *Caterer and Hotelkeeper* headlined 'Derbyshire Hotel for sale, by private treaty.' It had a small black and white picture of a multi-gabled half-timbered building. Unfortunately the magazine was ten weeks old, but we both thought it looked interesting. "Get on to it, ring them now" Jeanne instructed. It was a command not a suggestion. I was nervous when I rang. "Hello, Bentley Brook Hotel, how can I help you?" was the dull response. "Oh er, I was just ringing to ask if your hotel is still for sale, by any chance, I have just seen it in a magazine, but it is a few weeks old." "Well there's a thing," came the reply. "I've just been sitting with my head in my hands somewhat depressed, because the sale I expected to complete this week has just fallen through. I had sold to a couple of gays and they've had the most dreadful row, split up, and reneged on the deal." "Well," I replied, "I'm not gay, but I am very happy to hear that. Can we come and have a look round?"

The next day, a cold wet early October day, we made our first visit. I had travelled by train from London to Derby and Jeanne had driven down from Halifax to pick me up at the station. It was still just light, when we dropped down the steep hill into Ashbourne and drove slowly through the little market town. Cheery lights were coming on in the many shop windows with no sight of windows boarded up, or of more than one charity shop. Jeanne said quietly, "I have a good feeling about this." "Yes," I replied, "so have I, it looks prosperous enough."

We easily found the Bentley Brook because it is on a junction and the owner had given us good directions. We walked into the bar, without announcing ourselves as the prospective buyers. I bought a glass of wine for Jeanne and a pint of Marston's Pedigree for me and sat at an empty table. It was not difficult, all the tables were empty. The bar however was full, not of customers, just a hazy blue fog. This was due to the smoke from two dull fires failing to clear the chimneystacks. There was only one other customer, a jonty farmer, sitting on a stool at the end of the bar. He seemed affable, but odd, because he ordered a different drink from the top shelf each time his glass was empty. From time to time he broke into song, "Sugar in the morning, sugar in the evening, sugar at suppertime," the same song every time.

The furniture was tatty, and not appropriate for a bar. Age had worn all but one of the carpets threadbare; the decor was particularly grim. The owners had removed every second light bulb from the twin light fittings in an obvious economy drive. The garden was a wilderness and a glance into the kitchen showed the whole thing to be a health hazard of pandemic proportion. Not a sign of any stainless steel, no tiles on the walls, just crumbling plaster. Electric power cables hung in loops, suspended from metal ceiling hooks across the middle of the room. Worse still, it looked as though all the work surfaces had been bodged, using poor quality plastic, glued to chipboard. The edges of these crude tables were not protected and years of spilt blood, milk, gravy, soup and other liquids had caused them to expand, exfoliate and rot, making them a spawning ground for mould, botulism and pathogens of all types.

Rough-cut unpainted timber legs, that Hodge had nailed to batons of the same timber screwed to the floor, supported the cockling food preparation surfaces. This crude structure made it impossible to clean the floor. The floor was interesting in itself; in part made of tiles laid during the Middle Ages. Here the cockroaches battled for territory with the silverfish while keeping a watchful eye out for the rats. The mice had retreated to the bar, where they thrived on crisps and chocolate bars.

A few days later, during our second visit, we declared our interest. The owner, offering the hotel for private sale, was one Norris Sergeant, also a fugitive from his first profession of engineer. He told us that they were selling this 'little gold mine' only because they wanted to move back to the south of England.

Norris was pleasant and always helpful, but we could not help noticing that bright beads of perspiration often covered his forehead, even when he was not busy behind the bar. We never did decide the true cause of his cold sweats. We wondered if it was because he was nervous that we might not buy the business, or if it was due to his habit of topping up his glass from the whisky optic. We later learnt that the more likely explanation was that the criminal fraternity had been threatening to break his legs, adjust his face with a razor slashing and set fire to the place, with him tied up inside.

His wife Kath was agreeable, but it was obvious that she wanted to get away as soon as may be. Their son John was the nominated cook and they had a daughter working in the restaurant. After this second visit, we went to the Coach and Horses, the village pub, just a few hundred yards from the hotel. Here, warmed by a roaring log fire, we enjoyed a good meal in the cosy bar. We looked at each other and we knew that the Bentley Brook met our criteria and would suit our purpose. "Shall we buy it then?" "Yes it will do." We sealed the decision with a clink of glasses and a gentle kiss.

Because I was still working, Jeanne looked after the business of completing the deal. With her usual flair and the help of Michael Gledhill, an old friend and no-nonsense Halifax solicitor, the sale was completed. With great relief, I left my sinecure in the City and we took possession of the Bentley Brook Hotel. It was just three weeks after my telephone call in response to the advert 'Hotel for sale by private treaty'.

Our move to the Bentley Brook was interesting. We had

# It Could Be a Little Gold Mine

been back in England from Hong Kong for about six months, and Oscar, our ginger tomcat, had completed his quarantine on the Friday before we were due to take over. On the Saturday, we attended a wedding celebration in Sevenoaks, Kent. It was, therefore, quite a carload that I drove from Halifax to the cattery in Harrogate, then to Sevenoaks, before setting off for our new home in Derbyshire. We finally arrived, all of a tumble, at the Bentley Brook late on the Sunday evening, when we observed the ancient ritual of putting butter on Oscar's paws. It worked, he settled and never wandered. He brought us great happiness for the next three years until he died of a heart attack, doing what he enjoyed most, stalking birds in our hedgerows.

We had used every penny from the sale of our house and the provident fund, paid out by my old Hong Kong company, to purchase the 'lock' of the Bentley Brook. We had yet to purchase the 'stock and barrel'. What we had bought we hardly knew. No bank had an interest; consequently, we had not prepared a business plan, let alone a cash flow projection. We had not even decided who was to do what in our great new enterprise; we just felt that it was right for us.

Together and separately, we had searched for our ideal business. We had travelled up, down, and across the country, north to south, east to west. We had been to view many properties, all within our price range, all meeting our criteria in full, or in part. Many had appeared to be in better condition and trading more actively than the hotel where we sat on that first visit, in a smoke haze, listening to the jonty farmer's song. However, none of the others caught our imagination. It was only the partly derelict Derbyshire half-timbered folly, shrouded by trees and bramble that spoke to us, whispering,

# From Profession to Vocation

"Perhaps."

At 10am on Monday 26 October 1977, we signed the final documents and handed over a cheque for the purchase of the 'stock and barrel' to add to the 'lock' already paid for. It did not amount to much because Mr Sargeant, at his suggestion, had run down both the wet and dry stock as far as possible. It was, however, enough to break one of the ten criteria that we had agreed between us. It took our bank account into the red. I bluffed Jeanne, telling her the overdraft was simply working capital, not really a debt.

During the licence transfer proceedings, we took the opportunity to change the name from Bentley Brook Hotel to Bentley Brook Inn. We did this so that all would know they would be welcome. Who knows whether an hotel is private, licensed for residents only or even temperance?

On takeover day, the weather was worse than on the day of our first visit. This time sleet came in through the windows. We soon learnt from the locals that Derbyshire had 'Nine months of winter followed by three months of bad weather', or worse: 'Derbyshire only has two seasons - this winter and next winter'.

The week before we took over, Mr Sargeant, being a good scout, put up the price of Marston's Pedigree, by one penny, to thirty-one pence a pint, so that it was he, not us, who took the flack from the few customers. Although we were now the partner proprietors of The Bentley Brook Inn, it proved difficult to get rid of Mr Sergeant or more particularly his furniture. The missing light bulbs confirmed our suspicion that he was a bit overkeen when it came to economies. He had negotiated a 'special deal' with Pickfords, the removal people, to pick up his furniture, goods and chattels, but only when

# It Could Be a Little Gold Mine

they could use one of their pantechnicons returning empty from another contract, and passing nearby. It was well over a week before they came to relieve the situation of blocked corridors and stairs. No chance to arrange our furniture and the sadness of telling the time each day by the superb grandfather clock that dominated the staircase. This wonderful timepiece was the one thing that he had excluded from the sale. We still have not been able to afford to replace it and I feel a sense of failure each time I pass the empty place on the stair.

By 11 am the lawyers and stocktakers had consumed their share of our hospitality, leaving us alone and wondering what to do. We did not have long to ponder. Before midday, into the bar came our first customers. Quite naturally, as the consummate hostess, Jeanne went to greet them and offered to get them drinks. Feeling at a loss, I wandered into the kitchen. Quick as lightning, Jeanne kicked the door to behind me and the division of labour was established. I had left my profession of engineer and found my true vocation, as a cook. I did make one foray into the bar on our first day, Jeanne was nowhere to be seen, but clearly visible was a customer, standing at the bar, intent on being served. "Oh hello er... good afternoon," I ventured, "What may I get for you?" "A Hamlet please," was his gentle response. "Oh yes," I managed and then a long pause as my brain raked over long forgotten nights in hotel cocktail bars. Hamlet, no it would not come, a Manhattan I could remember, a Horse's Neck I was sure of, but a Hamlet – no. "I'm so sorry sir, a Hamlet has quite slipped my memory. How do make yours? I'm sure I can make one with your guidance." "Nay lad that won't be necessary, you see you are standing in front of the Hamlets." "What?" I asked. "Those little cigars behind you are Hamlets they are fifteen pence each," he laughed. "Don't look so flummoxed, you'll soon get the hang of things. I don't think you'll get much call for cocktails, we're all proper folk round here."

Over the next few weeks, several abject failures behind the bar convinced me that I was better working alone in the kitchen. My most frequent folly occurred when I would take an order from one party, then give the drinks ordered to another party and finally give the change to a third party.

The first thing I did in the kitchen was to remove and pack up in boxes all the tins of powdered soup that ranged along the kitchen shelves. Next, I threw away a huge Bonzer tin-opener. I was determined that soon, all food sent out from my kitchen was to be home-made. I took down the dartboard from the kitchen wall, and burnt it, along with the two leather armchairs and a coffee table that had been the chef's snug.

For the first few weeks, I had no alternative but to use the existing menu. It was very simple, using bought-in boil-in-the-bag things, beef and gammon steaks. We only had a couple of guests to feed on our first night as innkeepers and we coped; the only difficulty was finding things. After I had finished the two simple meals, one of the guests stuck his head round the kitchen door and asked, "Have you got a hammer?" This shook me a bit, but after a searching about, I found my tool-box and offered him a satisfactory sort of hammer. "What do you want it for?" I asked. "Oh, I just thought I would relay the stair carpet for you, it's in a bit of a mess. Don't worry, I've found some tacks."

The question asked by my second caller at the kitchen door also raised my eyebrows. "Have you got a bowl, mate?" "Er... why yes. Will this do?" "Just the job mate," and he was off to return twenty minutes later with the bowl full of black-berries. "I picked them all within a few feet of the front door." I was pleased to have the blackberries to make a pie, but a bit disquieted at the thought of the task ahead to clear the under-growth and overgrowth that almost hid our inn from public view.

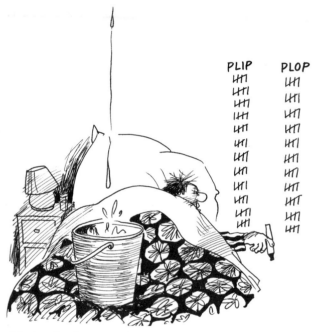

PLIP  PLOP

Obviously, the special ambiance of the place had seasoned both our guests. Each one asked for a bucket to go to bed with. "What for, you're not feeling sick are you?" I nervously asked. A dread thought had come into my overtired mind, had I given them food poisoning? or worse, poisoned them with some cleaning agent or pesticide? I reasoned that this was the more likely, as the previous cook had mixed up bot-tles of bleach with brandy, treacle with turpentine and rat poi-

# From Profession to Vocation

son with pearl barley, in what he told me was the larder. "No mate it's raining and the roof leaks. Mr Sergeant used to go mad if you let it drip on the bed," was his reassuring reply. Yes, we had serious roofing problems, seventeen major leaks in all, most from the old unused chimneystacks.

Washed up and cleared up, I joined Jeanne in the now empty bar for a well-earned pint of Pedigree. "Sorry David, it ran out an hour ago, we have some Guinness though." Can't be bad - I thought - sold out of Pedigree at thirty-one pence a pint and I only put the barrel on this morning, well that must be worth a bit. My dash down to the cellar to put on a new firkin set me back a peg or two. The tap I had inexpertly driven that morning had come out. All my precious beer, and profit, was soaking away into the mud floor.

After our first day as innkeepers, I felt totally exhausted as I lay alongside Jeanne in our bed, in a room above the bar, a cold room without carpet or curtains. Pins and needles ran from the tips of my fingers, via my scalp, down to the end of my toes. "Are you alright Jeanne?" I asked. "Hardly," was her reply, "I've got pins and needles, from head to foot." "We took sixteen pounds thirty pence today." "Good, and we've made some friends." "Yes." "We are on our way then." "I suppose so." "Who's doing breakfast?" "We are, go to sleep." "Yes Jeanne." I set the alarm for six thirty.

# CHAPTER TWO

# Getting a Grip

What we had bought and hardly knew soon began to reveal its mysteries. Each day exposed new problems, shortcomings, deficiencies and faults. We understood that we would have to put them right before we could even start to look for opportunities and carry out our planned improvements. Although subject to many setbacks, pitfalls and unforeseen constraints, we have never doubted that, one day, we would have our little gold mine. Each year only required one final effort and it would be ours. After twenty-eight of those quickening years, I still tell Jeanne that the next crest will be the summit. Each time, Jeanne's well-developed and practised old-fashioned look withers me, but she always proves strongest in our drive to succeed. As far as our ever reaching the summit, my best estimate, an estimate I keep strictly to myself, is that we have not yet reached the South Col.

Within the first few days, we knew that we had to sort out a contradiction. Even though we had few customers we realised that it was vital to get rid of the late night drinkers, if we were to succeed in running an inn that would and could welcome all. The contradiction was that, pretty well, they were our only customers. Each night they would drift in, just before or just after closing time. More often than not, it was after the few early doors customers had left. The early ones, some of whom had consumed a pint and a bag of crisps at best, complained about the prices, and satisfied themselves that 'the new folk' were not a patch on the previous lot.

The 'late ones' came in no particular order, each taking up their familiar places at the end of the bar. Usually there were five of six of them, never less than four. Night after night, seven days a week, they would arrive and stay until the early hours. Whisky was their drink. Woe betide any poor soul who had not left the bar before they came in. "You'll have a whisky?" would come the icy voice of the pack leader. "Er... pardon?" was the most frequent nervous response. Again would be heard the unwelcome, now apparent, rhetorical question. "You'll have a whisky?" Again, "Oh, er... no thanks we're just off." The pack leader, a thin flint-eyed man in his mid-sixties I would guess, would then call to me, "Barman, get him a whisky." The departing customer would plead, "Er... no, but thank you all the same, I don't drink spirits." The poor chap, or worse, couple, would sidle out of the door, further intimidated by the disdainful dirty looks that followed them, determined never again to come to drink at our inn.

Jeanne and I agreed a plan to put an end to the problem. On the next Monday night, following the script and stage direction we had worked out, I put the plan into action. Exactly ten minutes before closing time, I rang the great brass bell that hung in the bar and called "Last orders please gentlemen." I got no reaction from the 'late ones' at the end of the bar. In those restrictive times, 10.30 pm was closing time during the week, and there was no drinking up time allowed. At precisely 10.30 pm, I rang the great brass bell for the second time and called "Time gentlemen *please*." Once again, as expected, there was no reaction. They completely ignored the bell, the law and me. With a surge of confidence, supported only by my nervous system stimulating an adrenaline rush, I picked up their six half-empty whisky glasses and emptied them, one by one, into the sink and down the drain.

The shock of what I had done turned them rigid and for a moment speechless. Then slowly and quietly came the icy, gravelly dark voice, "You'll fill those buggers up." It was time to give a generous smile and assume an air of quiet determination. "No sir, you are out of time and out of order. If you can't drink here during licensing hours you can go elsewhere, I am not prepared to risk our licence." "You'll fill the buggers up, now," was the loud and menacing reply. Again, the stage direction called for a smile and the script a well-rehearsed response from me. "No, you know the law," and then a little white lie. "I've had a warning from the police." To which came a now mild response, as they tried a different tack. "Come on lad, we've been good customers here for years, fill them up, we'll pay." Again, I smiled, more strained than generous, but at last came a breakthrough. One of the group was muttering "Stuff him, I'm off." Then came the wheedling, "Just one for the road David," but I knew I had won. One more smile, or was it an inane grin and they left.

At least five times the flint-eyed pack leader came bursting back through the door with his index finger wagging like a more than usually demented Jeremy Paxman. Each time he had a different message. First, "You're a bloody young fool, we've spent thousands here, we've kept this place going," and he was off. Then banging back through the door again and storming the bar, "Nobody will come if we don't come," and off he went, only to return again in equal bad temper. "Norris relied on us." He was out and in again so fast I thought he must have found a revolving door. "I'll see to it that the brewery throws you out," and finally, as his curtain call, "You won't last six months." At least he had that wrong. I was confident that they would not come late night drinking again.

I finished clearing up, locked up the bar and climbed the now carpetless stairs to reach our bed. I was tired but exhilarated, as I stepped on beams where the electricians had taken up the floorboards to allow for rewiring. Jeanne, already in bed greeted me with the usual enquiry, "You all right?" Quite proud, I replied, "Yes, job done, it went quite well really. Damn it, I've got pins and needles again." Sleepily Jeanne replied, "Me too, go to sleep."

Pride does indeed often go before a fall. I thought I had it sorted, but I had not understood the nature of one of the late night drinkers. He was a small thin sharp-nosed ferret-faced man who was always on the outer fringe of the group. I don't think that I'd ever spoken directly to him, but felt that he had taken an active dislike to me from the start, let alone after I had poured his whisky down the drain. The first time that we heard from him, after stopping the late night drinking, was by letter. It informed us, in formal terms, that he now owned the five-acre field adjoining our property. The field had belonged to the inn until a few months earlier. Norris, the previous owner, in a stupid round of betting lost it, on the turn of a card, to one of the late night group. Apparently, after it had passed through different hands, ferret face had bought it. The letter stated, correctly, that we were using about quarter of an acre of his newly acquired land, as part of our car park. It went on to state that unless we purchased that small piece of encroaching land for ten thousand pounds, within seven days, he would erect a steel fence along the boundary line that divided our properties. For good measure, the letter advised us that the fence would close off the top entrance to our car park. He also demanded that we provide him with a gate and free access to his land as part of the deal and that we were to bear all legal costs. It was clear that this threat could cause us to lose everything.

The same day, I asked an Ashbourne firm of auctioneers and estate agents, to measure and mark the actual boundary for me. I needed to determine if, as stated in the letter, the top access to the car park would be lost. After a quick visit by a senior partner in the firm, for which he never charged us, a large-scale map of the area, an elastic tape measure and a following wind gave us hope.

We replied to the extortion letter, telling ferret face and his solicitor that the land had been valued at less than one hundred pounds and his fence, if properly aligned with the boundary, would not restrict our access. We added that if his fence were one inch out of line, we would take it away and charge him for the expense. At Jeanne's suggestion, the letter finished with an invitation to a site meeting where matters might be resolved. I was very concerned. Ten thousand pounds would have finished us, as would the loss of the car parking and the top entrance.

My concern increased when a local man, who in his youth had been an amateur boxer, engaged me with stories about some of the drama that occurred with the late night drinkers. When Mr Sergeant had the inn there had been such goings on, with threats of extortion, broken legs, and arson, that plain-clothes police attended for nights on end and there had been several fights.

After further exchange of letters, with even greater threats to our property, the site meeting did take place. However, it did not take quite the form that we had in mind. At the appointed time he came into the empty bar, alone. I was also alone. The ferret's blunt opening gambit, "Well, are you going to pay or do I fence you off?" was a mistake. The last time that I ever hit anybody was when I split a boy's nose and lip with a cracking straight left. He was then and he remains a good friend. That was thirty years earlier, in the schoolyard, when he was twelve and I was eleven. This little runt's cocky remark infuriated me and with the anxiety of the past few weeks grinding on my nerves, I lost my temper.

I grabbed his jacket lapels, shirt and tie with my left hand and pinned him against the bar wall with his shoes six inches from the floor, and his feet still in them. "Now listen, if you ever come near me, my land, or family, ever again, I'll crush your head," was the general drift of what I told him. I admit to having my free right fist drawn back, a fact that added conviction to my statement. I must have held him there for a good ten seconds before I slowly let him down. Without a word he was gone. He disappeared, as they say in Derbyshire, 'like a ferret up a drainpipe'. We never heard any more about boundaries and fences.

Some months later, I learned that the field now belonged to someone I knew who lived in the village and wanted to keep horses. He was a gentleman who was quite happy for us to keep on using his bit of the land as part of our car park. I am not proud of what I had done, but looking back, I don't think I would have hit him, and my undisciplined action did save the day. It was only later that I began to link him to the alarming incident of the diamond racketeers. During our twelve years living and working in Hong Kong, I had never felt to be in personal danger, nor had I concern for the well-

# It Could Be a Little Gold Mine

being of my family. In fact, I felt protected by the community around me. However, on returning to England and before finding the Bentley Brook, I worked in the City of London, and lived four days a week in a bedsit in Bayswater. Here experience taught me to take care when walking alone in the streets. I also took particular heed of the regulars when choosing restaurants and pubs to frequent. When we chose to buy the Bentley Brook, sheltered within the Peak District National Park, a rural idyll, I was sure it would be crime free and my family and I would be safe. I was soon to be disillusioned by events. Not many weeks after moving in, during lunchtime a bulky red-faced man came into the bar. He was dressed in a dark blue pinstripe suit, shiny with wear, the stripes of which were wide enough apart and white enough to be taken as tacking stitches. A loosely arranged white spotted red silk handkerchief spilled from the top pocket of his jacket. His blue striped shirt, Windsor knotted silver tie and an old-fashioned trilby hat perfected the image he presented as a provincial racecourse bookie. He asked for a whisky and told me that colleagues would be joining him for a business meeting. It was not long before the others shuffled in, one by one, all similarly soberly dressed. They each ordered their drink separately, some taking them to tables, others staying seated at the bar.

"You don't mind if we do a bit of business do you?" This rhetorical question came from the florid man who was still wearing his trilby. "No, no carry on, that's quite alright," I replied, smiling. I only began to worry when it became apparent what their business was about. First, out came strips of black velvet, the size of our bar towels. Fat hands with fingers full of rings, each set with what appeared to be a solitaire diamond, smoothed out the jeweller's velvet. I thought it curious that each of them wore a double-breasted waistcoat with at least four to six pockets on each side. Unknowingly the men answered my unspoken question by taking from their waistcoat pockets and from their briefcases, screws of tissue paper. When unrolled, these packets spilled diamonds onto the cloths, some as big as pigeon eggs, some cut, others uncut, all clearly spread out for inspection and dealing.

It seemed to me, an innocent in such matters, to be a collection to match DeBeers January Sale. Diamonds all around the room, on tables, on the bar, and amongst them were rolls of bank notes or stacks of the same, held with gold diamond-crusted clips. The wads of notes were, in the Derbyshire Dales dialect, 'thick enough to choke a donkey'.

Just then, the phone rang. I went from behind the bar to answer it in the office. We only had one phone in those early days. I was already in a mild state of shock and the anxious enquiry of an unfamiliar voice, "Is that Mr Allingham?" did not ease my mind. "Yes, speaking." Then the same voice, "Is that Mr Allingham, the new chap at the pub?" "Well yes." I did not have time to ask how I may help before the voice cut in. "Now listen, listen carefully, and do exactly what I am going to tell you. This is the police; you've got some right bad bastards in your bar, you have. Send your entire staff home now. Get your wife away quick, then go back into the bar, serve them what they ask for, but for goodness sake don't touch anything."

By now, my pulse was well ahead of Greenwich Mean Time and what came next did nothing but increase the lead-time. "Don't worry," he continued, "we have plain-clothes men in an unmarked car on your car park and two cars with

# It Could Be a Little Gold Mine

uniform branch standing by, just up the road, so just act normally." I was unsure how one acted normally when serving drinks to a criminal gang known to the police as 'right bad bastards'.

I did not have any staff to get rid of and so, as instructed, I went back behind the bar. There I gave the performance of my life as a bewildered catatonic chronic drunk, suffering simultaneously from delayed concussion and a bout of amnesia. One by one, on some excuse or another, they all left the bar. Some said they needed to go to the car to get a briefcase, others to go to the loo, others to make a telephone call. They left me alone with a roomful of what appeared to be several million pounds worth of diamonds and thick wads of folded money. The police warning not to touch anything was completely unnecessary.

Nervousness approaching hysteria had locked my hands to the bar. Firstly, this was necessary to support my body weight as my knees would not and secondly, to prevent the noise of my knocking knees alerting the 'bad bastards' that something was up. Thankfully, they must have realised that the phone call had alerted me because, on their return to the bar, each one quickly packed up his loot and melted away, as quietly as they had come. I have no recollection of whether they paid for their drinks or not. I was so pleased to see them go that I would not have noticed if they had nicked the till.

A minute or two after they had gone, in came another group, far more dangerous looking than the last. "Right lad, let's all have a cup of tea." It was the plain-clothes police. It was grand to have them with me, particularly as they were as relieved as I was that the 'bad bastards' had gone. "By hell! We don't want their sort round here, out of Birmingham they are. Between them, they have done years inside for drug offences, gun-running, shootings and the Lord knows what else. They must have heard you were rich, buying a place like this, and wanted to get you involved in a scam, or money laundering some of their ill-gotten gains." "What about the diamonds?" I asked. "Oh no, only one of them would be real, in case you had asked to look at one. It would all have been paste, or worse, with real bank notes only for the top and bottom of each stash."

A bittersweet conclusion came to my early confrontation with the pack leader of the late night drinkers. We met again, many years later, on the day of his second marriage. His new wife, knowing nothing of her new husband's falling out with me, insisted on the wedding breakfast being held in our restaurant, a table for four, the bride and groom, his best man and her matron of honour. He looked very smart, in fact quite dashing, in an obviously brand new, lightweight linen safari suit. They ordered drinks. Disaster occurred with an almost inevitable certainty. It was just too good an opportunity for my fun-loving god not to drop a pebble in my pond. The bridegroom ordered a pint of lager, an order that surprised me, as he had never drunk anything other than whisky. Along with other drinks, I took his pint to the table. As I put it down by his place setting, his new wife asked me something. When I turned toward her, my sleeve knocked over the full chill-cold pint. It must have been a cruel shock and dampened his ardour because it all went straight into his lap. His generosity in excusing my clumsiness, without any reference to past differences, gave me much to think about. After the event we used to talk happily whenever we met in town. But he never came back to drink at the bar.

CHAPTER THREE

# I'll Come Down and Have a Look at You

From the beginning it was obvious that a great deal of work was required to attract more paying customers to the inn. First, we would have to make safe the derelict state of the buildings and get a fire certificate. It was also evident that what the sale prospectus unashamedly listed as 'fixtures and fittings' needed urgent attention. The fixtures were on the move and the fittings hanging loose. We would also have to clear the rampant vegetation that shrouded the inn from public view. This introduced into our accounts the nominal item 'R & R', Repair and Renewals.

It was no use grumbling that the roof leaked or that the electric wiring was dangerous. All the old lead sheathing on the copper conductors had oxidized to white powder years ago. This caused short circuits and power failures every time we got busy. Our customers enjoyed the candlelit suppers, singing out each and every time there was a failure "Who's got a shilling for the meter?" In such well-rehearsed phrases decimalisation has no place. Nor could we worry about the plumbing, or rather lack of it. There were ten bedrooms but only two bathrooms. We just had to live with the fact that there was no heating in any of the upstairs rooms and worse,

# I'll Come Down and Have a Look at You

no proper sewerage. The clean drains ran with the foul, to empty together, straight into a ditch that ran into the brook, the Bentley Brook. We owned what we had bought. Had there been no dereliction or deficiency the hotel would have had star ratings and would have been beyond our means.

Our first move to improve the facilities was to turn to the *Yellow Pages* to find a local plumber to repair a leak in the one and only hot water tank, a huge copper tank that served the kitchen and the rest of the building. When I asked a listed local plumber if he could come and repair our leak, we heard, for the first time, the 'Ashbourne Anthem'. It ran as follows, "I'll come down and have a look at you." "Oh good, when?" "Well, let's see now... when I get down to have a look at you." I pressed for an answer, "Please make it soon, I'm not sure it's safe." "Right then," was his long drawn out reply and he put the phone down.

Some days later, a large elderly man loomed, unannounced, into my kitchen. It annoyed me that he was smoking a huge crook stemmed pipe with a bowl big enough to smoke a cabbage. He wore corduroy trousers with a wide leather belt and a vividly patterned woollen jumper stretched tight over his massive belly. Over his shoulders, as a backup to the belt, he wore a pair of wide leather braces. I knew who he was as soon as he opened the conversation with that long drawn out "Right then." "Oh hello, I'm glad you could make it, this is the leaking tank I was telling you about." There was no sharp intake of breath through clenched teeth for this fellow. Having cast his eye around the kitchen he sucked hard on his massive pipe, leaned against the door and went straight to the point. "Eee master, you've bought a ruck of trouble." "Oh! Can you fix it?" I asked. "That boiler needs coming out for

# It Could be a Little Gold Mine

a start," he replied, "Eee, you have bought a ruck of trouble you have." "Oh! Why?" "It's rammel, it's all rammel, I've told you, you bought a right ruck of trouble here, it will all have to come out." By now, I had had enough and suggested, with some asperity, that he take himself off and leave me to deal with my ruck of trouble.

I tried the *Yellow Pages* again, several times. Each time the Ashbourne Anthem had me dancing to its tune when I tried to get some sense from other plumbers. "I'll come down and have a look at you," was the by now expected response. "Fine, when?" I tried. "Well later, I can't promise anything." At last, a second plumber did come and he at least followed the courtesies by ringing the reception bell to announce his arrival. He seemed to be normal, and he was wearing engineer's blue overalls, but it did concern me that he did not appear to have a tool bag.

"What's the trouble mate?" "Well it's this leaking hot water tank I told you about, this one here." I had to admire his direct approach. "I'd heard you was a engineer, but yer don't know owt about plumbing do yer? Yer can't repair these you know, anybody can tell you, it will have to come out, you'll never get one this size, they don't make 'em any more, it's all rammel." My temper did not last as long as it had with the first plumber. "If you can't help, go away, I will find someone who can."

From these two failures, I learned that for matters such as this there was a much better source of information than the *Yellow Pages*. The answer was literally facing me across the bar. Friday night trade was increasing and I simply said, to no one in particular, "Does anybody know of a good plumber?" A customer who I had talked to once or twice came across and

# I'll Come Down and Have a Look at You

kindly said, "My lad Philip is an apprentice, he's with a good firm of plumbers. Would you like me to ask him to come in tomorrow morning and see what he can do?" "That's very kind, I'm stumped otherwise, and it does need sorting," I replied, hoping for the best.

Saturday morning, 9 am in came Philip, a fresh-faced young man, and joy of joys, he was in his overalls, plumber's brown not engineer's blue. Better still, he carried a traditional bas, a reassuring D-shaped thick brown canvas plumber's bag, full of plumber's tools. "Morning Mr Allingham, my Dad asked me to see if I can mend this leak of yours." Half an hour later, the leak was a leak no more and the tank was sound. I was thrilled and asked, "How much?" "Oh! forget it, it were nowt, buy us a pint tonight, I'll come in with my girlfriend."

Work often took Philip away from Ashbourne, so he was not always available to answer our plumbing needs. Customers recommended that we try a certain Mr Adams, known to all as Cliff. Now Cliff was a grand chap, keen to do his best, but totally disorganised. He turned out to be the perfect proof of the old adage that plumbers never arrive on their first visit with the proper tools for the job. He was a one-man band who frequently managed to ravel his control strings. During the early years of our planned and unplanned refurbishment of the inn, he did many small plumbing jobs for us. His good humour and gentle nature made us forgive him his many trespasses against us. The trespass was on our busy time. He never once brought the right tools for the job in hand. When Cliff was on site, he was a constant interruption to my cooking. "Oh! Er, Mr A... er have you got a three-quarter sprocket fangler?" or just as likely, being singularly single-handed, in he would come "Oh! Er, Mr A... can you just

# It Could be a Little Gold Mine

come and hold this while I er, fix the other end?"

However, as I have said, he was grand chap and we did get our own back when he brought his young wife to dinner. They came, as young couples do, one fourteenth of February, to celebrate Valentine's Day. His table was perfectly laid up for two, except his setting was minus a fork, and the table minus salt and pepper. Jeanne played her part beautifully. Said Cliff, all dressed up and anxious to impress his lovely wife, "Could I please have a fork?" Jeanne was waiting for his call. "Oh! didn't you bring one?" and when Cliff plucked up courage to ask for salt and pepper, she again sang out, "Oh! didn't you bring your own?" Finally, when serving the main course vegetables from two hot dishes, Jeanne pushed one into his hands, without a serving cloth but with a smile, and asked, "Excuse me sir, could you just hold this while I serve from the other one?" Poor Cliff, he was unable to respond when his lovely wife had happy tears of laughter in her eyes as she gave Jeanne a huge hug. "Oh poor you, I don't know how you put up with him, he's just like that at home, all the time."

Some answers to our problems were even closer to hand than customer recommendation. A new hot water system and gas central heating in the upstairs rooms finally made redundant the huge leaky hot water tank that had caused us problems. When we bought the inn, it had five large chimneystacks, each with several flues and chimney pots. Our builders carefully deconstructed three, pulling them down, course by course, through the loft and first floor, down to ground level. This had the advantage of increasing the size of the bedrooms and made them easier to furnish and eliminated the seventeen roof leaks. However, it had not been pos-

# I'll Come Down and Have a Look at You

sible to take out an enormous chimneybreast that still dominated the north wall in the kitchen. Many years earlier, to make room for a modern, small electric oven, the old built-in cast-iron range was removed, requiring the overhanging tons of brickwork to be supported by massive steel props.

With both the tank and potbellied stove gone, I was aware that the chimneybreast could be removed, but before I had the opportunity to take the initiative, Pauline, our housekeeper, taxed me about it. "When are you going to get rid of that lot? It's dangerous," was her blunt approach. "Er! Um? well er... as soon as we can afford to get the builders back, but I have not yet been able to pay them for their last job." She replied with that familiar long drawn out Derbyshire "Right then," followed by a sigh that said much. "We'll have to do it ourselves then. You go and buy a bolster chisel and lump hammer and we'll start first thing Monday morning, when we are quiet."

On Monday, with my new bolster chisel, lump hammer and wheelbarrow we were ready. Pauline clearly saw herself as foreman. "You get a beer crate to stand on, leave the props in place, then start at the ceiling to drop the bricks. I'll barrow them outside." I was getting into this and responded in the vernacular drawn out "Right then." It did not take long to dislodge the first brick, as the mortar was hundreds of years old. I thought, "If I can drive a hole through to the flue, I will be able to pull the bricks out without difficulty." Encouraged by Jeanne and Pauline, I easily removed several more outer bricks to make room to attack the exposed inner row that lined the flue. With determined resolve, aided by my newly acquired bolster and lump hammer, I made the breakthrough.

# It Could be a Little Gold Mine

I have never been too clear about what happened next, except that the world went black and I could not breathe. I could not see one inch, up, down or sideways but somehow found the open door and collapsed, choking and coughing, onto the back lawn. I was not alone. Already there were two black people, with only the whites of their eyes in contrast. They were both coughing, spluttering and, thankfully, laughing.

After half an hour, several glasses of water and numerous cups of tea we could see across the kitchen. What we saw was not encouraging. To Pauline's horror, the door from the kitchen to her domain had been open when the avalanche of soot struck. Fine dry soot, hundreds of years old, had plumed through the open door to settle everywhere, the bar, the stairs and the hall. Ever the stoic, Pauline simply said, "Ah well,

# I'll Come Down and Have a Look at You

that's a job for tomorrow; we had best finish the chimney today, but not until we have closed and sealed all the doors with tape." And finish it we did.

Working blind with a wet towel over my head and holding my breath, I was able to pull down several bricks each time I rushed to the breach. While I coughed and choked outside, Pauline worked like Hercules in the Augean Stables but without a river to help. Eventually she cleared the last of the rubble. There was only one thing for me to say, "Right then, let's all have a cup of tea."

We had another major problem that needed our urgent attention. It was the choking blue smoke haze we had noticed during our first visit. There were two fireplaces in the bar, each connected to a different chimneystack. The flues in these two stacks did not work as chimney flues should. Previous owners had made two small rooms, each with a separate fireplace, into one large room. They had done this by knocking out the brick panels either side of the chimney-breast that had been the dividing wall.

A room with two fireplaces connected to two separate chimney flues usually creates a problem and our bar was no exception. Depending upon the direction and force of the wind, either one or other of the chimney flues became dominant. The dominant flue drew smoke across the room from the other fire before it could go up the chimney in the usual way. Whatever combination we tried, with one or the other or both fires lit, we were living in a blue haze at best or a complete smog on bad days.

I took it upon myself to design the solution, sketching it out with a thick felt pen on a fragment of bloodstained peach paper, a material that butchers used to use to wrap meat,

# It Could be a Little Gold Mine

before the horrid habit of vacuum packing in plastic became almost compulsory. The sketch is now lost, but it showed a single central fireplace, open to both sides of the bar. It specified limestone cobbles set in a circular hearth with a dog-grate fire basket. Above the hearth, I indicated a bell shape of local rough-hewn limestone, with a contrasting stone mantelpiece wide enough to hold a pint pot.

Our builders introduced me to a master stonemason, a young man who had won competitions for his craft, and we engaged him to build the new fireplace to my rough design. He showed an immediate understanding of my ideas and suggested some excellent improvements. He found limestone cobbles for the hearth, granite sets for the mantelpiece and blocks of rough-cut limestone for the bell shape. The limestone came from Ballidon quarry, just three miles up the dale from the inn.

The master mason's apprentice thought it a 'stupid design' because he copped for the job of digging the limestone cobbles from a derelict farmyard and of washing off years of accreted cow dung. The poor chap also had the task of drilling a quarter-inch diameter, two-inch deep hole, into about fifty granite sets, to fit an iron peg that would bond them as the mantelpiece, into my dream structure. It took weeks to build. Each evening, to contain the dust, the builders completely shrouded the masterpiece with heavy tarpaulin taped to both floor and ceiling. Our customers began to speculate on what was going on that was such a secret. The interest became so intense that some of the regulars ran a sweepstake, the sought-after ticket being that it was a theatre organ that would rise from the cellar for nightly concerts.

While this major work had been going on, the builders

# I'll Come Down and Have a Look at You

had taken out the other fireplace, bricked up the flue and plastered over the hole. With only one flue to take smoke from our new central fire, I was confident that our days of eye watering discomfort would be over. When it was at last unveiled, our customers gave the construction their approval and settled all bets.

At last came the day when I could test whether the new fireplace would work and clear the air. Barry Potter, a local skilled blacksmith, hand-forged a fine large dog-grate for the new fire and delivered it on a day that was raw cold. I wanted a decent fire to test how the smoke would flow. I was anxious. With the grate opened to both rooms, there was no longer a fire-back. With no fire-back, I was aware that there would be no immediate Coander effect. This is the phenomenon that makes a gas stream stick to the first surface with which it comes into contact. In normal fireplaces, the projecting angled chimney back captures the smoke and guides it up into the flue. To compensate for the lack of a fireback, our mason built gently curved surfaces on all sides, to form a smooth throat to lead the smoke from the grate to the flue. I was confident that once captured by good old Coander, the smoke would have nowhere to go, but up.

I quickly found newspaper and dry sticks for kindling. I wanted a good blaze to get the cold chimney hot, as quickly as possible. I added a couple of shovelfuls of coal and a log or two to sustain the fire. At the strike of a match the blaze soon developed. Oh Joy! the fireplace and chimney I had designed was working. A sudden and terrible doubt then dampered my euphoria. Wisps of smoke leaked out beneath the mantelpiece into both sides of the bar. This shook my confidence, but I could not admit that I had it all wrong.

# It Could be a Little Gold Mine

"Don't worry," I told Jeanne and Barry who had stayed to watch, "it's just because the chimney is cold, it will soon clear." It was only when I heard Jeanne shouting "Stop it, put it out, it's ruining the new paint," that I conceded that something really was not quite right. The smoke did not seem to understand Coander.

Followed by Jeanne and Barry, I ran into the garden to inspect the chimney from the outside. Unaware of what I was doing, the builders were up there retiling the roof. To stop the rain coming in, they had fitted the tarpaulin, previously used to shroud the new fireplace, over both the roof and the chimney pots. Back into the smoke-logged room we ran, and with Barry's help, we used broom handles pushed under the new dog-grate, to carry the blazing brazier out into the back yard. Quite delighted with all the excitement and activity, our youngest son Bill, happily barbecued sausages over the dampened flames. We, soot blackened and weary, queued for the only bath.

The next most urgent task was to sort out the drains both clean and foul. Forgetful of our previous failures with the *Yellow Pages* I looked up and rang a local builder who claimed in his advert to be a specialist in drains and drainage. "Oh! Hello, is that the Direct Drain Company?" The curt reply depressed me, "Just a minute, I'll get him." "Thank you," then a pause followed by a blunt "What?" "Oh! Hello, my name's Allingham, we've recently bought the Bentley Brook Inn and our drains need sorting." "Yes, I know, I've heard you've bought a ruck of trouble, *right then*, I'll come down and have a look at you." I quietly replaced the receiver and made my way to the bar.

# CHAPTER FOUR

# Have You Got a Minute?

Within a few weeks of our early misadventures into repair and renewals, we realised that professional guidance was required. A few discreet questions to our customers led us to call on Anthony Short, a local architect. He was, and still is, a man of great good humour and rare talent. Understanding our needs, he prepared drawings to show how we might upgrade the dilapidated main building and the derelict coach house, to a standard where customers could stay in comfort.

Norris Sergeant, the previous owner of the inn, had made a steak bar from what had been a pantry and the housekeeper's sitting room. The bench seats were made of thin plywood nailed to rough-cut softwood supporting batons. These he covered, in part, with cheap shiny red plasticised fabric. Norris had secured his DIY benches in rows, back to back and either side of even cheaper fixed tables. The overall result was that they looked like a child's toy train ride at an undercapitalised fairground. The unfinished edges of the plywood snagged my blue overalls, let alone Jeanne's nylon stockings. The second pair snagged and the steak bar had to go. More seriously, during and after heavy rain, a three-foot wide, shallow stream came through the wall under the main window, to run diagonally across the floor, before disappearing under the far wall. It did this in a passing fair imitation of the nearby mysterious River Manifold. This boundary marker between

# It Could be a Little Gold Mine

Derbyshire and Staffordshire has a trick of appearing out of a dry gully to run full flood as a river, only to disappear again into sinkholes a few hundred yards downstream.

The decision taken, for once we had a stroke of luck. Richard Pullin, a designer with whom I had worked in Hong Kong, called to see how we were getting along. He agreed that changes were essential and prepared a design for a new bar. This we decided to call the Travellers' Room, as it would display some of our souvenirs collected during our trips around the world. Richard's agreed fee was dinner, bed and breakfast for him and his elegant wife Maggie.

Walker and Grounds, a local firm, won the contract to carry out roof repairs and to do all that was necessary to obtain the essential fire certificate. They also sorted out the drains and installed a huge fibreglass underground septic tank. Michael Gallimore, a local electrician, took on the unenviable task of completely replacing all the electrical wiring and switchgear throughout the whole building, in addition to installing a fire detection and emergency lighting system. For Michael it meant weeks of work to thread new cables through the unchartered walls, voids and floors of the old building. Generations of previous owners had extended, refashioned, added to and rebuilt what had been a medieval farmhouse, to create a complex gentleman's residence.

The plumbing was in such a parlous state throughout, that we had need of an almost resident plumber. After many trials, we finally found Stuart Helleby. Stuart was competent and reliable in all things except accounts. For this shortcoming, we were always thankful. Often he would not send his bills for work done for months or even more than a year after completion. He explained that, as most of his work was done

# Have You Got a Minute?

by order of local farmers, who did not pay him for months or even longer, and as he had been in business for many years, taken all together, it really did not affect his cash flow.

We gave the job of creating the Travellers' Room, based on Richard Pullin's drawings, to Alf Beetson, without tender or any agreed price. It was an inspired choice. Alf, an ex-army cook, and civilian painter and decorator, had worked for years for a company that specialised in hotel and pub refurbishment. For the very modest sums we paid him, we not only had a painter, decorator, and general maintenance man, but also a good friend and mentor. Alf, aware of our precarious financial position, never pressed for payment and because he was popular, his many friends brought us a lot of trade. At a moment's notice he even took over as chef for a few days when, once again, my innate clumsiness led to a heavy fall requiring hospital treatment.

Fortune favoured us in the choice of these contractors, all of whom worked hard, to make safe the buildings and to give us a firm base on which to build a business. However, the confusion of contractors working upstairs, downstairs, on the roof and in the garden did bring problems. At least once a day, often several times a day, I heard a call that I came to dread. "Mr A, have you got a minute?" For almost a generation I had been involved in the planning, development and construction of power stations. These were complex contracts, costing millions of pounds, but it was not my money I was spending. Oh those carefree days, when "I think we should have a meeting," was all that I had to deal with. Now each time I heard the dread call "Mr A, have you got a minute?" it was deeply personal. No longer did I have a team of able and willing colleagues to check details and come up

# It Could be a Little Gold Mine

with solutions. It was down to me. Each time I heard the call I had to drop what I was doing in the kitchen, go to assess the problem, wherever it was, and give an instant decision. It was not quite as disturbing as the most famous call ever made "Huston, we have a problem," but I knew that each time I authorised extra work, my decision brought us nearer to bankruptcy.

John Walker, a partner in the firm who did most of the early restoration, was a hard worker, and a skilled craftsman. He suggested that it would make food service easier if he moved one of the doors to the bar, to face the kitchen door. He explained that all that was required was to cut through one wall, brick up the other, and to re-use the existing door and frame. To me it all sounded a bit too reminiscent of the *Fawlty Towers* episode with the O'Reilly men when they moved a door, almost bringing the hotel down around Basil's ears, but, confident in John's better judgement, I agreed. The builders made an early start one Monday morning. One team took out the existing door and frame, bricked up and plastered over the hole where it had been. The other team busied themselves with hammer and chisels to cut through the wall where we wanted the door to be.

It was at this stage that John put his head round the kitchen door and said, too quietly for my liking, "Mr A, have you got a minute?" "Oh hell! What's happened now?" was my instant worry. I was already counting the cost of some terrible structural failure. "No, it's alright," said John, "I just thought that you might like to look at this." To look was not easy as the room was full of a floating, misty white dust. As it cleared, I could see what had interested him. It was a glimpse of history, an exposed part of a medieval wattle, daub and beam structure that had been undisturbed for hundreds of years.

Clearly, it had been part of the original farmhouse built around the time of Henry V and the battle of Agincourt. Across the exposed wattle, where the door was to be, lying at an angle, was a huge beam, at least a foot and a half thick. "Well, that's put paid to that idea then," I said and went on, "you had better re-plaster the wall and put the door back where it was." More money wasted I thought grimly. "No, don't worry," replied John, "can't you see? The beam is not doing anything. Sometime during earlier alterations they just left it." I stuck a screwdriver into the the beam and it sank easily to a depth of about an inch, but then it met firm, even iron resistance. John continued, "I'll get the boys to bring a two handled cross-cut saw and we'll just cut it through where the door is to be." The mighty saw, deep-bellied, more than seven feet long, resembled a huge blue whale, but its teeth were like those of a great white shark. Vertical wooden poles, each at least half a yard long, made the handles at each end.

The apprentices started the first cut at about eight the following morning. Back and forth, back and forth with steady rasping rhythm they toiled. It was just after noon when with a great cheer they were through. "Right then," John said, as he examined the teeth of the saw. "You've made a right set of old gums of this you have, you had better go back to the workshop to get it sharpened and reset. You can do the other half tomorrow." The look they gave him was at least equal to that given by the proverbial galley slave to the slave driver when told that the emperor wanted to try water-skiing in the afternoon.

The second cut caused equal toil and a deal of sweat but

# It Could be a Little Gold Mine

when completed it enabled us to examine the heart of oak at the centre of the beam. It was so tough that it showed no saw cut marks, even from those massive teeth, just a fine polish.

Even with all this mayhem, dirt, dust and noise going on around us, we had no alternative but to continue to be open to the public. We had a business to run. A few of the bedrooms were just about fit to let. We could serve both food and drink, provided the contractors swept up and covered up each evening. We had to keep going to generate a cash flow sufficient to stave off the worst demands of the bank. Our customers amazed us with their patience and understanding, forgiving our trespasses against them, and supporting us in all our endeavours.

A young couple who had occasionally been coming to have Sunday lunch best illustrate this tolerance of our failures. This time, as they were leaving, their bill already paid, they asked to see me. Again came the dread call, "Excuse us Mr A, have you got a minute?" It is my regular habit when faced with such a request from a customer to go all to pieces. The primary thoughts are always the same. Is it food poisoning, mistaken identity, overcharging or are they perhaps AA Hotel Inspectors. Then the synapses switch to secondary fears, that they are Food Police, VAT Inspectors, Inland Revenue enforcers or the local Mafia. All that I managed to squeak was "Er, can I, er, what? Er, is everything, er..." Then to my relief, "Oh yes, we have had a lovely meal, as we always do, but think you should know that we both had rhubarb crumble for pudding." By now, I had changed from panic mode to one of confused puzzlement. "Oh! I am sorry, were they not, er, what? Er..." Their sweet reply, "No, it was delicious," calmed me down but they went on. "But we had already had your cream of winter vegetable soup for starters." "What?" not pardon, I rudely interrupted. "Well your waiter poured the custard for us and er, er well, er, it was the soup again." "What?" I interjected again rising to panic. "It was the soup again," they said in unison. "But it tasted fine so we ate it." Back in my kitchen, I checked. Yes, both custard and soup were as smooth as silk, side by side in identical pans and both as yellow as, well, custard.

However, we could not please everybody with our amateur goings on. During the height of the reconstruction works, a well-known local hotelier came in with a couple of companions and stood at the end of the bar; clearly, they were taking stock. He was wearing brogues, green ribbed socks, plus fours, check shirt, tweed tie and shooting jacket, every inch from the soles of his shoes to the top of his head, a city man dressed for the country. We were somewhat taken aback when he announced, in plain speech, using a voice that carried to everyone in the bar, that as we were unqualified in catering and hotel management we had no right to be running this place. He went on to add that it was obvious to all, we were nothing but greedy property speculators. We took this, not as an insult, but a golden spur. Besides we were having too much fun to take any notice of him.

One factor that we had not fully understood was the impact that being located within the Peak District National Park would have on our business. The so-called Peak District National Park is not a park in any normal understanding or definition of a park. The OED has six definitions for park, none of which suit that which is merely a defined area where a government appointed authority has control over planning. When making the decision to buy, we had in mind that being

# It Could be a Little Gold Mine

in the Park would not only mean that we would be living in one of England's most beautiful areas, but also, it would be helpful to our marketing plans. As newcomers, we were completely ignorant of the nature and purpose of the Park Authority, but several of our customers had told us to beware of them, because they had the last word in planning issues. Mindful of what might become a problem, we asked the planners to visit the site so that we could discuss our ideas for future development and get their reaction.

Anthony, the architect we appointed, and Richard, the designer who had worked with me in Hong Kong, joined us for the meeting. The officers and members of the National Park Authority came by minibus, outnumbering us by more than three to one. The leader of their team introduced himself as the Board's Chief Planning Officer. He appeared to be a pleasant and apparently reasonable man. He then introduced his team, some professionals and some county and district councillors appointed to the Board. Their architect, who could not have been out of university for more than a few months, was a thin, poor specimen. He had a wispy goatee beard, an open-necked shirt of coarse material, brown corduroy trousers, open-toed sandals, no socks, and a limp handshake. Well it was the late Seventies and young architects seemed to have need of this image as a sort of green credential.

Before we had even entered the inn, it came again, "Mr Allingham, have you got a minute?" It was their little thin architect's equally thin voice getting to the point. "Mr Allingham, what are you intending to do with this building?" All eyes turned to view what in years gone by had been a fine coach house. The ground floor provided a stable for two carriage horses, a space for a carriage and in one corner a very small room, with a stove, for the coachman. Above, running the full length of the building, was what had been a loft for hay and straw. Lack of maintenance and the ravages of Derbyshire weather had brought it to ruin. The roof was falling in and the walls were falling out. Throughout the whole structure, dry rot was competing for supremacy with wet rot, and colonies of woodworm and deathwatch beetle fought for territory over the decaying timbers.

A curious "Pardon?" from me and then again from their Seventies-educated architect, this time more determined, "What are your plans for this building?" Prepared to be completely open with the planners I went along with him. "Well there are two thoughts about it. We either leave it derelict for a few years, until we can afford to restore it, or we knock it down now to provide extra car parking." "Oh no," he simpered, "the Authority would vigorously oppose any application to demolish it; after all, it is made of natural brick." For a moment, I pondered on these natural bricks. I wondered whether one could pick them off the branches of a brick tree or whether it would be better to search for and dig them out of the ground like precious truffles. My two professional advisors, seeing my stunned reaction and rising colour, signalled frantically to indicate that I should let it pass and not respond with my usual sarcasm. After a long pause, I did as they wished, but the look I gave him of the goatee beard and limp wrist, at least choked off any further involvement from him during the rest of the meeting. The sheer stupidity of his statement, unchallenged or corrected by any member of this unelected quango, marked down my opinion of their worth then, and nothing in my later experience has done anything

# It Could be a Little Gold Mine

to change it. The anecdotal evidence of ludicrous, vindictive and sheer barmy decisions made by the planners of the Peak Park Authority, trotted out almost every week in our bar, would fill a book of encyclopaedic proportions.

MORNING!
NATURAL OR FREE RANGE?

Not all "Have you got a minute?" moments were devastating. One day we received an unannounced visitor. It was at a time when we were deeply involved with our planned restoration of the fabric, fittings and fixtures of the inn. There was debris left by builders, plumbers and electricians everywhere, all adding to the usual mess in the kitchen. My visitor was smartly dressed in a suit, aged in his early sixties I would guess. He called to me while I was in the garden hacking down one of the many yew trees. "Mr Allingham is it?" "Er, yes, what can I do?" was all I could get out before he went on, "Sorry to interrupt, but have you got a minute?" Oh dear Lord what now, I was thinking as I came to meet the out-

# Have You Got a Minute?

stretched hand that shook mine firmly. I felt that I was being looked over very carefully, but somehow kindly, his eyes were as friendly as his greeting. "Hello young man, I'm Mr Todd, the Environmental Health Officer for this area, do you mind if I have a look around?" I gave a shaky response, "Er, no, glad to, but we are in such a mess, I've got builders everywhere." "Good, it shows you've made a start," was his brisk reply. Then again, I sensed the long hard look "You're Inspector Allingham's lad aren't you. When I first qualified I worked in Halifax and had a right adventure with your Dad, he was a grand man." So, I came to understand, was Mr Todd.

He told me that my father and he had together condemned an old multi-storey, woollen mill building as unsafe. Their judgement had proved correct, because its five storeys completely collapsed during the following night. I had heard the tale from my father many times and it was good to hear it again. "From our point of view it's a right nightmare of a place you've taken on," he said. "However," he continued, "I can see you have the right idea, and I promise, if you keep on improving things, we'll not bother you." He kept his part of the bargain and we kept ours. On each of his official visits, he was as excited with our progress as we were. Would there were more of his like.

Some of the best "Have you got a minute?" moments were those asked for by customers in our restaurant. One such was during the first wedding reception that we catered for after taking over the inn. The handwritten note, entered in the diary, was an irrevocable agreement to the menu. To start, *soupe du jour*, followed by roast beef and then apple crumble. We did not plan for this type of function, but the people were grand and it was what they wanted. It was only after the

# It Could be a Little Gold Mine

meal, leek and potato soup followed by roast sirloin of beef, then pudding and after the speeches, when the guests were drifting away, that the father of the bride sought me out. He was a thin wiry sort of a man, a Derbyshire hill farmer born and bred and well over sixty. "Nah then lad," he started "have you got a minute? You've done us proud, reet well in fact and we are well satisfied but I thought I should have a word. Tha sees, I've had two other lasses wed here, one when Master Sergeant was here and before that one with yon Rainbird fellow. Now I know that you are new to this hotel game and I thought it only fair to tell you, *soupe du jour* is tomato."

Even now, after twenty-seven years, the restoration continues and the merry contractor's song rings out "Mr A, have you got a minute?" Sometimes it is a builder as he stares thoughtfully into a hole where no hole should be. Perhaps it is an electrician as he waves the end of a potted off cable asking, "This is live, what is it for?" More often, it is when a plumber finds a leak in a pipe going nowhere and he asks, "Where is the stop tap?" Now, in the computer age, as our brand new state-of-the-art computer crashes yet again, a new call beckons, "Mr A, have you got a nanosecond?"

# CHAPTER FIVE

# A Good Pint

For twenty-eight years Jeanne has held a licence to serve *intoxicating liquor of all descriptions*. I have checked my Thesaurus, and my dictionary of English Etymology for a group word that embraces *intoxicating liquor of all descriptions* and found only the vulgar derogatory term, 'booze'.

I have often said, and meant it, that there is more nonsense talked about booze than about sex. For all but the first few weeks of the years I have spent dispensing booze, I have been bored stiff by those few but very persistent customers who feel it necessary to tell me of their special understanding and secret knowledge of beers, single malt whiskies and the only way to make a Martini. No food writer, wine critic, or CAMRA member, can know if the first sip of a recommended spirit, liqueur, beer, cider, perry or wine will trigger the synapse of the drinker's brain to stimulate a response of pleasure or disgust. The persistent few bored me because booze has no benchmark; one man's meat being another's poison.

During our early days at the inn, the worst of the bores were ex-landlords. As newcomers to the trade, we were obvious targets. They seemed determined to seek us out, usually before we opened for the lunchtime session. "Cleaning the pipes lad, you take it from me, I'll tell you, you mustn't use that stuff the brewery sends. Oh no! You do what I did, just ordinary common salt in warm water." Some varied this to Epsom salts, bismuth, caustic soda, baking powder, toothpaste powder, bleach, or some other infallible solution. "Mark my words, I used to serve the best beer in the county, it were well-known." "Oh thank you." I learnt to reply, "Why did you give up?" Invariably came the reply, "I couldn't make it pay, it were in wrong place."

It was usually early evening when the other 'mentors' came, when they knew the bar would be quiet. Typically, it would be a middle-aged stranger. The script and business were always the same. The stranger would lean over the bar and pause before murmuring, in low tones, like some conspirator, "Your Pedigree, it's not bad, but I can tell you, it's nothing like the stuff they brew for the pubs in Burton-on-Trent, now that's the real Pedigree." "Oh is it? I must try to get hold of some. Do you work at the brewery?" I would sigh. "No, but it's true," they would say, "I know it for a fact, my brother–in–law lives in Burton and he has a friend who works for the brewery." If time allowed, I would lead them on: "He does, what does he do then?" Then would come the evasion, "Why he's summat big in the office now, I don't know just what." I never had the heart to argue and would let it pass. It was soon beyond counting the times that these chaps, who were always on their own, revealed this particular secret to me. That they were on their own was understandable.

Even more common is the mantra, "Of course, the Guinness we get here in England is completely different from the Guinness in Ireland, it's the water you know." Once upon a time, it may have been so, but not now. Science, water treatment, and brewing have progressed. Any competent chemist can now modify water from any source to replicate water from

# A Good Pint

any other source. For some months, sometime during the first or second year we had the inn, the Guinness delivered to us was brewed and sealed in its keg in Dublin. The reason was that the workers at the Park Royal Brewery in London were on strike and our supplier had found a route through Liverpool, to beat the picket lines. Not one of our Guinness drinkers noticed any difference; nor have I, since the beginning of September 2005 when all Guiness sold in England is brewed in Dublin.

A two-week visit to southern Ireland, during the summer of 2003, confirmed my conviction that there is no constant difference amongst the draught product of the many Guinness breweries worldwide. In any case, who could now tell? Pubs and bars worldwide serve the black stuff pressurised with a mixture of nitrogen and carbon dioxide, and so cold that all taste buds are neutralised.

Now that we have our own brewery, Leatherbritches, we attract what are known in the trade as *Tickers*, mainly middle-aged solitary men who travel many miles to drink a half pint of every known real ale, so that they may tick them off their list and write tasting notes and comments alongside each entry. I have my own name for the extreme collectors. I call them *Fivers*; fifty-five, five-foot five, five-foot five round the middle with an IQ in the fifties. Fortunately, they are a very small minority amongst the growing number of real ale drinkers who are good company, coming in groups, drinking in pints, and taking turns to be the driver. Many are members of CAMRA, the Campaign for Real Ale, a lobby group about which I have some reservations. However, I fully support their campaign to keep cask-conditioned and bottle-conditioned ales available throughout the country and their efforts to stop

# It Could be a Little Gold Mine

the more easily managed pasteurised denatured keg beers and lagers driving out real ale from Britain's more than 70,000 pubs.

Marston's Pedigree had always been the best-selling beer at the Bentley Brook before we bought the inn, lock, stock and barrel. We were determined to be as good as the best, and to find the best, we followed every lead our customers gave in answer to our question, "Who serves a good pint round here?" A consensus soon revealed that Mr Castledine, landlord of The Gate in the nearby village of Brassington kept a good pint. After washing the glasses and clearing the tables left by our few lunchtime customers, Jeanne and I took an early opportunity to visit him, to sample some of his well-kept beer. We arrived at The Gate, a wonderful unspoilt village pub, just five minutes before the then mandatory closing time after the midday session. We introduced ourselves, as the novice newcomers from the Bentley Brook and explained that we were here to learn what Pedigree should taste and look like.

Mr Castledine, a gentleman landlord of many years experience, pulled a pint for me and a half pint for Jeanne. He would not take a penny in payment and wished us well in our new venture. It was a good pint and although it had slipped past closing time, I ventured to ask, "I know it has gone time, but you have been so kind, will you please have a drink with us?" "Why thank you, of course, why not." However, as he replied I noticed that he dropped the latch on the bar door. What happened next was just cruel. As Mr Castledine was gently pulling his pint I heard him mutter under his breath, "Drat, drat and double drat." The Pedigree had taken on the appearance of well-used coconut matting and it was as thick as

# A Good Pint

porridge. When pulling his pint he had drawn the sediment and yeast from the bottom of the cask into the pipe and beer engine. Despite our protests that we would come back again, his reputation for keeping a good pint was at stake. He insisted on pulling us another and to save time flushed the line through using beer from the new barrel instead of clean water. Just how many pints he poured down the drain to clear the pipes and engine of the dross, I could not bear to thing about, but it must have lost him all profit on that barrel.

During a period of several months, Pedigree caused us more trouble than enough. Some change in the ingredients, the finings or the brewing process, caused the beer to turn cloudy if one just coughed, sneezed or, excuse me, broke wind in the cellar. An overhead thunderstorm had the same disturbing effect on the lees at the bottom of the barrel, as a tornado has on the dust of the Kansas Plains.

I kept to the Head Brewer's written cellar instructions about how to keep Pedigree with almost fanatic zeal. Even so, during this period, it was our third or fourth summer at the inn, I had to return gallons of beer to the brewery because I could not get it to clear, or it went cloudy partway down the barrel. Although the brewery representative certified that the beer returned was not fit for its purpose, I still had to throw away too many pints without compensation.

One morning an aggressive briefcase carrying, belted blue raincoat wearing little Gauleiter from the brewery came to tell me off, in no uncertain terms. "It is your fault the beer is cloudy; our beer is good. No other landlord is complaining; you cannot be following the set down procedures. You must improve your cellar management." My tense warning "I beg your pardon?" went unnoticed or ignored. He went on, "You

# It Could be a Little Gold Mine

will be given no further credit on ullage returns; I suggest you clean the pipes for a start. Good morning," and off he went. I cannot remember being quite so cross and consequently rang the brewery. In a put-on, clipped upper crust voice I said, "Duty Brewer please." My bluff worked, getting me past the usual screens of telephone operators and secretaries. "Duty Brewer here," was the welcome response. "Oh good, sorry to bother you, but I have a free trade account with you and have been having a lot of trouble getting your Pedigree to settle. Am I the only one?" "Good heavens no," was his spontaneous response. "For the past month or two we have had more sent back than we have sent out. In fact it's so bad, Customs and Excise owe us money this quarter." "Thank you, thank you very much," was all I needed to say.

After a quick telephone call to Mr Andrews, the Free Trade Sales Director, a gentleman of the old school, he restored credit on our returns. Whatever the problem had been was resolved and the beer returned to its usual superb quality. I learned later, that the man who told me the cloudy beer was all my fault had been 'moved on'.

For a few wonderful moments, one golden summer afternoon, this same Pedigree temporarily cost me ownership of the inn. We had been most fortunate in that Bill Richardson, a near neighbour, had come to work for us. Bill was unique. He was born at Alders Farm, once part of the same estate as our inn. After leaving school Bill worked on the farm before serving in the Royal Air Force. He completed a tour of twenty-seven raids over Germany, as a rear gunner in Wellington Bombers. He used to delight in telling visitors from Germany that he had visited their country many times, never adding that he only stayed long enough to drop bombs. After

# A Good Pint

the war, for ten years, Bill kept the Nag's Head in the nearby village of Hulland Ward, before his wife Norah, a nurse, fearing for his health, insisted he leave the trade. He then worked full-time, as an assistant in a high-class grocer's shop, until he retired aged sixty-five. With Norah's permission, he came to the inn, as our lunchtime barman. His gifts were many and he demonstrated great courage, never backing away from a challenge. He was also one of the best tellers of tales since Chaucer. Best of all, Bill was a perfect Romeo to all our lady customers. He soon built up a faithful following of blue-rinse ladies who came from all over the counties of Derbyshire, Staffordshire and Cheshire to simper and coyly respond to his patter. "Madam, what little libation can I get for you this fine spring morning?" "Oh! Just a small sherry if you don't mind." "A sherry, why of course dear lady, for you I would pluck a star from the sky were it in my power."

It was on that golden summer afternoon, with the bar and garden full of folk, when a fellow marched in through the door from the garden. He was dressed as though Ealing Film Studios had fitted him out for a comedy role as an archetypal retired army major. Loud Norfolk tweed jacket, cavalry twill trousers, suede chukka boots, check shirt and of course, a cravat with matching top pocket handkerchief rather than a tie. Bill, from behind the bar, forever the genial host, asked, "What may I get for you sir?" The man replied in a supercilious voice, pitched for all in the bar to hear, "A brimful pint of your best Pedigree with a tight head, in a clean glass, a glass with a handle, if you don't mind." Bill the barman drew the pint from the engine with the Pedigree clip stuck to the handle signifying its provenance. As always, he used a clean glass and as requested, screwed up the sparkler on the beer engine

# It Could be a Little Gold Mine

to get a tight head. Bill set the beer on the bar. With a theatrical gesture, the pseudo major raised the glass and looked at it against the light from the window. He sniffed the beer, he sipped the beer, he ran the beer round his gums, as though it was great claret. Then he put the beer, hardly touched, back on the bar in front of Bill our barman. "That is not Pedigree," he declared. "You are passing off, now get me a pint of the proper Pedigree." I was in the bar, in full chef's fig, serving food and was therefore of no consequence to this arrogant fool. Not having Bill's courage I went to hide in the corridor, just behind the bar, making sure that I could watch unobserved and that I could listen to an experienced expert dealing with a silly customer.

I was not disappointed. Bill our barman, taking issue with the toff, "Sir, I am not passing off, the drink that I have just poured for you is very fine Pedigree, now you will do me the favour of paying your dues, drinking up and pissing off." The man was holding his ground but turning apoplectic, "Now look here my man, I happen to be a shareholder and friend of the Managing Director of your brewery, I shall report you to your manager and have you discharged." Bill was up like a bantam cock, "You'll find that quite a hurdle to jump; you see I own this hotel, lock, stock and barrel. Now drink up and bugger off." The clever pun was that Mr Hurdle was then Chairman and Managing Director of Marston's, the brewery whose flagship beer was Pedigree. The slow handclap of derision followed the fellow as he made his retreat, back through the garden doors. Once he was out of the door, the customers gave Bill a resounding round of genuine applause. Ever gracious, he popped his head round the door, knowing where I would be hiding, "Hope you didn't mind my borrowing your

# A Good Pint

pub for a few minutes?" "Not at all Bill, not at all," I chuckled, as I went to find sanctuary in my kitchen.

Another Pedigree incident occurred a year or two later. Unusually, I was behind the bar getting or returning something for the kitchen. I was never any good at serving customers with drinks. Two men brought half-finished pints of Pedigree back to the bar, stating very emphatically, "This beer is crap." Before I had time to respond, came a quiet yet commanding voice with a Black Country accent, "The beer is good." I realised that a small, slightly-built middle-aged man, with a thin heavily-lined nutbrown but strong face had said this. I did not know him, but did know that he had been staying on the nearby caravan site for a week and drinking his fair share of Pedigree during both the lunchtime and evening sessions. He was sitting on one of the high stools at the end of the bar but had not turned to look at the men, or their pints. "We are not talking to you," replied the men who had brought the beer back. Then they tried again, "This beer is crap." Again came the quiet commanding voice, "Be told, the beer is good." Again, the man who spoke had not turned to look at the men complaining. This time the two men complaining about the Pedigree spoke together with some aggression directly to the man at the end of the bar. "Just who do you think you are?" Only then, did he turn to look at them. Although they were two, and both bigger than him, he faced them down. "I'm the one you should be taking notice of. I work for Marston's, the brewery that provides this pub with Pedigree. My job, each day that I am at work, is to prepare the samples for the Head Brewer and Shift Brewer's morning tasting and for the laboratory's quality assurance tests. I am also one of the tasting panel. I have told you, the beer is good. Now be good lads, sit down and finish your beer," and they did.

Not that passing off and fraud does not occur in some ale-houses and pubs where there are few regular customers. Regulars will soon spot changes and let you know if things are 'not quite as they should be'. This is because regular customers have a stake in keeping the goodwill of the landlord, just as the landlord has a stake in keeping his regulars happy. Because of this mutual, almost symbiotic dependency, problems are usually resolved without fuss.

Not so in the pub where my elder brother John worked for two summer vacations whilst a student at Birmingham University. This was a large corner pub on the sea front in Clacton. The majority of customers were Londoners who visited the pub when on day trips to the coast. They could never become regulars. Two old men, early doors drinkers, ordered a pint of mild apiece and took them to a table in the window overlooking the cold grey sea. This pub did not clean the beer lines from one end of the season to the other. The manager gave instruction to all the bar staff that, at the end of each shift, all the slops from the drip trays, whether lager, bitter, mild or even orange juice and lemonade, must be poured through a huge copper funnel, into the barrel of mild beer. This was a special barrel of enormous proportion, well big enough to house Diogenes. After some discussion between themselves, one of the old men brought both their beers back to the bar. "Excuse me, this beer's cloudy," he said in polite, hesitant manner. "Yes sir," was my brother's tutored reply, "there's a high spring tide today." The old man returned to his seat in the window, with the two glasses of cloudy beer, to stare again at the cold grey sea. Content with my brother's

# A Good Pint

invention, they both drank their warm cloudy, adulterated, mild ale and another secret mystery about beer was set loose. In truth, there are no secret mysteries about keeping a good pint. All that is required is careful stock rotation, quick sale once a barrel is broached, constant cool cellar temperature, time to settle the beer before sale and beer lines cleaned once a week according to the brewer's direction.

Recently, we were once again reminded that even in the best-regulated houses, including those with a determination to keep a good pint, there are pitfalls and traps waiting round every new corner. Even though we had been in the business for more years than most innkeepers manage, we fell into one such trap in sure proof that experience is no protection against human frailty. We had advertised for a bar person. The use of the word *person* always irritates, as what we need is either a barmaid or barman to suit our particular need. The mongers of politically correct speech heighten my frustration by their call for the use of the word *person*. To people of my generation the word is exclusively the euphemism used for the unmentionable organ in cases of indecent exposure reported from magistrates' courts.

What we did wrong was the sin of omission. We did not check the CV or take up references from previous employers about the youth who came for interview for the position of *Experienced Bar Person*. He told us that he had a deal of experience, working in bars from the busy town pub to the up-market hotel and knew all that was needed to be known about real ale, lagers and wine.

My two days observation of him at work caused me to worry. He was just too flash. His third day at work justified my concern. When I came into the bar, it smelt like a car

# It Could be a Little Gold Mine

breaker's yard. It was that unmistakable reek of penetrating oil. "What's that smell?" I asked. "Oh! I knew that you would be pleased gov, this morning I brought in a can of this stuff, it's marvellous," he said, waving a can of WD40. "It's stopped the beer pumps squeaking, it's worked really well." It was as bad as I feared, a rainbow film on each beer that I pulled. All six beer pumps in need of complete overhaul and gallons and gallons of beer wasted. We exchanged his gift to us of WD40 with our gift to him of a UB40.

# CHAPTER SIX

# Accidents Will Happen

My life almost came to an abrupt end, just a few days after we took over the inn. By good fortune, what occurred turned out to be an early incident not a fatal accident.

Although I have always been accident prone, I do not think, for one moment, that my ever-loving parents thought me an accident, although I was the youngest of their three children. However, I remember my mother telling me, many times, that I was born awkward. This was not to do with a breech birth, but to my innate clumsiness. My awkward and maladroit behaviour seldom embarrassed me, as I usually found my worst transgressions to be the best part of the day.

My propensity to accidents did not pass with the teenage years but remains with me to this day. With a track record proving that I was an accident intent on finding somewhere to happen, it was probably not a good idea to become a chef. I soon found kitchens are dangerous places, quickly earning the badges of rank of the professional chef: burn scars on the forearm from oven doors and grill plates, cut fingers from blunt knives, for they are the ones that cut deepest, and of course scalds. Chefs and kitchen workers take these accidents lightly and usually pass them off without fuss.

The early incident that nearly finished me started with Jeanne's early morning command, "Stop what you are doing, go and fix up a washing line." The command had a certain

# It Could be a Little Gold Mine

forcefulness to it that brooked no denial. Jeanne had her priorities right. There was a great deal of hotel linen to wash, also our family laundry to deal with, but nowhere to hang out the washed clothes to dry. "Right oh!" I said, "it won't take long." Outside the kitchen door was a regular tip of old equipment and tools, slates, bricks, rubble, broken concrete slabs and chimney pots. I soon found what I was looking for. It was a heavy steel tube, about four inches in diameter and more than ten feet long. 'If I can get a foot and a half of this into the ground,' I thought, 'it will stand firm and take one end of a clothesline.' I reckoned it would then be easy to tie the other end of the line to a convenient tree or drainpipe. I soon found the ideal place and as all sensible husbands do, I checked with the wife that I was on the right lines. "Good," was the curt response, followed by an unnecessary exhortation, "That will do, get on with it, I've a load of washing to hang out and for once it has stopped raining."

At first I scratted about like a demented hen, trying to dig a hole for the post but I had no pick, nor yet a shovel, let alone a post hole digger or cement and aggregate to make a concrete foundation. I did however stumble across a fourteen-pound sledgehammer. 'Eureka,' I thought, 'I have found it, the tool I need to drive my tube into the ground and turn it into a post. All that I now need is height.' The height problem I solved with a six-foot stepladder. Without thought for safety, I was soon standing on the top platform of the stepladder, banging away at the top of the post with the sledgehammer I had christened Big Bertha. To my great satisfaction, with each blow the tube was sinking, by fractions of an inch, into the approved spot. After about a hundred pile-driving hammer blows I went back down the steps to feel if the post was firm enough, but was not satisfied. I sensed however, that if I could drive the tube a couple more inches into the ground, I would have a post. Back on the top platform of the six-foot stepladder, I gave the steel tube a few more carefully aimed blows, right on target. It was then that I reverted to type, and committed the near fatal error. Casting caution aside, I convinced myself that I could settle the matter with just one single mighty blow, one hearty whack, one final blistering bash. I raised the by now very heavy sledgehammer, high over my head, and swung it down, full force, for the coup de grâce. I missed.

Not arrested by any impact with the tube, Big Bertha's massive head followed her natural inclination. The wedge in the thick end of the long wooden handle held the fourteen-pound lump of steel secure. Foolishly, I still held fast to the other end of that same handle. Big Bertha's head swept past by my feet with a force the equal of a scratch golfer driving off the tee of a par five hole into a strong headwind. Following Newton's Law that action and reaction are equal and opposite, and not having spikes in my shoes, natural science took its part in my downfall. Momentum overcame inertia forcing my mass to rotate around the fulcrum of my middle to be disposed in a horizontal attitude, at an elevation more than three feet above the top platform of the six-foot step-ladder. I did not have the time to calculate that this positioned my centre of gravity more than nine feet above ground level, before Newton's Law of gravity took over. With no alternative available to me, I fell to the ground. Not having a cat's ability to turn in free fall, I dropped, still in horizontal attitude, until my descent was checked by Mother Earth. It all happened so quickly that I did not have time to be con-

# It Could be a Little Gold Mine

cerned for my welfare.

On impact, I lay winded, laughing with relief that I was unhurt. Once again, my luck had held. I had not broken anything; Jeanne need never know. I was about to get up and go back up the ladder to finish the job, when the enormity of my foolishness came home to me with a force greater than gravity. As I lay, flat on my back, I saw I had cheated death by less than four inches. Sticking vertically out of the ground, halfway between my elbow and chest, was a concrete reinforcing rod. It was a frightening ten inches of high tensile steel, as sharp as an assassin's dagger. I dare not tell Jeanne about it, if I had, she would probably have killed me. I demurred; to risk a violent end twice in a morning would have been leaving too much to chance, even with my luck.

My second memorable accident at the inn occurred in my kitchen. It could have been serious but, once again, I was lucky. It was all to do with chivalry, vanity, inexperience, my stupidity and a pressure cooker. All accidents are the result of many circumstances.

Once they had settled in, I found the first two young ladies who we employed direct from college a delight to work with. I do not think they felt the same about working with me. On a good day, both girls thought me to be a direct relative of Mr Bumble, the workhouse master in Dickens' novel *Oliver Twist*. On normal days, they rated me to be worse than Wackford Squeers, the horrid Yorkshire headmaster, in *Nicholas Nickleby*.

One day, when I came into the kitchen, I knew straight away, from the unmistakable smell, that one or other of the two little maids from school had let a pan boil dry. What concerned me more was that one of the girls, Caroline, was strug-

# Accidents Will Happen

gling with the handles of a pressure cooker. "Stop." I bellowed, "leave it; I will deal with it." Careful of the power of steam, I filled the main kitchen sink with cold water and completely immersed the pressure cooker, adding some weights to keep it submerged. Once I was sure that it had all cooled down and the steam pressure gone, I thought it would be a good idea to teach the girls a lesson in safety. I asked them to watch carefully. "You see you will be able to tell if the pressure has gone if you can gently and without applying any force, slide the handles apart. Whatever you do, don't try to force the handles apart like this."

The flash and bang were impressive. A sheet of scalding steam caught me across the eyes, nose and forehead. I immediately plunged my head straight into the cold water still in the sink. This limited the scald, but what a sight. Blisters covered all the upper part of my face. The following morning, I was due to pick Jeanne up after a few days holiday she had spent with her mother. I looked like the *Mummy's Return*. Sheets of pure white dead skin sloughed from my face. It was like a rerun of the *Quatermass Experiment*.

I rang Jeanne to warn her that I looked like an exfoliating Dead Sea parchment scroll, and to remind her that beauty is only skin deep. I must have looked terrible. More than twenty years later, when I went to the local surgery for a routine test, the clinic nurse gave me a friendly greeting. She told her colleague that I had given her the biggest fright of her nursing career when she was a young student nurse, and I had stuck my exfoliating head round the casualty room door to ask, "Can you do anything with scalds?"

For the accident-prone, it is reassuring to learn that other unfortunates also suffer from the condition, sometimes to an

# It Could be a Little Gold Mine

extent worse than their own.

Pasquale Mazzerella came to work with me in the kitchen and stayed for about three years while he saved money and searched for a business of his own. He is a truly great chef who has never received due recognition. Pasquale, from the deep south of Italy, had worked in kitchens in most European countries and could cook in any style asked of him. When he joined us, he agreed to cook strictly according to my style, using my recipes and methods. He never failed me. He was at least ten years younger than me, but his dark complexion and face, riven with deep lines, made him look a good ten years older, but he was easy going and easy to work with. Sometimes, during the quiet of an afternoon, while he got on with prep for the evening rush, he would entertain us with stories of his life in continental kitchens. His tales of drama and accidents were endless, but one still gives me nightmares and reinforces my conviction that management theory has no place in running any small unit catering for the public.

He told us of a club dinner that he cooked for, in Germany. It was at the lower end of the price range, a simple meal; soup, followed by a plated roast pork knuckle with sundry vegetables, then gateaux for the dessert. From the kitchen, he could see the waiters serving the soup when his commis chef called to him, "Eh! Pasquale, the oven, he go out." The oven referred to was the gas fired hot cupboard in which were stacked over one hundred plated meals. Aluminium rings separated and stacked the meals ready for service, piping hot, in a few minutes time. "Don't" was all that Pasquale had time to shout before the commis chef, acting on his own initiative, did exactly what Pasquale had tried to stop him from doing. He bent down to relight the gas with his cig-

# Accidents Will Happen

arette lighter. The explosion took the windows out of the kitchen, left the commis hatless, with singed hair and no eyebrows, but no serious injury. Inside the cupboard, however, the main course was now just slurry. It was an unrecoverable mess of pottery shards, twisted aluminium, meat and three veg all tangled with sauerkraut.

Many times, I have tried to think of what I would have done, if faced with Pasquale's dilemma, but always failed to find an answer. It is a salutary tale that confirms the obvious to those of us who cook for the public. You only get one shot and you are only as good as your last meal.

The more difficult accidents to deal with are those that Jeanne and I, or members of our staff, have inflicted on our customers. One of my most spectacular involved a tray of drinks, with two pints of beer, an ice-cold lager, two gin and tonics, both with ice and lemon, a glass of red wine and a Coke with ice. I failed to lift the tray high enough to clear the top of the beer engine handles when I passed it over the bar. This tilted the tray and cascaded all the drinks, as one supercocktail, over the grey shirtfront and white, starched stiff, back to front collar of a visiting vicar. This cold douche occurred at two o'clock in the morning when the visiting vicar had called for "Just one more round please landlord." Did he suspect that it might have been deliberate? It was not, it was just me.

Jeanne dropped a huge bowl of scalding hot chips into the lap of a customer who had arrived for a late dinner. He told us his party had, that evening, walked out of the restaurant where they had originally booked their meal, because the service had been so bad. Did they possibly think we were conspiring with the first restaurant? No, it was just an accident

# It Could be a Little Gold Mine

and they became regular customers and firm friends.

Thom Olshansky, a young Dutchman with a talent for dealing with customers of all ages and types, showed us the professional approach to dealing with minor accidents. Thom had circus in his blood and could perform wonderful acrobatics. He told us that his name came from *Circus Olshansky,* who had fostered, or perhaps kidnapped, his Danish father and brought him up to work in the circus. After the war, the Iron Curtain had trapped the circus in Eastern Europe, leaving his father in the West. Thom's father left circus life to become a restaurateur and Thom was determined to follow in his footsteps.

A young area sales manager, offensively loud, was at the head of a table for eight, where he had seven of his older colleagues under his screw. He was all modern management speak, demanding sycophantic attention from his underlings. He was boring them, and me, rigid, with tales of his superior sales technique and about the better class restaurants than our crummy joint that he normally frequented. Thom, while silver serving a richly sauced dish, spilt a small bead of the sauce onto the immaculate sleeve of the Young Turk's suit. The suit was a silver shiny lightweight job typical of those worn by the young lightweight sales managers of the time. His reaction was as expected: "You clumsy fool, you incompetent idiot, you've spilt on my sleeve, you have ruined the suit. It was brand new, you'll have to pay me for a new one." Thom, playing the continental accent to the full, "Monsieur, my pardon, I am so sorry. Please do not worry; in my country, we have a special way to treat this. Please let me take your coat, I shall see to it, immédiatement monsieur."

In the kitchen, Thom, using a nailbrush, simply scrubbed

# Accidents Will Happen

and rinsed the spot under cold running water. Then he was off upstairs for a coat hanger. Quickly, he tucked two inches of the scrubbed and rinsed sleeve back up into itself. Holding the coat on the hanger, high over his head, with one sleeve now apparently shorter than the other, he grabbed our largest pair of poultry scissors. With his left hand now holding both the coat on its hanger and the huge poultry scissors, he noisily burst back into the restaurant, drawing the attention of everybody to what he was carrying. It worked, I am sure that it worked every time he did it. The young manager, for a few seconds only, lost his cool. He was halfway out of his seat, intent on murder, when the wave of laughter from the other diners penetrated his inflamed brain and stopped him. He resumed his seat and ruefully returned to his meal but, for that evening at least, Thom's little act had punctured the sales manager's super-inflated ego. The seven colleagues, previously his menials, were now at least his equal, and harmony came to his table.

Some accidents are pure serendipity. I had a poor start with the planning officers of the Peak District National Park, but we did get their consent to convert the derelict coach house, into two modern flats. However, the nit-picking planners, unable to give a straightforward approval, had insisted that we alter our design. They specified that the three simple vertical first floor bedroom window gables should be haunch and tile. All of the eight gables in the main building are simple, not haunch and tile. A quick drive around the town of Ashbourne and the neighbouring villages of Fenny Bentley, Thorpe, Tissington and Parwich revealed all gables, whether on cottage or mansion, are of simple vertical construction, not built in the haunch and tile design the planners wanted for our conversion. Working unilaterally, I altered the approved working drawings back to the simple vertical design. The building inspector came on site and said to Stan, the builder's joiner, "You can't have these gables you know, you'll have to get 'em changed to the approved drawings. They've got to be haunch and tile they have." "Well you go and tell him then," says Stan, "I'm not." "Not me," said the inspector. "I'm told he's a bloody tyrant, I'm not risking it. I'll have to report it to my boss, the Planning Control Officer and let him deal with it."

I thought no more about it until I had a telephone call from the head of the Peak Park's Planning Department asking for a site meeting. Obviously, planning control officers, at various levels, had ducked the issue. "Oh! All right then, when?" I replied. "Monday morning, ten o'clock suit you?" "Yes that will do." I was determined not to give in on this issue, as their planners were plain wrong and acting outside their brief. I was fully prepared and had my opening gambit planned. I would offer to amend the gables but only if he could show me evidence of haunch and tile construction in the local villages, where I had already established that there were none to be seen.

At the appointed time for the meeting, I was fully charged and ready for a vigorous debate. I was already in the bar when he walked in and he opened without ado, "Mr Allingham, how many cars can you park on your car park?" I felt as though he had pulled the carpet from under my feet. I was rattled, I could not see where he was coming from and had no idea what may be coming next. My carefully rehearsed plan for dealing with the Head Planner was not working. "Well, if the first one parks tidily, about thirty; why?" With a

# Accidents Will Happen

resigned shrug, he continued, "Well there is only one car parked today and I have just destroyed it. I reversed into the side of it, bending back the door pillar. I am afraid it's a write-off. I have left my name, address and insurance details under the windscreen wipers. I have to go now I'm afraid; I have a student with me on work experience. Can we leave it at that?" I just smiled and said in the local vernacular, "Right then." It was no accident, I was sure that the Supreme Architect, with his omnipotent view from heaven, had seen the good sense of my argument and settled the matter in his own way.

There is often comedy associated with accidents. There was even a funny side to the accident that had a profound effect on my family, our business, and me. It was an accident for which, just for once, I was blameless. It happened early in the morning on Sunday 18 October 1987. I had already been to Ashbourne to collect newspapers for our guests and was about to go into the kitchen to cook their breakfasts and prepare for the Sunday Special Carvery Lunch. Unfortunately, I noticed a small calf had got through the neighbouring farmer's fence and was grazing on the roadside. The farmer just happened to be coming down the track in his tractor, complete with muck cart, so I hailed him and pointed to the calf. "Damn it" he said, "I've no time to bother with it now, can we put it in your paddock?" "Surely, I'll help you," I agreed. When I opened the gate, walking backwards with arms outstretched, the ground under me opened. I crashed into a concealed steel-rimmed brick-built manhole. I knew immediately that I was badly hurt.

Jeanne, alerted, somehow got me to bed and said, "Stay there and behave, I'll do breakfast." A little later, having been to Ashbourne, Jeanne was back with a full set of Sunday

# It Could be a Little Gold Mine

newspapers. "The doctor's coming; I've brought these to keep you quiet." By mid-morning, I had picked up the *Sunday Express*, still a broadsheet in those days. All my life I have been agnostic about fortune-telling, but bored, I turned to read the printed half page of horoscopes, particularly the bit about Aquarius, my so-called ruling sign. In an instant, I was on the phone to Jeanne, to read her the forecast. "I take it all back about horoscopes," I said. "I'm a believer, I'm a convert." When I rang my mother, as I always did on Sunday mornings, I told her about my accident and the horoscope. All she said was, "Eee David, you were born awkward."

This accident changed my life, not just my week. My knee and hip had to be fitted with prosthetic joints and it irrevocably damaged my spine. I never worked again in my beloved kitchen. This was the never to be forgotten text of my Aquarian future, predicted by that day's horoscope: "Your plans for the week will fall through, early in the morning."

# CHAPTER SEVEN

# Sex, Politics, Religion and Money

Until the second half of the twentieth century, sex, politics, religion and money were taboo subjects for discussion in polite society. Following convention, publicans and innkeepers of that time decorated their quaint parlour bars with pokerwork plaques, brass castings or skilfully worked and framed needlepoint and tapestry samplers that politely requested their customer to refrain from such vulgarity.

In these first few years of the twenty-first century, things are different. Radio, television and the newspapers distort and debase natural behaviour and people freely and unashamedly talk about all four topics. A couplet, of which I am quite proud, taken from my book of light verse, runs

> *I'll start them talking, sideways if I must,*
> *Their MP paid to touch our vicar's bust.*

There is a tale of politics, money, religion and sex, in just one couplet. I never talk about sex because I do not understand it. About religion, I am unable to offer any opinion. I believe in one God, but have no religious conviction because my intellect points me in one direction but my instinct in the other. Until I know the truth of the path not taken, I shall

# It Could be a Little Gold Mine

stay silent on both sex and religion.

Happily this still leaves two vulgar topics open to me. I will talk of politics and about money with anyone who has a point of view and is prepared to express it. Mind you, Jeanne complains that I do not engage in conversation with our customers. "No," she says, "like Gladstone in audience with Queen Victoria, you address them as though they are a public meeting." As always, she is correct, because deep down I am a frustrated politician.

I took my first direct action in politics when I had a run in with the trade union movement. This was about their peculiar understanding of what they called *Station*, meaning *Class*. After leaving school, aged sixteen, I spent my first year as a student apprentice engineer working in the floor moulding foundry of a north-country boiler works. During my second year, I had to learn something of the work done in the fitting shop with machine tools, spanners, files and micrometers. Here, unlike the foundry, all the workers were members of the GMBU, the General Manufacturing and Boilermakers Union.

It did not take more than a few weeks to learn that the so-called fitters, with whom I now worked, thought themselves to be superior to the foundry workers. They went so far as to believe that they were stationed in a class above them. As I watched the way the fitters and machinists worked, in relatively cool comfort, in comparatively clean overalls, I could not understand, for one moment, their demeaning attitude to the foundry workers. The cupola masters who rendered the pigs of iron into molten metal, the moulders and core makers who fashioned the iron into castings, and the labourers who toiled alongside them, I rated not far short of heroes. I had learned that those grime blackened foundry workers were men of quality. They coped, every working day, with danger and the searing heat of molten iron, as they laboured in choking acrid gloom. Their footing was precarious on the loose, burnt black, powdery, no longer green sand of the foundry floor. There were no pithead baths. All went home with their dirt. They had looked after me, openly taught me their skills and protected me with both kindness and generosity. They were my true friends. I made no friends in the fitting shop.

Mr Hind, the owner of the firm that employed me, took a keen interest in my work. Understanding the pauper state of apprentices, he supported my social life by giving me tickets and cash so that I could go to the local charity balls, dances and concerts. He took me, with his wife and Harry their only son, to events that would extend my education and give me an insight into different ways of life. Altogether, he gave me an education far superior to that which the sixth form of my old school could have given me.

One late afternoon, while operating a large radial drill, I had been talking with Mr Hind for quite some time. This was too much for the small-minded shop stewards of the GMBU. The senior steward, attended by his acolytes, came and stood close to me while I worked. Above the noise of the huge single electric motor that turned the lay shafts and belting that drove the machines, he shouted, "You must not talk to that man again; you are getting above your station." "Oh! what is that to you?" I asked, sure of my ground. "I am not yet eighteen and as an apprentice I am nothing to do with you, nor have you anything to do with me." "Oh is that it, you cheeky young sod, you'll bloody well do as you're told or we'll have you out of here," he shouted. By this time, I had stopped and

# It Could be a Little Gold Mine

locked the drill and was facing him. He looked the image of Peter Sellers in his best film, the black comedy, *I'm alright Jack*. His pressed blue tailored engineer's overalls and leather belt around his waist, picked him out as one of nature's little Hitlers. I was as thin as a rail, but very strong after my year in the foundry. With the supreme confidence of youth, certain of my legal position, and sure of my physical strength, I took him on. "Is that your last word on the matter then?" He, faltering and looking for support from his henchmen shouted, "I've told you, you are getting above your station, we've decided, you're to have nowt to do with him, do yer get it?"

I do not think that he ever fully understood what happened next. Crossing my arms, I tucked my thumbs under his belt, either side of him, and taking a firm grip lifted him clear of the ground, then swivelled him round to invert him. His knees scuffed around my ears a bit, but he was not a big man, and I found this no hardship. I looked round, wondering what to do with him. His colleagues had formed a close tight-knit horseshoe round me, in solidarity with their squealing leader. "Catch," I called, as I threw him the three feet of so, towards them. As one man, in unison, they stepped back. His luck ran out, the horseshoe parted. He hit the floor head first, tearing his scalp quite badly. Only then did they scoop him up, to rush him to the accident room. I heard nothing further from him, the union or Mr Hind, but I was not off the hook.

The hook landed days later. It struck while I was having a quick bite to eat before going to night school. My police inspector father, a handsome man, well over six foot tall, came home after a 10am to 6pm shift, resplendent in his uniform, with cape and cane. His sharp right hook across the back of my head with his pair of tan leather gloves drew to him my full and undivided attention. "What was that for?" I asked, laughing. "That's for throwing the shop steward halfway down the fitting shop floor," he said. "How did you know about that?" His reply to my question, "It's the best piece of gossip for years, it's all round the town," astonished me, but I was not at all contrite. "Well, he deserved it," I said, a bit stubborn like. "Yes; happen he did, good lad, now get off to school." From the look in his eyes and the tone of his voice, I knew that he was proud of me. This little incident cast me in the mould of a true blue Conservative, as strong and enduring as the castings made by my friends in the foundry.

Some thirty years later, an incident at the inn reaffirmed my conviction. The area organiser of the GMBU, the same union who had told me not to get above my station, asked if we could accommodate evening meetings of the senior shop stewards of his area. I agreed they could have the Travellers' Room, free of charge, any Monday night. I thought it only fair because we had given the same facility to the local Conservative Party. My offer was not altogether altruistic, I was sure we could sell them a few beers and perhaps a sandwich, to remind them of the Wilson years at *Number Ten,* and Mondays were always quiet.

The top man became a good cheerful friend until his all too early death a couple of years later. However, his shop steward colleagues were just the same dull bigots that I met all those years ago. They had a meeting on the night that Terry Marsh, a London fireman, became the first British boxer for many years to win a world title. As soon as their meeting finished I went into the room to give them the good news. To a man, they chorused, "He'd nowt to beat." I with-

# It Could be a Little Gold Mine

drew, depressed as Churchill with his 'Black Dog'. Once again, I was sure of my conviction that men of their ilk will bring our once great nation state to darkness, for even on a good night they cannot see the stars.

When Jeanne and I came home to England from capitalist Hong Kong, our shared belief in conservative values gave us the confidence to go into business on our own behalf. What we got wrong was the capitalist bit. I failed to realise that we did not have enough of it. Knowing no other way, we determined to run our business on proper business lines, fiddle free. There would be no cash in hand transactions, no undeclared staff, nor any separate tills or books. We both came from families that taught us to abhor such fraud. My father would not get off a crowded bus until he had paid his fare, however long he delayed its onward journey.

Jeanne's father, Jack Edwards, a land agent's taxation accountant, was scrupulous, not even allowing his aristocrat clients to pass off their hunters as farm animals. He was also Secretary of the Market Harborough Conservative Club for a record forty-four years. Although sometimes it caused problems, the long-term proved that our policy was the right one for us. With an open book, we have been able to secure support from banks and breweries, even though their loans were not always to our best advantage. However, over the years, we have seen many an apparently more successful business than ours suddenly go bankrupt after a VAT or Inland Revenue investigation. During the hard times, it did not help that so many people gave us nods and winks and tried to barter by offering cash. "No need to put it through the books old boy," was the usual suggestion. On one occasion, the manager of a large London branch of one of the *Big Five* banks tried to arrange a function by offering to pay cash, if we would give him a receipted bill for more than it cost and lose our copy. "You see," he said "that way is fair, because we will share equally in the saving on tax and VAT." We refused and lost a function that would have helped our cash flow and would have been profitable even with all tax and VAT paid.

I understand that in the years just after the war, fraud in the pub trade was rife. The joke going the rounds amongst publicans was "Have you heard about Fred at the Red Lion? Poor fellow has gone doolally; the men in white coats came and took him away. He got confused and banked the fiddle instead of the take."

We chose a bad time when we bought the inn. It was during the Labour Government's Callaghan, then Healey years. They were in a deep hole and kept on digging. The Midland Bank imposed interest charges on our account that peaked at 24 percent and stayed over 20 percent for three years. This was at a time when we were committed to paying private school fees for the three boys and huge bills for restoration of the fabric of the building, particularly to meet the needs of health and safety. The bank did what banks do in these situations. They put a limit on our overdraft facility. They demanded business plans and complicated cash flow projections. Worse, they charged huge sums for their trouble when they returned cheques or wrote us unnecessary letters at £50 a time. Inevitably came the day when the bank had had enough of us and we were *called in*. The manager of the Midland Bank in Halifax, where we had kept our account, summoned us to appear before him. He was a certain Mr Twyte, who, more to his embarrassment than ours, had a son in the same house as our three boys at Uppingham. It was a cold

# It Could be a Little Gold Mine

and bleak journey north, made more miserable by Mr Twyte telling us that he held the deeds to our property and had no alternative but to put the inn up for sale. We realised that a forced sale by the bank would leave us with nothing and probably still in debt to our suppliers and contractors. When we left I did manage to say, "Well we'll just have to go to another and better bank, we are not going to give up now." To this he replied "Yes, I know that you will make a success of the business, I'm sorry, it's the bank, my hands are tied."

Out in the cold, we got straight back into the car and set off for home without even calling on mother or brother John, always our custom when visiting Halifax. In the car, always considered the board room, we confirmed our intention to go ahead. I said, "I'll go and see Eric." In Eric, we found a completely different attitude. Customers, who sensed our difficulty, told me that the hard-pressed local farming community called him Santa Claus.

In just a few months, his lending strategy had raised his branch from being a minor player to undisputed lead bank for local businesses. I rang to make an appointment hoping to go to see him. "Better if I come and see you," he said, "how about tomorrow, about eleven, so that I can get a feel of things." I was surprised at the prompt response and replied "Good, I will have the books ready for you and we can have a look around." His visit took hardly any time and very soon we were sitting with cups of tea and coffee, facing each other. He opened the formalities with "Well, as it is, things could be better," and then it came. "But we shall come through," Churchill's inspiring phrase from his famous speech 'Let it roar, let it rage...' given in a radio broadcast in May 1941. I could hardly believe what I had heard. "We shall come through." A bank manager who was with us, here there was commitment, what a difference from Twyte's trite remark "I'm sorry, it's the bank, my hands are tied."

With the breathing space given to the business by the bank and the passing of the Labour Government, the interest rates eased. Turnover increased and our profit margins improved. The improved economic climate allowed us to carry out further improvements to the all-important fabric and buildings. However, cash is king and we never had enough of it. Eric retired and the new incumbent manager did not have the same control over funds.

As a policy, we operated close to the overdraft limit, intent on investing to achieve the property we wanted. The swings

# It Could be a Little Gold Mine

of seasonal variation in cash flow every winter led to problems. An opportunity came up that we had to seize or lose forever. I heard, through local gossip, that the adjoining five-acre field might be coming on the market. The field was the same that had been lost on the turn of a card a few months before we bought the inn and had brought us so much grief with the boundary dispute. I did not want to risk a public auction so immediately called the owner. To my relief she agreed to sell us the field at a price set by a local land agent. The agent came, walked the land and the price was set at £5000. I rang the new manager at the bank and asked to see him as soon as may be convenient. In his plush office, after a general chat, I came to the point. "I need another five thousand to buy the five-acre field of adjoining land." "Sorry David," he said looking a bit grim. "It's just not on. You're not the only one at your limit. So am I." I am not authorised to go above certain values and your account is already there. You are on what they call *special watch*." I was now a little anxious, "But you must realise that we should buy it," I replied. "Of course I do," was the immediate response and he went on, "Do you have any other loans that I don't know about?" "No," I replied, "we used to have one with Lombard but it's paid off." "Then for God's sake let's ring Lombard, I'm sure they will come through." There we were, at his desk, scrabbling for the number through the local telephone directories, he with the main directory, me with the *Yellow Pages*. "Here we are" he said, scribbling down the number and passing me both the paper and phone. "Ring them now." "Hello, my name's Allingham, we once had a loan with you and I would now like to borrow five thousand pounds." Across the desk, our bank manager was all excited. "Tell them it's to buy land." I did as he suggested. "Hello, Mr Allingham, we have you on record, yes your credit is good, that will be fine, on a personal basis, and as it is for a land purchase we will knock half a point off the interest. Come in tomorrow when we will have the cheque ready for you."

"Damn good, well done," said the manager, as he left his desk and went over to his elegant sideboard. "This calls for a celebration. Sherry, sweet or dry? Let's sit in comfort, I've got a few minutes." We two sat smiling at each other, like Ratty and Mole, snug in the comfort of the deep leather armchairs, pleased at our shared adventure. As I sipped the warming sweet rich Bual, my thoughts drifted back to that cold, cold day in Halifax when we had been *called in*. I was sure that although at times the pressures were great and the way through hard, I would not change places with any manager, bank or otherwise, for all the tea in China or sherry in Spain.

Fed up with reporting to the bank each month and with their quarterly review meetings for little purpose, irritated by the burden of their charges, we finally arranged a soft loan with a brewery. This type of loan arrangement is not as good as being debt free, but has the advantage of no interference in the day to day operation of the business and of greater help; no meetings, no reviews, no hidden charges and with our latest arrangement no interest charged, providing we sell an agreed quota of their product.

I still buy my weekly lottery ticket and play the football pools using the same numbers each week. I dream that one day, one day soon, I shall be able to take Jeanne into the garden to look at the inn with its restaurants, bar, brewery, the beautiful gardens, and say, "All this is ours. Now what are we going to do?"

# CHAPTER EIGHT

# For the Love of Cooking

*For those who cook with love, they have rewards on earth,*
*Simple satisfaction in culinary art.*
*Their partners do not stray; they know each other's worth,*
*And young cooks find the way, to win their fancies heart.*
*The best is yet to come, when cooks this earth do part;*
*For there's a special place, kept in heaven above,*
*Air-conditioned kitchens, for those who cook with love.*

An enthusiasm for food and my love of cooking, drove me for the ten years that I was chef at our inn. Given half a chance I would talk, to anyone who would listen, about my food philosophy, my kitchen commandments and cook's proverbs. Even so, I did have doubts. Was my passion truly a love of co.oking, for its own sake? Maybe not; perhaps it was more to do with my bursting pride when occasionally I heard guests say, "That was good," after they had eaten a meal I had prepared, cooked and served. The act of cooking does have pleasures of its own relating to all the senses. It also has excitement and satisfaction when an untried recipe turns out to be just right. There is also fun to be had when creating a new dish, or presenting an old dish in a new way.

"Who me? I can't boil an egg, I can't be doing with all that mess," is the usual response when I ask a customer, "Do

# For the Love of Cooking

you like cooking?" When pressed, the more considered reply, from those who will engage in conversation, is the flat statement, "Oh no, I only cook when I have to. I havn't the time." Then, perhaps adding by way of a defence, "All those pots and pans, all that washing-up." If I press on and cajole them to describe a meal or just a simple dish that they have prepared for friends, more often than not there is a great change. "Oh! that was different; yes, I'll admit I was ever so pleased when they said how much they had enjoyed it." They invariably go on to say, "and do you know, I didn't have a thing in the house and I didn't use a recipe."

Is it only the plaudits of our guests, or even better our families, that drives some of us to say that we love to cook? Are we who declare our love of cooking, no different from old impoverished thespians, who, when friends suggest that they should try for other work, having not been offered a part for more than ten years, declaim "What, and give up the stage?" Is it all just pure theatre, in four acts? Shopping, Preparation, Cooking, and Presentation.

I was a fifteen-year-old boy scout when, for the first time, recognition of my cooking skill delighted me. The whole troop of thirty or so boys, and half a dozen masters, enjoyed a simple meal I prepared and cooked for their lunch. The compliments from masters and boys alike made me realise that cooking was both fun and rewarding. I was camping in North Yorkshire with the school troop when early one morning, Old Bill, one of the schoolmasters, a veteran worker from the Middle East oilfields, called to me, "Nah then Allingham, why don't you cook a good dinner for the whole troop today?" The previous day he had seen me prepare a simple supper for my patrol of ten boys. Dinner was of course lunch,

# It Could be a Little Gold Mine

the main meal of the day, he was suggesting. "But I cooked yesterday," I replied. "Good," he chuckled, "you've had some practice then." I was secretly pleased and sure that, given some help I could do it. First, I would need a big fire and with Old Bill's help, I collared all the juniors and had them scour the riverbank to get firewood. I then explained that the cupboard was a bit bare and asked him to go shopping in the village of West Tanfield. "Will you get some beef suet please, the stuff in a packet already minced and floured, and baking powder, and oh, some dried mixed herbs; you know, the sort that come in a sort of tea bag sir." I knew we had potatoes, onion, carrots, swede, flour, salt, tins of corned beef and a small carton of Oxo cubes.

It was obvious to me that the solution was a stew as it would be easy to cook, but I thought stew on its own to be boring. However, I was sure that a herb pan dumpling would make all the difference. I had often watched my mother make small individual dumplings to drop late into a seething stew, but occasionally, as a special treat, she made what she called a pan dumpling. For these the suet and flour, mixed with herbs and moistened with water were rolled out, as one piece, shaped to exactly fit the pan and so completely cover the stew. This neat arrangement forced the steam from the simmering stew to pass up though the dumpling duvet. This arrangement forces it to rise and enriches it with wonderful flavour. Such a dish was for me a clear choice. My pressed men, having found a stack of good dry wood, were set to peel and prepare the vegetables. My cooking pot was my secret weapon. It was an ex-army fire blackened nine-gallon dixie, oval in shape, with a tight fitting lid designed to prevent spillage. The army used these dixies to carry water in their

# For the Love of Cooking

hard-sprung vehicles over the rough desert sands of Africa and the rutted fields and ditches of Europe. It was ideal for my purpose.

Once my sheath knife had proved that the vegetables were nearly cooked, I added the cubed corned beef and gently laid the rolled-out suet and herb dumpling mixture to float over the stew. I had mixed and moulded the single dumpling to match the oval shape of the dixie to make sure it would seal at the edges. Finally, I fitted the lid, swung the dixie over the fire for the last time and gave the young scouts the task of stoking the flames. Less than half an hour later, the result was perfection. The stew was tasty, the suet crust as thick as my wrist, and as light and white as swan's-down.

The whole troop sat or lay back, well-full and satisfied, in that quiet mood of contemplation that follows a good meal. Old Bill broke the spell, "Well done lad, what's for dinner tomorrow?" I knew that I had succeeded and was as pleased as if I had scored a winning try or taken all ten wickets in a school match. It was the start of my love of cooking, but it was to be more than a quarter of a century before the pecuniary bonds that tied me to my profession of engineer were broken and I found my true vocation as a cook.

My departure from Hong Kong, where I had worked for twelve years, was marked with a headline in the *Hong Kong Standard*, 'Engineer leaves on highest note'. I was Ir Allingham, Immediate Past President of the Hong Kong Institution of Engineers, CEng, HonFHKIE. FIMechE, F.Inst.Arb, and a few more letters besides and I held a Diploma in Management Studies. I was well enough experienced and qualified to further my career in the Middle East where a multinational company had offered me a senior management position.

# It Could be a Little Gold Mine

However, being qualified and experienced in that field, I could see pitfalls in such a career move.

Fortunately, I had never taken any lessons in cooking. I was totally unqualified in catering, hotel management, or inn-keeping. I had no certificates in book-keeping, hygiene or in the dark arts of the sommelier or cellar management, nor for that matter any other qualification of academic or practical relevance to the hospitality industry. Therefore, it was with a clear sense of purpose and total confidence that I assumed my duties at the Bentley Brook Inn. I was to be Chef in charge of the kitchen, Cellar and Bars Manager, Wine Buyer, Chief Accountant and Financial Controller. I also had the sideline jobs of gardener, tree mortician, and maintenance superintendent. Jeanne had the far more complex and difficult front of house duties; housekeeping and dealing with customers. All these duties she had to manage at the same time as looking after our home, our three growing sons and me.

It was just as well that I did lack the basic prerequisites for success in the trade. If Jeanne and I had paused to work out a business plan or measured our skills against those that Management consultants set out as essential for success in the hospitality industry, we would have baulked at the opportunity and not bought the Bentley Brook Hotel.

The division of labour was an easy choice. With no cash reserve, there was no chance to experiment, there were no funds for research, and there was no time for planning. Within two hours of our taking over the inn, I had gone into the kitchen to cook and Jeanne had served our first meals. The customers paid for the meals and did not send them back. Base instinct, a little Yorkshire cunning, and twenty years' experience on the other side of kitchen counters around

# For the Love of Cooking

the world, were all that I had to guide me.

Jeanne was much better prepared to deal with what the hotel trade call *front of house*. Her nursing career, and later in Hong Kong, bringing up our three boys almost single handed, had honed her natural ability to cope with people, however peculiar. Jeanne also brought the invaluable assets of her beauty and gifts as a charming hostess.

It was the kitchen and cooking for me. Dead easy I thought. All that I would have to do would be to copy and recreate the very best of what I had eaten during my travels around the world. I picked up my early culinary education in England, first in Berni Inns and Bradford baltis, then with my regiment where we dined very well. My expense account with Hongkong Electric covered the cost of learning about exotic dishes that I ate in fine and humble restaurants and kitchens from Hong Kong to Hawaii, Belgium to Brazil, Lebanon to Los Angeles and Ghana to the Ginza.

My travels had given me well-founded confidence and a clear understanding that 'nothing to do with cooking is difficult'. It is my creed, formed long ago, but which I believe in to this day. This clarity of purpose and understanding came from observing cooks around the world. I saw cooks working with what I thought to be strange exotic ingredients, but which to them were just local produce, which they daily used to create their regional cuisine. Some may consider my creed that 'nothing to do with cooking is difficult' is nonsense, but I affirm it is true; I brook no contradiction; I have it on the best authority. During the early years of the twentieth century, Auguste Escoffier, known as the Chef to Kings and the King of Chefs wrote, 'I never found cooking difficult. It is choosing the menu that is hard'.

# It Could be a Little Gold Mine

I soon understood that there are only six ways to cook: to roast, bake, boil, steam, fry, or grill. Similarly, I learned that there are only six ways to make a sauce: to aerate, reduce, coagulate, liaise, purée, or bind. I realised that all I had to do was to master these simple tasks and the rest would be easy, just common sense. Most of the time I got things about right. Sometimes, however, I lost all sense, let alone the common one. On one occasion, when required to prepare a dinner for about twenty-five ladies, I thought, to give them a treat, I would cook a hot salmon mousse with a crayfish sauce. It would have been perfect had I not served it as a main course. It was so rich that two small spoonfuls as a starter would have satisfied the best of trenchermen. For the ladies, as a main course, it was sickening. It nearly all came back, fortunately to the kitchen not the bathroom, virtually untouched. The dish was a triumph, the menu a disaster and I was a sadder but wiser man.

The desire to produce the best possible meals for our customers was part of my love of cooking and led to many a cross word from me when I did not get a satisfactory answer to my question, "Who is it for?" when Jeanne put up an order. I felt it was imperative to know for whom I was cooking. I was always sure that I could make a dish better fit for its purpose if I knew who was going to eat it. I could make subtle changes if it were for a hearty man in the prime of life, or if I thought the dish overrich or overfacing for an elderly lady. This overwhelming desire to prepare the best for everyone, led inevitably, to costly overspends on ingredients and errors in projected profit. Thus, as with other passions, the path of my true love of cooking did not run smooth.

In any restaurant kitchen, there are good days and bad

# For the Love of Cooking

days. Our worst days were when we tried, of necessity, to do everything ourselves. Sometimes sheer exhaustion took all the pleasure out of cooking and when a complaint came to me in the kitchen about an over or undercooked dish, or more usually of the time a customer had had to wait, it was difficult not to feel totally crushed. Our livelihood was at stake.

The absolute nadir came early. We had taken over the inn late in October. Mr Sergeant, the previous owner, had already taken the bookings for Christmas Day lunch. All tables on the ground floor, both sides of the bar and in both restaurants, and more besides, had been reserved for small family parties. The menu was simple, soup, a plated meal of roast turkey, followed by Christmas pudding, all at very little cost. It was not at all the sort of meal we would have offered, but we were committed. Worse, the previous owners had not passed on the deposits they had collected, so we would be working for next to nothing.

I planned to do all the necessary preparation on Christmas Eve, during the day, because we had a full house of residents to feed in the evening. I had been up *betimes* as Samuel Pepys says in his diary, and with Jeanne's help was just halfway through cooking breakfast for the guests, when click, the electricity failed. This made life a little difficult as much of the preparation for the Christmas lunch needed heat. The power failure lasted a full twelve hours, until eight in the evening, giving us just a chance to cook and serve dinner to our resident guests. That done, I worked all through the night playing catch-up. Then breakfast for the house guests and turkeys in the oven, with all the trimmings. The records show that, by four o'clock in the afternoon, we had cooked, served, and cleared one hundred and thirty Christmas dinners and we still

# It Could be a Little Gold Mine

had to do the washing-up. I sat down for the first time in thirty-three and a half hours and felt so exhausted that I told Jeanne I thought I might be having a heart attack, but a few cups of tea later, I realised I was to live to fight another day. We vowed, then and there, to go a bit more up-market. No more than fifty at a sitting, but all at four times the cost.

The busy evenings spent in the kitchen, with my friend chef Pasquale, were the good times for me. Together we would go at it, hammer and tongs, preparing, cooking and presenting, our *Innkeeper's Table* dishes. We offered the customers a choice of eight first courses, four soups served as a separate course, five fish dishes that they could take as a separate or as a main course and eight main courses. It was a logistical challenge on our limited equipment, our memory and stamina. I now tease the chefs, telling them that all we had was a Bunsen burner and a Baby Belling cooker. It is an exaggeration but not much. Even so, we talked as we worked, happy in each other's company. "What are you doing?" I remember asking, one very busy Saturday night. I was surprised because he was pouring out flour from a three-kilogram bag, without measuring. "I make a few apple pies for tomorrow," he replied. He was doing this at nine o'clock in the evening, during the height of service with the whole kitchen as hot as an oven. Dover soles and steaks at risk under the fierce salamander grill, soups seething in pans over gas rings and main courses in and out of the oven or frying pans, ready for Jeanne's call. Pasquale carried on calm and assured adding, when a few seconds allowed, butter, eggs, sugar, and milk, all unmeasured into the ring he had formed of the flour. No bowl, no blender, just his hands; never a drop spilt and perfect pastry every time.

# For the Love of Cooking

When the last dish had gone out and we were told that the atmosphere in the restaurant was good, it gave both of us a deal of satisfaction and we would nod to each other in recognition of each other's worth. We did not go in for any of the hysterical back thumping and jigging foolery of athletes and soccer players, though we had played longer and harder than athletes do for most sports. I would head for the bar to drink a pint or three, Pasquale headed home to his family, leaving the juniors to wipe down the tables and mop the floor.

Pasquale left us to set up in a restaurant of his own. We were sad to lose him but encouraged him in his desire to have his own family business. I was proud to learn that on his menu, he featured some of the dishes we had cooked together. In his choice of restaurant he made a serious error by not picking the right location. The resort he chose on the Lincolnshire coast is the last refuge of those who know the price of everything and the value of nothing. On his annual visit to his family and friends in Ashbourne, he calls on us and we sit together, he with strong black coffee and me with a pot of tea, and compare our prices. For the same dish cooked in the same way, Pasquale has never been able to get his price to more than two thirds of what we charge at our inn in rural Derbyshire.

Yes, there is a love of cooking for its own sake. Love is sensuous and the tasks of the cook lead deep into all five senses. As I worked alone in the late afternoons preparing for the coming evening's dinner guests, I had these senses all to myself. The intoxicating smell of simmering red wine from a casserole, mixing with the softer yeast odour of baking bread rolls was worth a pound a minute and that of bacon in the

# It Could be a Little Gold Mine

pan at breakfast, twice the price. The sight of a golden roast turkey, or a perfect crust on a pie, or better still the almost luminescent sheen of a well-made sauce were magic to me. Touch had its place. The soft yielding of rising dough when it was being knocked back by my floured hand, the strangely sensuous tactile feel of the knife cutting pastry to shape round the top of a plate pie. The texture of well-made crumble topping, rubbed between thumbs and fingers, ready for one of our Sunday lunch puddings. Sounds brought their own pleasure. Who would not enjoy the rustle of whitebait cooked just right, as it cascaded into a large silver dish, or the glass-like shattering of salted roast pork crackling, being cut by the carving knife? Then of course taste, the most exciting of all. Every day brought new flavours to test and savour, to delight the palate if all was well, or to signal for emergency corrective action if it were not. Finally, for the loving cook, there is yet one more sense, the sixth sense of the cook, that sense of satisfaction in a job well done.

Cooking is also drama; certainly it was for me on those few occasions of precious memory when, with the last of the main courses away, I threw down my kitchen cloth, donned a clean apron, walked through to the restaurant to be greeted by a spontaneous standing ovation. On those nights I was certainly sure I was where I should be, happy in my true vocation; a cook.

# CHAPTER NINE

# Marketing and Media Matters

It was my own fault; I should not have suggested it in the first place. Unknown to me then, my remark was the first step along a path that would to lead me from my profession as an engineer to my true vocation as a cook. I let it slip during a management meeting when the subject was the need to build a new electric power generating station to meet the rising demand. My comment, "We should start a marketing campaign," first caused silence, then uproar, then laughter. At the time, I was Assistant Chief Engineer of the Hongkong Electric Company. Before the incredulous laughter from my colleagues finally subsided the Chief Executive broke in, "What are you on about? We are having enough difficulty keeping up with demand as it is." "Well," I replied, "a properly directed marketing campaign could influence the peak demand problem we have. This would save fuel, increase our efficiency and possibly delay the need for capital investment in new plant." The response from my peers around the table was unanimous ridicule. I did not mind that, but I did mind their complete lack of understanding of the powers of marketing. I therefore held my council thinking I would hear no more about it. Discussion moved on and the meeting broke up at about 6 pm. First thing the following morning an internal open memo, without envelope, from the Chief Executive,

# It Could be a Little Gold Mine

landed on my desk. Printed on the back of an old fan-fold computer report, cut down to A5 size, it did not look as important as it was. I had forgotten management's golden rule: 'If anyone suggests anything new, make them responsible for it'. The message was stark, short and simple. In addition to your present duties as Assistant Chief Engineer you are now *Marketing and Public Relations Manager*. As usual, there was no mention of a change in salary. I rang the Chief Executive and said "Yes I'll do it, but only if you change the title to *Marketing and Public Affairs Manager*." Public relations people have always irritated me. Later events proved my dislike of their kind well-founded. My alteration of title was agreed but the substance of the job remained.

With one additional memo, telling me that the directors wanted me to appoint a public relations consultancy, the brief note was, and remained, my only guidance. It was obvious that I would need to appoint an advertising agency to help me and the few staff I recruited, to run the campaign. The first task was easy. I invited six internationally famous advertising agencies to make proposals. All came up with relevant, competent and professionally worked out strategies. I judged the Australian branch of Ogilvy, Benson, and Mather a clear winner and appointed them our agents. Once they understood my style of direction, their work was outstanding and they never let me down.

Conscious of the old adage - *Never ask a consultant the time, for he will ask to borrow your watch so he may tell you*, I gave them their brief in the shortest possible terms. Thereafter, I provided no further clue to my ideas, nor did I give them a hint that they may be on the right lines when they were making good sense. Until they made proposals that I was confident would work, my only comment on their storyboards and strategy statements was simple, Clem Atlee's; *Not up to it*. I would not entertain further discussion as to why. When they got it right, they had my unqualified, unequivocal approval.

I had no such luck with public relations companies. I invited six firms to propose how they would manage my company's relations with our more than one million customers, the public in general and the media. All were incompetent, but one was outstanding in its complete lack of understanding of the role of a public utility. This firm invited a colleague and me to witness a presentation at their head office in Central Hong Kong at the unusual hour of 6.30 pm. We arrived promptly, at the appointed time and rang the bell in a deserted reception lobby. An untidy youth showed us to a bare room with a single lamp hanging low from the centre of the ceiling. Scattered around on the bare wooden boards of the carpetless floor were a dozen or so plastic beanbags.

After about ten minutes, their chief honcho hove to, dressed in jeans, a loose shirt, no tie and the inevitable sandals with no socks. "Hi guys," he said. "Good to greet you, I thought we would just shack down with a beer or two and toss a few ideas around to get a handle on what you want." "No" says I. "Unless you can arrange for a proper table and chairs the meeting will be cancelled and your company will not be considered." "OK guys, sure thing, why don't we chaps go to the Captain's Bar and have a little libation while my girlies get a room ready." "No, we will come back in half an hour," was my frosty response.

On our second visit, our honcho host took us to the same room. Now there was a table, there were chairs and there was Gloria. The odious fellow introduced Gloria as their *Executive*

# It Could be a Little Gold Mine

*Assistant for the project.* Gloria was a twenty-something Chinese. From the ground up, she was wearing white high-heeled slingback shoes, a pencil slim, very short black skirt, and a diaphanous, transparent light blue blouse. No other garment was visible. She had a very pretty face, framed by long straight jet-black hair.

Clearly hoping that I would be distracted, the odious agent sat Gloria, the *Executive Assistant for the project*, in a chair immediately opposite me. Throughout the meeting she spoke not a word. From the start however, she played her part. With her right hand she slowly undid the two middle pearl buttons of the gossamer light blouse and all the meeting long, gently stroked her left breast, teasing her nipple to the state that would have allowed one to hang one's hat on it. I was intrigued but not distracted because I suspected worse was to follow. My poor colleague was mesmerised and took no part in the meeting. I realised that the centre light contained a microphone and I began to suspect the purpose of the long horizontal mirror on the wall. Making an excuse to go to the lavatory, I opened an adjacent door in the corridor and saw, as I suspected, that the mirror was a one-way window on the group discussing my company. A large old-fashioned tape recorder was running. I persuaded my board not to appoint any public relations company. The whole affair confirmed my instinctive dislike of these parasites.

I have only prattled on with these stories because I want you to know that before Jeanne and I bought the inn I had had almost three years' experience of dealing with advertising, the press, television, and with public affairs on the grand scale. As with the management theory, learned so diligently at the Hong Kong Polytechnic, I soon found my experience in marketing to be worthless in the small business world of a country inn. The million-dollar budget I had controlled was not my money. In Hong Kong, I had secretaries and departmental heads to assist me. I knew the editors of the colony's main newspapers personally and had funds to carry out research to determine whether a campaign was effective or not. None of these luxuries are to hand for a country innkeeper with little or no funds.

From the start, lack of funds meant that we were unable to advertise with any commercial enterprise and this state continued for the first three or four years. With no accreditation by the national or regional tourist boards and without a star rating with the AA or RAC, we did not qualify for inclusion in their guidebooks. The cost of advertising with the

# It Could be a Little Gold Mine

local newspapers and magazines was prohibitive. Our only propaganda was that which we could generate in-house. Here again there were difficulties because we did not have a typewriter or anyone who could type. Science had not then developed personal computers, e-mail or the World Wide Web. The only broadcast advertising available to us was the best of all advertising, word of mouth, but this takes time to develop, a lot of time.

We never did buy a typewriter, we took our business, with one mighty bound, from script to computer. Pre PC, my handwritten menus and notices had been a bit of a problem. This was because I cannot always recognise word form or number form. I can write 363 as 636 and never see the difference. My elder sister Pat, an excellent nurse for all her working life, tells me the medical profession know the condition as dyspraxia. During national service, the War Office Selection Board, after I had taken a particular aptitude test for a second time, rated me educationally subnormal. This twenty-minute test, one of five, examined word and number recognition and manipulation. How I managed to point my battery of field guns in the right direction remains a mystery. My deficiency meant that my menus and notices were full of errors in spelling, and worse, they had many back to front figures giving wrong prices for the dishes.

Then, one wonderful day, I realised I was not alone; I had support. I found an ally and a defence against the pedants who regularly ridiculed my errors. It happened one lunchtime, during our second winter at the inn. A very attractive lady with pretty legs and attractive shoes, was perched on a stool at the bar calling out my spelling mistakes. Her high-pitched teacher-like tone was clear for all to hear and she was obviously enjoying the audience she had attracted. In front of the fire, unnoticed by her, was a newspaper with boots. I knew it to be a very venerable Roman Catholic priest, well into his eighties, who was acting interregnum, until his Bishop could find a new priest for Ashbourne. Despite knowing my far right English protestant leanings, he occasionally came to the inn for a sandwich and a pint of Guinness. He always pulled a seat close to the fire so that he could prop his boots on the hearth while reading his broadsheet newspaper.

Prompted by a particularly arcane point made by the lady with pretty legs and shoes, the newspaper with boots stirred. The rustling paper lowered to reveal the collared priest with his shock of snow-white hair, his saintly rosy smooth skinned face, part shielded by rimless spectacles. He coughed gently, then in a soft but penetrating pulpit-practiced voice that carried the room enquired, "Pray madam, by what authority are you making these definitive criticisms? In our free independent and democratic country there is no canon law, statute law, or common law to regulate how a word may, or may not, be spelt. Your plagiarisms are merely the pedantry of a particular publisher whose dicta are compromised by commercial consideration." The newspaper with boots then resumed its state of grace.

Sometimes my errors were of meaning rather than simple mistakes in spelling. From time to time, we have advertised with Derbyshire's glossy *County Magazine*. We did this because the people who enjoyed our type of meal use the magazine's *Dining Out* feature, as a restaurant guide. This magazine targets the As and Bs of the socioeconomic mix, so we have to be careful to state, in all our adverts, that our restaurant is part of a busy country inn and not of a country house

# It Could be a Little Gold Mine

hotel. We needed to make this distinction for the sake of profitability. I would rather have a cheery market stall trader bring half a dozen of his family and friends to eat and drink, than have a baker's dozen velvet-jacketed men, with their partners all pearls and twinset, coming to dine, intent on comparison.

In one advert, my choice of words was spectacularly wrong. Paul Jones was our restaurant manager. He had a talent for working the restaurant to create a good atmosphere. Thinking to give him a boost, I paid for an expensive colour advert, which included a photograph of him in the restaurant. In the text with the advert, I wrote, "Paul, our Restaurant Manager, will take care of you in his 'inimical' style. I thought I had typed 'inimitable'."

Because the word inimical exists, my knowledgeable but brain dead computer let me down. Worse still, the magazine editor failed me by publishing the text as I had written it. (OED 'Inimical' – Having the disposition or temper of an enemy. Unfriendly, hostile. OED 'Inimitable' - Incapable of being imitated; surpassing or defying imitation - peerless). These two words follow one after the other in my hefty but treasured two-volume edition of the Shorter Oxford English Dictionary, waiting to snare the innocent. The sad thing is that no one called; we received no letter or e-mail pointing out my heinous error. That month's issue sold more than twenty thousand copies and no one noticed. Clearly, the As and Bs were not minding their Ps, and Qs. Either they had not read my advert, or they were not literate. It seemed to me that this lack of response to our one-off advertisement proved that great advertising man, David Ogilvy's advice, *Never advertise unless it is part of a campaign.*

Lack of funds put advertising campaigns out of the question. We had to find another way. A unique selling point was required that could be given to the papers as news. This was difficult as the competition is fierce, but the idea suited both Jeanne and me. We took every opportunity to be a little different, if not unique. This sometimes had far-reaching effects.

It was a quiet early evening when they came in. Two of them, one a typical middle-aged English management consultant. He was all pin stripe dark blue suit, protruding shirt cuffs, shiny black Oxford shoes, white shirt collar on a coloured shirt and spotted silk handkerchief spilling from his striped jacket pocket. The other was a Chips Rafferty / Crocodile Dundee type, a slouch-dressed, raw-boned Australian with an accent that left no doubt about his origins. The consultant type asked, in soft well-modulated tones, "Do you have a table in your restaurant tonight?" The Australian chipped in, "Course he's got tables, but can he feed us? I only have tonight before I fly on to the States." "Of course, would you like to look at a menu sir?" I got in, before things got worse. The Australian looked askance at the dishes offered and said, "Kee ryste, I'm only here with you poms for a few hours and the only thing I wanted was proper fish and chips," and he went on "yer see, we don't do 'em right in Oz." "Yes sir, of course, but first let me take your colleague's order." I then called "Darren, have you got your motorbike handy?" I was relieved to hear him reply, "Yes, it's on the yard." "Right then" I said for all to hear, long and drawn out in Derbyshire dialect, "Fish and chips for the gentleman. From Bright's only mind, if you have to let someone go in front of you so that you get the fish fresh fried, never mind. Must be cod, do not be put off with anything else, double wrapped, and oh, bring a tub of their mushy peas please."

# It Could be a Little Gold Mine

Twenty minutes later, I served the fish and chips on a large oval plate, in the newspaper that had insulated them on the draughty two-mile ride from Ashbourne.

The far-reaching effect was not realised until many years later. A small minibus drew up on the yard and in tumbled seven or eight Australians. "Yes, I reckon this is the fella" said one. "Too right" another, "Tall enough is he?" from a little one, "Shall we try him then?" from one at the back. "What are you lot on about?" was my quizzical, puzzled response. "Well it's like this; the boss fella of our company has banged on about you and this drinking hole of yours for years. He has promoted your pub all over Western Australia. You had a lad go on his motorbike, to get him proper fish and chips, and you served them in their paper. Yer see; we don't do 'em right in Oz." It was then that I remembered the phrase and the Chips Rafferty / Crocodile Dundee Australian. "We're at an exhibition at the NEC in Birmingham, but just had to truant to come and see if it was true." They ate from the bar menu and drank well. More funds in the kitty, this time from a very long shot.

Local radio gave us the occasional plug if we had something to say. We had a five-minute spot each day for five days in one week when BBC Radio Derby broadcast a series about people at work. Edward, our second son, has a talent for generating a happy atmosphere wherever he goes. He is a bit like Sammy Davies Junior in his prime. The little compulsive entertainer admitted that he would go into a routine whenever the lights came on, even if it was only when he opened a refrigerator door. The Irish redhead who interviewed Edward, trying to add some depth to the interview about working conditions asked, "What is it like working for your father?"

# Marketing and Media Matters

His immediate response, broadcast loud and clear across Derbyshire: "An absolute bloody nightmare, he comes in when I have the place going with a swing, turns down the music, puts on his beloved Beethoven and clears the bar in minutes. It's so bad the staff and I have clubbed together to buy him and Mum a motorhome so that she can take him away at weekends." I did not hear the broadcast and for a long time could not understand why so many people, even those I hardly knew, greeted me with a smiling, "Been off in the motorhome recently?"

I have a hit rate of about one in eight with my letters to the editor of the *Daily Telegraph*. One that the paper did publish led not only to some small increase in customers curious to see if it was true, but also, to my delight, to my being reunited with some old friends with whom we had lost contact years ago. It all started with a letter in which I admitted that our customers, locals and staff alike, know me as *Mr Grumpy*. In the letter, I pointed out that only owners of restaurants and hotels could, like Basil Fawlty, reply in like kind to customers who are rude. All others who toil in the hospitality industry in this country as managers, have to bite their tongue when abused, as they often are.

*Today,* BBC Radio Four's main morning news programme picked out the letter and had me on air for a light-hearted interview. Several regional radio interviews followed, including an astonishing twenty minutes on the English channel of Radio Spain. The *Daily Express* followed by publishing a full two-page spread about *Mr Grumpy*. Simon Edge, their young but very experienced reporter was bright. He could have been brutal, but I think in sympathy for Jeanne, his report was entertaining. We had enjoyed his company; he enjoyed our

# It Could be a Little Gold Mine

beer and dinner. Better still, the paper paid for his accommodation and meal. More was to follow. *BBC Prime*, looking for a new approach for yet another relaunch of the *Fawlty Towers* series, this time in Northern Europe and the Middle East, used the *Mr Grumpy* bit. They filmed for five hours at the inn to get twenty seconds of Mr Grumpy. This they spliced together with twenty seconds of scenes from the *Fawlty Towers* series for their trailer. The exposure brought contacts from Greece, Spain, and Ethiopia. Altogether, *Mr Grumpy* had, for nothing but a few hours fun, bought the equivalent of many thousands of pounds of advertising space and it was both entertaining and rewarding.

# CHAPTER TEN

# Leatherbritches Brewery; a Wish Fulfilled

*The sun, caught by late summer's barley tops,*
*Phoenix like, glows again in golden ale.*
*Sweet wort of malt grains with Kent's bitter hops,*
*By yeast's alchemy transmutes without fail,*
*To that proof spirit of the brewer's art,*
*Alcohol, perfect in moderation,*
*An elixir for a generous heart,*
*Open minds and happy conversation.*
*Away with whisky, brandy, rum and gin,*
*Away with cider, port wine and sherry,*
*They are the hard stuff of skid row and sin.*
*Lager is only bottled up worry.*
*Conditioned cask ales are best for good cheer,*
*There's only one choice, English Ale and Beer.*

Other than Nurse Harvey's Gripe Water, or Dinnefords, many a mother's salvation before today's Calpol, I was fourteen before I had my first alcoholic drink. The memory of that drink is as clear today, as though the bubbles are still tingling on my tongue. On a clear summer's evening, my Uncle Clifford sat me, alongside my Aunty Nellie, (all children should have one), on a simple bench, before a scrubbed white wooden table, with my back resting against a whitewashed wall. This was no ordinary wall. It was a wall still warm from

# It Could be a Little Gold Mine

the daylong sun. It was the front wall of a small thatched cottage pub on the north Norfolk coast. My Uncle, who had gone inside the dark pub to get drinks and crisps, came out to set before me a full glass of clear sparkling amber coloured liquid. "Drink that lad," he said, "It will do you good." I am sure that it did. That one drink set me on a lifetime habit that has brought me no end of pleasure and within a few years, it helped to change me from a sickly child to a skinny but healthy youth.

This uncle of mine, who owned a high-class grocery, knew a deal about food and drink. He had a certificate to prove it. It was our good fortune that his shop was only a few doors away from our family home in Halifax. Rather late in his life, to his regret, he had married my mother's sister. His regret was not the marriage, but in having taken so long to find her. As they say in Yorkshire, Aunty Nellie, who was a little older than my mother, was a wonderful woman. She had long been my favourite aunt and that summer long ago, they had volunteered to take me to the seaside, 'to do me good'. I was the sort of child who my parents' friends, neighbours and relatives alike, took it in turns, 'to do me good', to nurture me back to health after one illness or another. I like to think that it was so, but on reflection, after more than half a century, I now have doubts. My holiday excursions were probably more to do with giving my mother a rest after she had spent nights and days with little sleep, coping with me, the runt of the family, at the same time as looking after my healthier elder siblings and her policeman husband, who worked shifts.

That first drink outside the Norfolk pub was of real cider. It was well-made and sparkled from the bottom of the glass like premium champagne. I have learned, over the years, that real cider, just like real ale, should not be dull, cloudy and flat. Such so-called scrumpy is just an excuse for poor craftsmanship. The cider for this first drink of mine was in a half pint, thick dimpled glass, a glass with a handle.

In my life, there have only been two changes in my drinking habits. The first from drinking cider to drinking beer and the second from drinking from half-pint glasses to drinking from full pint glasses. I have never changed my preferred type of glass, thick dimpled and with a handle. As my hands are like JCB shovels, thin glass vessels without handles, such as Nonics, Worthingtons, Wellingtons, tubes, sleeves, straights or whatever, make me nervous. I would as soon sip warm champagne from a plastic toothbrush mug as drink over-chilled beer from a wafer-thin glass. Such a treacherous smooth-sided thin glass tumbler full of beer slipped from my fingers to reinforce my peculiar preference. It happened when, as a young bachelor, I behaved in my usual clumsy manner during a chance meeting with a delightful girl at a barn dance in the Cotswolds. Sometime during the winter of that year, she had asked her father to ask me to be her escort to the North Warwickshire Hunt Ball. She was young and lovely, dressed in a daffodil yellow dirndl skirt separated from a Tyrolean white scoop neck, puff sleeved blouse by a hand-wide, deep green, patent leather belt. "Damn and blast the bloody glass," I muttered, too loud, as it slipped from my grasp onto the cobbled floor. Both the glass and my temper exploded. The foaming beer drenched us both, and quenched the spark of romance before it could rekindle.

Powerful positive advice from an elderly colonel of the Royal Army Medical Corps reinforced my strict adherence to beer. The colonel had an honorary attachment to the regi-

# It Could be a Little Gold Mine

ment in which I served. He had noticed that I had taken to drinking the odd gin and tonic or two. One Sunday lunchtime, acting like a latter day Mr Chips, he took me, by the ear, from the mess anteroom into the corridor. Turning me round to face him, he simply said "Stop It." My stuttering perplexed reply was "Me, er... what I have I done now?" His measured response, delivered in beautiful upper crust English tones has stayed with me to this day. "It is not what you are doing now, it is what you may do in the future that concerns me, and must now concern you. When you first joined the regiment, you drank beer. Then occasionally you drank a gin before dinner; it then became a gin before lunch and a gin before dinner. Today you drank two gins before lunch. You are an enthusiast in all that you do, therefore, drink only beer. When pressed, you may allow yourself a glass of wine or a port or perhaps a small liqueur after dinner, but nothing else, certainly no gin, vodka, brandy or whisky. In old age you may become, in medical terms, obese, and you may die of a heart attack, but you will not have destroyed your powers of reason." As befits a colonel this was not advice, it was a command. I owe him much. Apart from an occasional lapse, when on advice I did have a gin to ease back pain after playing hockey, I have obeyed his eloquent command.

I was forty-one years old when we took possession of the inn and that day I made to myself a new vow, a pledge that I would not drink gin or any spirits until I was sixty. This new intent, now for the first time time-limited, was based on the old Scottish adage *the whisky you are drinking afore you're sixty is killing ye; the whisky you're drinking after you're sixty is keeping you alive.* However, the good colonel doctor's advice proved the more powerful when I passed my sixtieth birthday and no

# Leatherbritches Brewery; a Wish Fulfilled

hard liquor has yet passed my lips. Real cask ale or bottle-conditioned ale, always poured into a thick pint glass that has a handle, remains my evening habit and pleasure.

Despite my enthusiasm for real ale, it took me until I was well beyond sixty to become the licensed brewer of our own craft brewery with the capacity and capability to produce beer to my taste. What wasted years; wasted because I have a positive dislike and distrust of pasteurised keg beer, chemically engineered lager, or worse, the double gassed so-called smooth-flow beers. These are not the natural time-tested product of genuine brewers. They are the artifice of smooth-talking, beanbag-seated marketing men. As a daily beer drinker, I should have seen the wisdom of brewing my own years ago. William Pitt the Younger, Prime Minister at twenty-four and dead at forty-eight was on the right lines but with the wrong drink. He was famous for oft declaiming, 'A day not spent drinking port is a day wasted.'

Well then, how did it come about that, after the wasted years, both Jeanne and I became the licensed brewers of *Leatherbritches*? our very own, though very small brewery. Well the truth is it was not my idea, nor Jeanne's. However, once put to me, the sublime inspiration made such good sense that, like Oscar Wilde, I took it as my own. From a business point of view, it would provide vertical integration, cut out the middleman, and give the inn another focus as a destination. From my personal point of view, it was a dream come true.

That the inn should have its own brewery was the idea of Bill, our youngest son. Timing his moment to perfection and with no alerting lengthening of his opening "Dad" to Da—a—d, he simply asked, "Dad, what name would you give to a new

# It Could be a Little Gold Mine

brewery?" His direct and easy opening to conversation, as I slouched in my easy chair, the right and proper thing to do after a good Sunday lunch, did not alarm me. Like all fathers, I've learnt that the longer drawn out and the more wavering the opening "Da—a—d" the more money it is likely to cost me, so I was still composed when I offered *Leatherbritches* for consideration. There was no immediate response, just relaxed silence. I had offered *Leatherbritches* because my father had told me about the Ale Conners, the King's excise collectors of medieval times. To assess the strength and quality of an ale, they would spill a little of it on a bench and then sit on it while they ate their snap. How sticky it felt when they stood up gave them an idea of its strength. Worsted, shoddy, nor even moleskin trousers could stand the wear and tear so the ale conners took to wearing britches made of leather. The leather britches they wore became the mark of their profession and just as the blue sash, the cordon bleu, worn by the knights of the order of Saint Esprit, came to mean those who prepared and appreciated good food, so *Leatherbritches* came to mean good ale.

I did think it a bit odd that Bill should ask me, of all people, about names. At his birth and at his christening we had named him, William Charles Baden. He has discarded all three, only responding to Bill, or occasionally allowing Billy, the preferred address from Mr Green, his housemaster. His was always the reproachful triple, Billy, Billy, Billy, when he was caught, as he so often was, behaving like *Just William* in Richmal Crompton's books.

After a while I thought to pick up the conversation with, "whose new brewery is it that you are on about?" said in a mumbling sort of Sunday afternoon way, thinking that it

# Leatherbritches Brewery; a Wish Fulfilled

must be a venture of one of his rich friends from school. "It's the one I am going to build in the old washhouse and vegetable store outside the kitchen door." At this, I was instantly wide-awake and fully alert. My mind raced over the many ramifications that such a venture would involve. For certain, it would require capital expenditure, and bring problems with cash flow, licences, bureaucracy, Her Majesty's Customs and Excise, officialdom and all the rest. Honed by military training and years of business and engineering management, my response was direct and incisive. "Oh is it?" Then I followed with what most sensible fathers say in times of crisis, "What does your mother say?" "Mother's all for it" was the solid response. I often wonder why I bother to ask.

# It Could be a Little Gold Mine

We spent the next few weeks visiting what we came to know as brewpubs. This was a bit of research I could readily put my mind to and found it to be most agreeable. Bill selected a small company and paid them to build a two-barrel brew line in the old washhouse and vegetable store outside our kitchen door. He assured us, and he is persuasive, that he would produce two barrels, that is five hundred and seventy-six pints, each time he brewed. He told us that if he brewed two or three times each month, this would keep the inn supplied with sufficient of our own real ale. With a deal of financial help from his late godfather, Arthur Darryl Alexander George Mosley, who had also discarded his four given names, answering only to Bill, Leatherbritches Brewery became a legal entity, separate from our inn. Bill became the sole proprietor and licensed brewer.

The first brew day was one of great excitement and delight for me when the glorious steamy wet smell of the boiling wort and hops drifted over the boules court and skittle alleys, now renamed the brewery yard. The people who had installed the brewery equipment helped Bill with his first brew. When I asked, "When can I have some of your beer then?" their curt reply was "When it's ready." A couple of weeks later, one evening when I was in the bar gossiping with, or as Jeanne has it, intimidating the customers, Bill came over with a full pint of beer in his outstretched hand. "Try that then," he said with a confidence verging on youthful arrogance. I queried, defensively, "Try what?" "Come on, try it Dad, and tell me what you think," he pressed. The penny dropped, this was it, the first Leatherbritches brew. It looked bright and clear and had a good tight north-country foaming head. I was proud when I first took little sips that I swirled round my mouth as I had seen wine connoisseurs do on the television and then relieved when I took a great beer drinker's draught, for undoubtedly the beer was good. Customers in the bar shared several pints, that were passed around for tasting. They agreed, unanimously, that Bill had created a distinctive new real ale. It was a beer well and truly fit for its purpose. The name just came to me, "By heck Bill, that's real good beer, well done son, it's tailor made this is," and thinking of the britches connection I added, "Perhaps you should call it Bespoke." And so it was. "Bill," I said in front of them all, "this is good beer, go and do likewise, brew another, just like this one." This time Bill was on his own, and all credit due to him, three weeks or more later, he produced the second brew. "Try that Dad," he commanded. "What is it?" was my genuinely curious response, for although bright and clear, it clearly was not Bespoke. "Well it is supposed to be Bespoke, but it's developed an identity problem," said Bill, clearly a bit worried. A squint against the light and a couple of good pulls at the pint offered, confirmed that the beer was paler in colour, the alcohol not as dominant and it was more highly hopped than his first brew. "Well you've no need to worry," I was relieved to say, "It's still good beer," and mindful of the sartorial connotation said "Perhaps you should call it Belter, because it really is a belter of a beer." And so it was.

The third brew, again an attempt to replicate Bespoke had completely different characteristics. Light, bright and with a good feel on the tongue. Again, the anxious look as Bill said, "Try this one Dad." Once again, I was relieved to respond, "Well it is nothing like the other two but it is very acceptable, no it is better than that, it's a great backup to the others. Perhaps you should call it Belt 'n' Braces." And so it was.

# It Could be a Little Gold Mine

An infection contaminated the fourth brew. It was an expensive failure that went down the drain, literally. I am sure that fate had a hand in this, because it turned out not to be a disaster, but a push in the right direction. It showed us all that anyone can brew beer, but it takes an expert to brew the same beer. Consistency was required and consistency we did not have. The next brew and all subsequent brews have been exactly as meant to be. This change in the fortunes of Leatherbritches came about because Bill knew David Corby Bsc. Msc., a professional brewer, and somehow he persuaded him to take on the job as Head Brewer.

Both of David's degrees are in brewing and he brought with him seventeen years' experience as a brewer with one of the country's biggest brewers. Employing Dave, a name he prefers to his given name, created a need to brew more beer than Bill originally planned. In fact, in order to pay Dave his reasonable fees, it was necessary to brew a lot of beer. This, in turn, meant selling Leatherbritches' beers to other pubs as well as over the bar at the Bentley Brook Inn. Bill took off his brewer's apron and went out to sell beer. He quickly built up a core of good customers, while also learning hard lessons about bad payers, problems of cask recovery and the difficulties of trading with wholesale distributors.

At the beginning of the new century, Bill rang me from his home in Leicester where his young family and his pub *Time*, a very busy drinking hall, fully occupied his time. At *Time*, he had about as much chance of selling real ale, as a pork butcher would have of selling sausages to a synagogue. "Dad - I'm too busy with *Time* to deal with Leatherbritches; why don't you and Mum take over the brewery?" Without hesitation or reference to Jeanne, my reply was, "Yes, provided

# Leatherbritches Brewery; a Wish Fulfilled

we can have it as part of our business. Tell you what, we will write off all your debts to the inn in exchange for our taking over all the equipment." Bill's debt to the inn was not very significant and what with the written-down value of the seven-year-old brewing equipment, it was a fair deal. The land and buildings were ours anyway. After a quick burst of correspondence with Her Majesty's Customs and Excise, they gave both Jeanne and me a licence to brew and Leatherbritches became an integral part of the business of the Bentley Brook Inn. Pensioners both, we had a brewery of our own and were happy to face the new challenges that this brought.

We were not all that brave because Edward, our second son, had returned from seventeen years' golfing and car parking in the United States. He took over beer sales and distribution, and on 1 November 2004 he became sole proprietor of the brewery.

Not content with what we had from the takeover, Jeanne decided we should bottle some of our beer for sale. This was to be bottle-conditioned real ale, different from the pasteurised denatured beers sold in cans and bottles currently dominating supermarket shelves. Jeanne was sure there was a market for good honest preservative and additive free, bottle-conditioned beer.

One of the greatest pleasures of being involved in the business of microbreweries is that nearly all brewers are keen to help each other. Another delight is that so many brewers, who produce good beer from microbreweries, are characters as unique as the beers they brew. I spoke with Brendan, of Icini Brewery, who agreed that bottling our beer for sale at our inn and through other pubs, restaurants, and specialist off-licence shops would be a sound proposition. He suggested

# It Could be a Little Gold Mine

that I should speak to Wellington, the Head Brewer at the Museum Brewery in Burton-on-Trent. Brendan told us that they had recently purchased an automatic bottling plant to replace their hand-bottling device, because their bottled real ales had been so successful. It was a good tip. We bought their redundant hand-bottling machine for not much money. It is a simple stainless steel trough with a float valve regulating the level of beer fed to it by gravity from a high-level conditioning tank. It has six pivot mounted siphon heads that when dipped into the trough siphon beer into bottles. All that is required to fill bottles to a full pint, half-litre, or any other standard bottle size, is a simple adjustment to the shelf on which the bottles rest. Simple it may be but it is a wonderful tool.

The brewers at the Bass Museum Brewery assured us 'No fibs', that with the device we had just acquired, using one man rinsing the bottles, one to put them on the siphons, one to take them off and one to clamp on the crown corks, they had filled at the rate of 850 bottles an hour. They assured us that they had filled a million and a half bottles on the device, mainly their excellent Worthington White Shield. Their shiny new automatic bottle-filling machine can do the same 850 bottles an hour, but it still needs to have at least one man in full-time attendance.

Well, we have not got up to their speed, but Edward with his wife Sandra and his children helping, managed to bottle a full four barrels at a time, more than twelve hundred bottles, in just over three hours. Each time I witness this, I cannot help but question if the Museum Brewery invested wisely in their shiny new 850 bottles an hour automatic bottling plant. What with the capital lockup, depreciation costs, maintenance and electricity bills and the fact that the machine still needs an operative in attendance, I wonder if they will ever get a payback.

I have taken to myself the task of conducting what we call Brewery Looks. Leatherbritches is too small for brewery tours. I welcome the opportunity of addressing a captive audience and hope, occasionally, to convert some mindless gin drinker to the reason saving habit of a daily quart of cask ale, or a couple of bottle-conditioned real ales.

# CHAPTER ELEVEN

# Better than TV

Our decision that any business that we started must be to do with people, was far-sighted. The fun, interest, and friendship that our customers, suppliers, and staff brought to our lives gave us the will to persevere when events went against us.

Neither Jeanne nor I enjoy theme pubs: places designed to attract a particular section of society, social class, or age group. It was always our intention that our inn should be open to all. We sought to attract and mix with individuals and groups of all ages, class, gender and race, including those of different religious or political persuasion. We have been successful in attracting a general mix of customers and in general, I have enjoyed the company of all except sports fans and motorcyclists. With them, I find it increasingly difficult to be sociable. The sports fan is infinitely boring to anyone other than a co-fan of the same team, or worse, individual. They seem unable to understand that the minutia of team selection or Beckham's boot, or Botham's bat is of no interest to rational thought. Soccer fans, particularly those who follow teams in the Premier Division of the so-called 'beautiful game' are the worst, and increasingly so. Some years ago, when Derby County were playing Manchester United, the police imposed a lights out and locked doors curfew on us for two hours after the match, until they were sure that they had shepherded the last coachload of the Manchester United supporters past us along the A515 and safely out of Derbyshire. Their hostile reaction to any fan supporting another team or those with no interest disgusts me.

In contrast to the football fans' intransigence, I witnessed a wonderful example of rational behaviour during the height of the Iran Iraq War, a war in which hostilities killed over a million people. I noticed a very tall and distinguished character with Arab features seated alone at a table in the bar. I asked the man, as I often do when we have foreign visitors, "Where are you from?" "Iraq" was the friendly response. Across the room, at another table, a newspaper was shielding another gentleman, also alone. He lowered his paper to reveal himself to be equally distinguished and obviously of Middle Eastern origin. "That's interesting," he said, "I am from Iran." After a few polite exchanges and questions the two joined each other on a larger table to have lunch together. Their only disagreement was when each one tried to insist on paying for both meals.

Being an innkeeper, on home ground, I can prompt reaction, from customers with uncalled for comments. The ensuing conversation and debate is so much more fun than watching TV. I like to think of it as throwing my pebble into their pond, just as I am sure my god throws some of his pebbles into mine. It does not mean that I necessarily like people, and for sure not many like me, but I am intrigued and fascinated by them. It is my hobby, more satisfying and cheaper than bird watching, fishing, golf and philately and certainly more worthwhile than morris dancing.

Observation of our staff provides most of the good copy for my people-watch diary. This was a surprise, as I thought watching the behaviour of our customers would be more

# It Could be a Little Gold Mine

interesting. However, just as there are no scripts for running a country inn, there is no reliable casting list either. As a result, although some like Edna, Vernon and Stephen have stayed the course during our twenty eight year sojourn at the inn, many more cooks, waiters, bartenders, cleaners and housekeepers have come and gone. Throughout the industry, few young people, despite two years spent at catering college, survive the culture shock of their first job. Even fewer young people survive if their parents push then into catering without college training. Too many parents have approached us along the following fixed lines. "We thought that dear Jane, because she is not academically as clever as her sisters, might do well helping out in your hotel." Those anxious mothers and fathers come to ask that we take on to our staff one of their children, usually a girl about seventeen. Never do the parents use the common word inn or pub; they always refer to our inn as an hotel and never do they mention the sordid word work; it is always 'helping out'. I cringe when I hear such mothers saying to their friends, "Yes, dear Jane is helping out at the such and such hotel."

The hospitality business means dealing with people. That is a difficult job at the best of times and when the people you are dealing with are paying for your service it is often a challenge, requiring a quick wit, a deal of tact and a world of experience. This makes it almost impossible to recruit and retain even those with the appropriate qualification and experience. The few who endure to gain a few years' experience often find that it all becomes too much for them. They leave and flee to seek refuge in other jobs. Jobs not necessarily better paid, but where the work is less arduous and not as unsociable. They find work in industries such as coal mining, nursing, the fire brigade, the police, or active service with the SAS or mercenary armies. It was ever thus; the Victorian adage still holds good. 'She was a good cook, as cooks go, and as good cooks go, she went'.

From the beginning, we tried to recruit young people in the hope that we could mould and encourage them to adopt our ways, rather than the accepted deadhead mores of the English catering and service industries. In those lively heady early days at the inn, Jeanne could say, with confidence, to any new young member of staff, "Don't be nervous, just do it as you would at home. It is no different just because we have paying customers." Now, in the twenty-first century, the totally unreceptive and uncomprehending young, simply do not understand. Modern times have made nonsense of Jeanne asking a newcomer to set a table "just like you do at home." Few have ever sat at a dining table at home, let alone set the table with napery, cutlery, crockery, glasses, butter dish, salt, and pepper. To most young people, 'formal dining' means taking the pizza out of its cardboard box, and putting it on a plate. Jeanne's instruction; "Just make the beds as you do at home," means nothing. Not even a quizzical or even a blank stare is forthcoming. Sheets, blankets, and eiderdowns are foreign objects today. The young sleep under Scandinavian duvets on Japanese futons and boxed corners are only to do with football.

The high rate of young people leaving hotel and restaurant work is not usually to do with poor wages or lack of opportunity. In the main, the cause is glandular fever. The fever I refer to is not the debilitating disease that swells the neck and needs a physician and time for efficacious treatment. It is the untreatable, unquenchable fever of young love. Boy meets girl,

# It Could be a Little Gold Mine

girl meets boy and the one working the unsociable hours of a restaurant, bar or kitchen is cajoled, nagged and pressurised to "Get a proper job. You never take me out, why won't you take me clubbing on Saturday; all you ever do is work." Even if both star-crossed lovers work in the same bar, restaurant or hotel, as likely as not, they will be on opposite shifts. Because love / lust is a natural state of human behaviour, the entire industry has the same problem.

To an extent, we have lost patience with the young and now tend to favour older people to fill staff vacancies as they occur. Andrew, who was over sixty, and has a lifetime's experience working in restaurant kitchens and bakeries, came to join us as a production chef, on a part-time basis. After a few days, he asked me if I was satisfied with his work. I was pleased to say, "Andrew, you are just what we have been looking for; you haven't learned a thing in forty years." "Thanks Mr A" was all he said, but his smile and nod of understanding told me that we were as one in our understanding of good food.

As owners of our business, we soon learned that the buck stopped with us. Not available to the owner operator is the comfort zone of explaining away poor service, poor food, a draught, no paper in the lavatory, slow service, a light not working or shabby furnishings with the excuse, "I'm so sorry, it's the management you see, they won't ... if it were me ... personally I would ..."

As I have already mentioned, our first recruits were the two little maids from school. "Actually," they were primly quick to point out, "Not school Mr Allingham, college, the Catering College at Buxton, if you don't mind." It is now called a university. Barbara was first to join us, Caroline followed

# Better than TV

a few weeks later. Both had newly printed City and Guilds 761 and 762 certificates to show that they had successfully completed a two-year course in catering. Oh, what joy! qualified professionals come to teach me, the enthusiastic amateur, the proper way to cook and manage a kitchen. We gave both girls the title of General Assistant, because we did not want, nor could we afford, any demarcation between the kitchen, the bar, the restaurant, or housekeeping. Barbara was so thin she told us she had to run around in the shower to get wet. She was as quiet and timid as a mouse when she came to us and had neither strength nor stamina. After each shift, morning or late, Barbara would crawl away to her bed to sleep until her next shift. Her life was just work and sleep, work and sleep. Many times during those first few weeks, Jeanne and I would say to each other, "We will have to ask her to leave, the job's just too much for her, it's killing her," but fortunately for us we held our nerve and Barbara stuck to the last. Caroline, in complete contrast, was the quintessential blonde bombshell with bumps in all the right places and a bubbling laugh that rang round the kitchen.

In that kitchen, I soon learned that the catering college had probably done their aspiration to succeed in their chosen career more harm than good. It was hardly their fault because almost all their college work had been theoretical and forgotten the moment they handed in their dissertations for marking. I still find it odd that during my lifetime stories became compositions, a composition became an essay, then essays became dissertations and dissertation became a thesis.

With little flour on their hands and no dirty pots and pans during their course work, the two of them initially were, well, it is difficult to find the right words. Useless comes to

# It Could be a Little Gold Mine

mind, as does incompetent, inadequate, ineffective, but never hopeless, because both were, in their different ways, super girls. Most modern 'uni' graduates have all those negatives described, and few of them have enthusiasm; bleating, "I have not been trained to do that." Barbara and Caroline were always punctual, clean as new pins, keen to learn, willing to tackle anything and most important, forgiving of my frequent and unreasonable irascible outbursts. Within six months, they were on their professional feet, up and running, able to turn out a very high standard of work. At the same time, they searched for, found and enjoyed a busy social life after their long working day. They still visit from time to time. From their visits, we now learn how little we knew then, about what they used to get up to both during work and on days off. Not only governments use the thirty-year rule to keep their secrets.

Whenever and however often I recollect the memory of one incident concerning Barbara and Caroline, it remains to cheer me. We had invested in a Kenwood mixer with an attachment for mincing meat. I had set Caroline the simple task of mincing about five pounds of raw beef and had left the kitchen to fix something or other in the beer cellar. This took longer than expected. After about half an hour I needed a spanner from the tool shed. To get it I walked quickly into the kitchen and out through the other door to the yard. In the kitchen, Caroline, red in the face, was on a stool trying to force the beef through the mincing machine with the blunt end of a rolling pin. "Caroline, you've got the cutter blade in wrong way round," I sang out, without breaking step. Returning with the spanner, I heard Caroline running up to her room in floods of tears. Barbara was sitting on the floor with her back to the wall having slid down in helpless laughter. "Now what have I done?" I asked. "Oh don't worry, it's just you, your timing was perfect. She has been trying, for almost half an hour, to get the machine to mince properly and all it was creating was a sort of streaky gooey whitish paste." Barbara went on to explain that she had just said: "That bloody man will come waltzing in and say, "'Caroline, you are doing it all wrong.'" Of course, that's when you came back in." Half an hour later Caroline was back in the kitchen and the two little maids who had made friends for life, were working, hard, effectively and happily.

Before we bought the inn, the senior partner of a firm of head-hunters took me to lunch in one of London's most fashionable restaurants, just behind Kensington Palace. He knew that I was considering buying a hotel or restaurant at the same time thinking about a job opportunity he had in mind for me. He introduced me to the restaurateur and said, "Do you have any advice you can give this chap if he decides to give up engineering and buy a restaurant?" "Yes," was his immediate response. "Simple, get a first-class washer-up, pay him well and make sure you keep him, it's the only way to keep the rest of your staff happy and the business profitable." His man, who could speak no English, was just huge, well over twenty stone. He sat on a pivoting high stool, like a benign octopus, collecting, sorting, stacking and feeding the maw of his stainless steel dishwashing machine, then filing the clean, plates, pots and pans neatly away.

Our first and best washer-up was Mary. In Ashbourne, and all the villages around, everyone knew Mary as *Copley Buttercup*. Well over sixty and twenty stone, with rosy cheeks, and a bit lame, she was a most gracious lady. To her the work seemed effortless, everything always in its place and never a

# It Could be a Little Gold Mine

pot or glass chipped or broken. Her hands were even bigger than mine were but they were as light as the tip of the fabled Angel's wing when she made pastry. Each Saturday she would come to work with six or more of the most beautiful plate pies, filled with fruit, that ever graced a table. She had one quirky habit that bothered me. Several times a night, in response to a request for a clean pan or grill-plate, she would repeat her mantra, "You'll miss me when I'm gone." She was so very right. Sadly, Mary died within a couple of years of joining our little team of workers. We often remember her, not only because she was such a good old-fashioned cook and conscientious worker, but also because her nature seemed to me to be thoroughly and completely good.

Another great find for the washing-up job was Janette, a women in her early thirties. She had two children and a hus-band who became violent from time to time. We knew of this because of the black eyes and the tell tale thumb and finger-print bruises on her upper arms. At first, we employed Janette to wash up. The catering expression KP, Kitchen Porter, was not in our lexicon. One evening, when I was single-handed in the kitchen and very busy, with rather more people in the restaurant than I could cope with, Jeanne brought in another check for six more starters and six more main courses, for a chance booking. In a bit of a flap, or to be honest, a blind panic, I shouted, "Janette you do the starters." In hardly any time at all, they were set out ready for Jeanne to take them to the restaurant, all beautifully, even artistically presented. I continued with my work to finish cooking the remaining main courses. It was only when the last meals had been sent out, and I was calming down, that I realised what had hap-pened. This remarkable person put into my hand, when needed, the correct knife, sieve, ladle, ingredient, or whatever else. Janette had taken on the role of assistant to the chef in the way that an experienced theatre sister assists a surgeon with a complex operation. Jeanne, who saw this happen, promoted her in the field, by giving her a rise in her hourly pay. For the first time, with a change in our policy, Janette also had the qualifier (Kitchen) added to her previous job title, General Assistant. I thought her new title should have been Fairy Godmother because, for once, I was in clover.

The next day we advertised for a new washer-up. On a dark day, about a year later, Janette asked to see us both. Seated with a cup of tea she depressed us by handing us her resignation. "Thank you both," she said, "you have given me confidence in myself which I never had before I came to work here. I am now so assured about my own ability and worth that I have started divorce proceedings against my husband. I am taking the boys to live with me in Derby where I have found a house and a good job as a cook." Although we were sorry to lose Janette, we were proud of her. With no formal qualifications she had beaten several other candidates for her new job because of her natural talent and because, in panic, I had shouted, "Janette, you do the starters."

Recognition of good work does not always come to those who deserve it. We took James on during his summer holidays simply because he came, knocked on the back door and asked for work. This is a rare approach in modern times. He was a long, skinny youth, with a quiet temperament. We were unsure of what to give him to do. For a long time I planned to build, or have built, a retaining wall to hold back the terrace, to provide a safe path to the bottom lawn and get rid of the dangerous old rockery steps. I planned a massive wall of

# It Could be a Little Gold Mine

limestone blocks, buttressed at the highest end by a huge old Derbyshire gritstone gatepost we had, that weighed well over a ton. The problem was that both the limestone and the old gatepost were a long way from the proposed wall. To my surprise and delight, James said that he would take on the task. Throughout the long summer months, he worked alone, never complaining, never asking for help or for instruction. Occasionally, I found time to go and see how he was getting along, and to watch how he worked. I was impressed. He moved the massive gatepost, inch by inch, using a crowbar and for a pivot, some of the wooden wedges we use to chock the beer barrels in the cellar. He had an innate knowledge of the power of levers. He raised the heavy stone pillar to the vertical in the same way that the builders of Stonehenge raised their massive stones, and the ancients built the Pyramids of Egypt. He built the necessary earth ramp with such precision, levering and filling earth under the stone until, at last, it slid into his carefully prepared foundation hole to rest exactly vertical, in precisely the right position.

Then over the weeks, the wall, with properly positioned drainage holes, was completed. I was not only impressed but also excited for him. "Has your dad been to see this?" I asked. "No, he's not interested," was the flat-voiced reply. I was far from content with this, and though I did not know his father, I rang him at his home. "Mr Green, my name is Allingham, your son James has been working for us during his holidays, he has built a fantastic retaining wall, all by himself, it really is wonderful what he has achieved. Will you come and look at it?" His reply chilled me to the bone. "No I will not, wasting his time when he should have been working." It seemed that Pharaoh had hardened his heart.

# CHAPTER TWELVE

# The Staff of Our Life

Of all the staff we have employed over the years, for interest, Kathy was the star. In the few short months that she worked at the inn, she gave me enough ideas to write a book of its own. Such a book would find a worthy and honoured place in the British Library section on *Modern Heroines*. It would also command space for a copy in the reference section of the Institute of Clinical Psychology.

The first we heard about Kathy was in a letter from the employment office in Liverpool. They wrote asking us to fill in a bundle of forms that would authorise them to advance to a young woman the bus fare she would need, if we would agree to interview her for a job. We had advertised for a General Assistant with the local Jobcentre because I was in dire need of help in the kitchen. Disliking paperwork and ignoring the forms, we phoned the Jobcentre, more in hope than expectation. "Send her tomorrow and tell her we will pay her expenses and pick her up from the bus station." Because most enquiries from Jobcentres usually come to nothing, it was a surprise when next morning the phone rang and a girl with a Liverpool accent said, "I'm at the bus station, can you pick me up?"

Kathy was a good-looking girl with dark Spanish eyes, a finely featured face framed with long black wavy hair and the whole made more intriguing by a well-defined jagged scar

# It Could be a Little Gold Mine

high across one cheekbone. My immediate thought was that a survivor of the Spanish Armada, wrecked long ago in the Irish Sea, must have been amongst her forebears. We never learnt much of her history. She did, however, tell us that both her parents had died when she was very young. Having only one known relative, an elderly aunt who lived in the Isle of Man, a local authority children's home in Liverpool was her only home during childhood. At sixteen, free from local authority care, she told us that she had gone to Amsterdam. What happened there we thought it best not to ask.

From the first day that we worked together in the kitchen, it became clear to me that there had been violence in her young life. As I reached to tear some paper towel from the drum dispenser above her head, she sprang away, so fast that she hit the far wall, without her feet touching the ground. In an instant, she turned to face me, arms behind her with hands pressed against the wall eyes blazing. Elizabeth Taylor in the film version of *Cat on a Hot Tin Roof* was never so dramatic. It took a few moments to understand what had caused this explosion. "Kathy, has anyone ever hit you?" I asked. There was a short pause and then "You are joking," said with such sadness that I never again raised the matter.

Kathy was a good worker but had the characteristic spiky Liverpool attitude to bosses, doubled in spades. After a few weeks working with me in the kitchen, I was sure that my strict authoritarian manner had convinced Kathy that, even when I was in a good mood, I was the second son of Satan.

"Mr A, there's a bus goes from Ashbourne to Manchester?" was her greeting one morning. "Yes it does Kathy, everyday," I replied. "Do you like Manchester?" Her reply, spoken in a heavy Liverpudlian accent, "I've never been," astonished me.

# The Staff of Our Life

Kathy, now in her early twenties and brought up in Liverpool was quite sincere and unaware of my thoughts. "Would you like to go? I asked. I'll take you to the bus station on your next day off." So it was agreed. I made sure that she got on the right bus and waved her off, thinking she would have a great day out.

The following day I wondered why Kathy was not bubbling with stories about her adventures in Manchester that 'No Mean City'. By mid-afternoon, I could no longer contain my curiosity. "Kathy, did you like Manchester?" "It was OK" was her brief dull response, followed by more silence. I was puzzled, then a dread thought came to mind. "Kathy, when you got off the bus and came out of the bus station, did you see a large white building on your left?" "Yes, a big white thing with a clock tower." "Sorry Kathy," I owned up, "You spent the day in Stockport, it's my fault. I forgot to tell you not to get off the bus at the first bus station." Having owned up and mindful of her temper I quietly slipped away.

Although she only worked for a few months at the inn, she was with us over one Christmas holiday period. As usual on Christmas Day morning, soon after breakfast, we all gathered round the log fire in the bar, staff and family together. This followed our tradition to exchange gifts before we opened for non-resident customers. Kathy was very excited and although our gift to her was only a token, she was very determined to give me a present. "Wait there Mr A, I've got yours outside, I won't be a moment." In she came, pushing a huge parcel. Ominously it was a parcel with wheels, a parcel fully wrapped in newspaper, newspaper stuck together with wide brown parcel tape. Obviously, Christmas wrapping was beyond her budget. All excited she said, "Go on, open it, it

# It Could be a Little Gold Mine

will be a great help to you when you have to bring in the cash-and-carry stuff from the car." I pulled at the paper and my heart sank when it revealed a brand new supermarket trolley, stolen from the store recently opened in Ashbourne. Poor Kathy, for once thoughtful, she had pushed it the two miles from Ashbourne in foul winter weather. She could not understand that I was shocked and told her it must go back. To Kathy, I was no longer the second son of Satan; truly, I was the heir apparent.

Kathy occasionally worked on the bar and was a magnet for the local young farmers. We watched as a romance blossomed and were pleased to see that she was making friends, but we could not agree to her beau sharing her bedroom. I suffered the same doubts and worry that many a parent does

# The Staff of Our Life

when faced with a daughter who brings home her 'steady' for the first time, to stay the night. I tried to explain that although I was not loco-parentis I did not think it would be right, but Kathy was both spirited and determined. She went straight to Ashbourne, bought a tent, then booked in at a local campsite so that the bliss of cohabitation could be realised.

The young farmer wooed and won her and Kathy left us. We read in the local newspaper that they were married in great style, with Kathy attended by many of his family as bridesmaids, and taken to church in a coach, drawn by four grey horses. Alas, we were not invited. I do not think she ever realised how much we liked her and how pleased we were for her change in fortune.

Recruiting people to work with us at the inn has always proved difficult and I own to being difficult to work with. It is all so very personal in a small country inn. During formal interviews, I have never been able to find out whether the person applying for the particular job, if employed, would be successful. Too many variables face a newcomer. They may not fit in with our existing staff; they may not enjoy working the hours peculiar to our business, or may not be sympathetic to customer needs. Worse, they may not understand that it is the customers, not Jeanne and me who pay their wages. This is not a particular grumble; I realise that all employers in the hotel, restaurant and pub business face the same common problems when trying to recruit workers, we are no exception.

A frequent unsolicited telephone call I answer goes something like this: "Hello! Is that the pub at Bentley?" "Yes, can I help you?" "Have you got any jobs going? My husband has

# It Could be a Little Gold Mine

been made redundant, I'll do anything, I'll do anything at all, honest, anything." I have learned to reply, "Good, we do need a kitchen cleaner, can you start this coming Sunday morning?" The reply is always the same, "Oh! I can't work Sundays." I go no further and put the phone down.

These little difficulties with recruitment have meant that we have had all sorts of misfits and ne'er-do-wells come to work for us over the years, but they have never lasted long enough to bother us. On the other hand, we have been very lucky, as some of those who have joined us have stayed the course to help us to build the business and they have become good friends.

Sometime after injury forced me to give up cooking at the inn, I worked for three and a half years for Nottingham City Council. While there, I learned about the working ways and habits of local government employees and the reason why our council taxes are so unreasonable. I knew that my mother would not approve, so I told her that I was playing piano in a brothel in order that she would not be embarrassed. I had worked for twelve years in Hong Kong where the work ethic was everything. I had been ten years self-employed at the inn, working a minimum twelve-hour day, without any holiday. I could not reconcile the two completely different attitudes to work. I found that in local government, the mantra of their employees 'don't work too hard now' is the accepted credo; they think time off for 'sickies' is a right and 'stress leave' gets the home decoration done. The only person I ever employed, who had previously worked in local government was a lady, who mercifully only stayed a few weeks. For her sake, I will use the pseudonym Mrs Buggins. Local authority mores and indoctrination had so deeply affected her habits

# The Staff of Our Life

that almost daily she made entries in our accident report book. This paperback document had previously lain undisturbed and covered in dust for years. Her entries in the accident book caused me to call in our Head Chef for a telling off, but I could not keep a straight face. His offence had been to write in large thick red felt pen letters across the front cover of the accident book 'Mrs Buggins's Diary'. What a woman, what an attitude. How different the attitude of other and better members of our staff.

In the early days, to bring some order to the undergrowth and overgrowth surrounding the inn, we had taken on Paul Holt, a qualified and experienced gardener. He came from a good family, who loved him dearly, but he liked to boast that they considered him the black sheep, a wastrel, a dropout. He was none of these; it was just his odd sense of humour. We named him Blot after a gardener character in a then current TV comedy series. He was a character full of interest, always great fun and when pressed into service to work on the bar during busy bank holidays, a riot. The first time this happened, I was astonished to see that he did not seem to have any difficulty working the till or adding up the amount for each round ordered by the crowds of drinkers swarming around the bar. He seemed to be relaxed and competent and to be enjoying himself. The following day I congratulated him. "Well done Blot, you were very good on the till yesterday and with the customers, a great help, thanks." Blot laughed, the quiet laugh of a true countryman. "You still haven't got it have you boss?" he said, smiling. "What! What do you mean?" I shot back, now nervous about what he would say next. "I can't fathom that new-fangled till of yours, I don't add up your silly prices and complicated figures, I just

# It Could be a Little Gold Mine

charge all drinks at a pound apiece, coke, beer, lager, whisky or gin, it's dead easy." "But didn't you get any complaints?" I choked. "Course not, they had waited so long to get served they wouldn't dare, anyway what are you worried about, there isn't a drink in the bar that costs as much as a quid."

Later that year, walking past the derelict coach house, I noticed a pile of dry rotten floorboards on the cobbled floor. "What's that Blot?" I asked him when he came over to ask me what I was looking at, "that pile of rotten wood." "Oh, sorry boss, I was upstairs yesterday getting some boxes for Mrs A and I fell through the floor, I forgot to tell you, I'll get a brush and clear it up now, sorry." It was only then that I noticed the new hole in the ceiling. What a man, what an attitude.

Stephen Lawson came to us as chef, sometime after injury forced me to relinquish kitchen work. He is a true 'what's the fuss?' man. Even better, he is a Yorkshireman. He took on all of the tasks that we set him, however demanding, with complete composure, only raising a quizzical eyebrow if asked if it was all right by him. To Jeanne's anxious enquiry "Stephen are you ready?" the answer has never changed, however big the occasion. A shy smile and always the same reply, "Mrs A, I was born ready."

I like to think that Stephen puts up with me well enough. We occasionally find time to gossip, and put the world to rights. He amazed me with revelations of his prowess as a racing cyclist. He had every right to be proud, he had been part of the England youth team until, on his sixteenth birthday, his mother locked away his bicycle in the garden shed and told him to go out and get a proper job. It was on a day long ago, when my mind was wandering, my chin cupped in my

# The Staff of Our Life

hand as we talked that I broke into his side of the conversation with the uncalled for and unrelated remark, "By God Steve, you are ugly." "Yes," he said, "it's my harelip and cleft palate, I got fed up after about ten operations to correct it, I may go back and let them finish the job some day." He reacted without rancour or hurt feelings, just a natural continuation of our chat. Although I had known and worked with Stephen for more than two years, I had never before noticed his hare lip. This and many other like incidents convince me that we do not observe the features of our true friends at all, we only recognise the whole person, their personality and worth. Only those to whom we take an instant dislike register their features in our consciousness, eyes too close, narrow forehead, clammy handshake, dirty nails and BO.

It is common to the catering vocation for some of those who accept a job to leave it after a few weeks, a few days or even on the same day. Many fail to turn up at all. Most of our early leavers go when they realise that we will not pay them cash in hand, without deducting income tax or national insurance. "I've worked in pubs all over," they blurt, "they have always paid cash in hand, so you can stuff your job."

It is difficult to know how to deal with the problem of staff retention, as being human, we are all so very different and have different expectations. Vernon, one of our longest serving colleagues, lasted just one hour on his first shift as washer-up. He threw down a pot cloth and, as he rushed out of the kitchen door he shouted, "I'm not doing this, it's woman's work." Furious, I threw down my oven cloth and went after him, chasing him up the car park. "Just where do you think you are going?" I shouted. "You told me you

# It Could be a Little Gold Mine

needed to work to get some extra money, get back in the kitchen, finish the washing-up and stop wittering." This textbook technique of modern human resource management worked wonders. Vernon stayed and became a friend. He still works one or two evenings each week and washes the huge pile of pots after Sunday lunch. It is now more than twenty years since he threw in his towel and I chased him up the yard.

Some new recruits, who seemed promising at interview, exhibit unacceptable faults once in post. One such was John, a well set up young man who turned up for work on time looking smart in chef's whites with his name embroidered in neat small blue letters across his top pocket. For the first week, his shift started at three in the afternoon and all went well. He exhibited both sound practical skills and organisational ability. I was very pleased and congratulated him but I noticed that he was never without a plain white china pint pot of steaming strong black coffee. For his second week with us, he was required to do the morning shift. This starts early to prepare and cook breakfast for the guests and staff and then to prepare for the day's lunchtime and evening meals. For three mornings running, John arrived in a furious temper, banging about the kitchen and crashing the pots and pans like a demented pop group drummer. I was on hand to make sure he cooked to our standards. On the third day I asked him to correct some small detail only to have the pan thrown at me with the simultaneous outburst, "If you think you can do it better, cook the bloody breakfasts yourself." "I take it that is your formal resignation?" I questioned. He was off, out of the kitchen, into his car and away. Jeanne, attracted by the noise and as ever the accurate diagnostician

# The Staff of Our Life

remarked, "It's the coffee he drinks, when he has had a few hours sleep he suffers from withdrawal symptoms." It makes me wonder if Gordon Ramsay is a coffee drinker.

Some memories of staff and their contribution to the script are but fleeting moments. Peter, straight from college, was not a natural, but a splendid young man all the same, though I had the feeling he thought me a tyrant. "Peter" I called, "bring the rollmops," and so he did: the patent floor mop and bucket with the two rollers that squeezed the mop head dry. It was my fault, how was he to know that I meant the pickled herring.

Darren, who was with us many years, had an acerbic wit that sometimes upset customers, but one Sunday lunch he got it just right. All three of our sons happened to be behind the bar when an elderly lady, who was a regular customer, called to Jeanne, "Oh, how wonderful for you, all your boys at home together, Christopher, Edward and Bill." Quick as lightning Darren stepped behind the bar and piped up, "And I'm up for adoption."

# CHAPTER THIRTEEN

# To Serve Them all My Days

Most customers who come to our inn pay their way with more than cash, cheque or credit card. They add interest. As a genus, they are enthralling, as a species fascinating, as a variety intriguing and as individuals beguiling. They feed my hobby of people watching with endless copy. Those who share this hobby and work in public bars, restaurants or *front of house* in hotels, need no cover. Unlike bird-watching twitchers, we do not need a hide or powerful binoculars; we are already invisible and close up to the quarry. This is so because the middle-aged and elderly of the British Public believe that all barmen, barmaids, restaurant managers, waiters, receptionists and hall porters are inanimate; younger customers believe them to be cyborgs.

Customers feel free to pass whatever comment occurs to them, giving no thought that they may be overheard. Equally, as they are not conscious of our observation, they have no inhibition about expressing their feelings with intimate physical behaviour. From our unhindered vantage, we observe much: we get news, views, and opinion of far better value than we can glean from newspapers, radio, or television. Their overheard humour, both conscious and unconscious, makes our days merry and gives us ideas that we use to develop and grow our business. Best of all, a few special customers, those who saw us for what we are, and engaged with us as fellow human beings, have rewarded us with lasting friendship.

We have not pleased all our customers, nor could we. Being human, we sometimes fail to cope with events; we misinterpret people's wishes, neglect our duty, or despite using our best endeavour, get it all wrong. Rightly, they complain. When we have let customers down, we do what we can to compensate them adequately, but this is rarely possible. If we provided a poor meal on their birthday we cannot rerun it on another day, the moment has passed. If, in error, we have double booked a room for which a couple have special memories, we cannot eject the current occupants. No alternative room, however superior its furnishings, can recapture the original magic of a special moment they have shared.

One couple always asked for Room 2, a room that we did not consider anything near our best, but for them, Room 2 it had to be. At last, some years on, we were able to afford to completely refurbish the room and were proud of the result. However, unknowingly we had spoilt its special magic for our regular 'Room 2 couple'. On the morning after the first visit they made after the refurbishment, I met them while they were having breakfast. "Do you like the new decoration and furniture in your room? We think it has turned out rather well." I was proud and expecting an enthusiastic response. "Well, it's all right," was the apathetic reply, "but it is a bit disappointing for us." "Oh, What have we got wrong?" "Well, you may not have noticed but I have always ordered cheese and biscuits instead of a pudding after dinner. You see the cheese was to feed your mouse; he used to come out of that hole in the floorboards where there had once been a radiator pipe. You've blocked it up and covered it with carpet and we've lost him, he was always there and he was such fun."

# It Could be a Little Gold Mine

Another of my tales of friendly pets almost belies belief, but it did happen, just as I have told it many times since and as I now tell it again. Fatso was a very ordinary sort of pet rabbit, a silky smooth light brown huggable bundle with large bright eyes, pink nose and sticky-up ears. Our youngest son Bill and his lovely girl Cindy left him, for us to look after, when they decided to up sticks and go to set up house and home together in Leicester. They thought it would upset both him and us if they took their charge with them, away from the country into the city.

Every now and again, to give him a bit of exercise, I took him out of his small cage in our garden and let him loose to flop about in the bar and restaurant. On these rare occasions, he caused much merriment as customers laughed at my clumsy and futile attempts to recapture him when it was time for him to be back in his quarters. Their pleasure, at my expense, always improved when Jeanne would come and catch him with no difficulty, by bribing him with a sprig of parsley. I retaliated, if customers told me his presence was unhygienic, by telling them he was a very clever rabbit. If they asked how I knew this, which they usually did, I would delight in telling them that he was an expert in currant affairs.

One dreadful November day of fog and ice, I did not expect many, if any, customers. Feeling a bit lonely, I went to fetch Fatso for a bit of company and gave him freedom of the house. Only one couple came as customers that day. Tired of driving in the bad weather and not knowing precisely where they were, they came to the inn for rest and recuperation. While the man, a stranger to us, was at the bar ordering drinks and food, Fatso, unseen and unbidden, hopped up onto the bench beside his wife, and then onto her lap where

# To Serve Them all My Days

he settled himself down quite happily. So charmed was the lady by his affectionate welcome that she stroked and nursed him for an hour as she ate a leisurely lunch. Clearly, both could not have been happier.

The following February, I received a telephone call asking if ours was the inn, somewhere in Derbyshire, where a tame rabbit was allowed the run of the bar. The male caller said he had suggested to his wife that they deserved a weekend away and that she had agreed, but only if he could find the inn where the rabbit sat on her lap. He went on to explain that because of the fog on that day he had no idea where he had been and no idea of the name of the inn but thought it was somewhere in Derbyshire. However, when he called the Ashbourne Tourist Information office, luck was on both his and our side. Hillary, a friend of ours, was the Information Officer on duty and she was the one officer who knew about Fatso. It was because of this string of happenstance that we got the booking, and bookings in February are doubly welcome.

The magic moment came later. I had forgotten about the booking but again, by rare chance, I had brought Fatso across to the bar for his constitutional, when I noticed a lady nursing him and shedding a little tear of pure joy. It was the same lady and she could not stop repeating, "He remembers me – he remembers me." With that one booking, Fatso paid for his lifetime keep many times over. The lady was supremely happy, the husband well-pleased at the success of his forensic efforts and I was content with the way of the world.

Occasional failure is inevitable in the hospitality business. It comes unexpectedly and cannot always be foreseen or avoided. Thankfully, few of our guests abuse our hospitality

# It Could be a Little Gold Mine

with behaviour that is unacceptable when we have failed them. Nevertheless, when we are subject to unkind, thoughtless, or arrogant behaviour, such incidents have a deep and damaging effect on us all. A famous restaurateur who visited us shortly after we took over the inn, knowing that we were new to the trade, gave good advice. "You will do well, you two, but from time to time you will be knocked back by outspoken criticism, some valid, some not so, some due to their ignorance. Do not let it get you down. Do what you do, do it honestly and as well as you are able. Let such criticism pass; you may learn from it, but do not dwell upon it. Remember always, it is your business and your home. Customers, good and bad, albeit that they pay and are important to your cash flow are invited guests." We try to follow his advice but still feel hurt and above all an acute frustration and sense of failure when our best-laid plans go awry.

Against all odds and common perceived wisdom, I have long argued that the customer is not always right. I usually cite the tie-less, gold medallion, gold Rolex wearing braggart who lit a cigar in our non-smoking restaurant, claiming immunity from the no-smoking rule by loudly declaring, "What's the fuss young man? Everyone has finished eating," and then calling out to all the other guests, "You don't mind if I smoke do you?" "They may not, but I do," was my measured reply. We lost that customer, but many of the other diners took time to thank me for standing up to the arrogant bully.

Sometimes customer complaints are unjustified. At the inn, this has been the case when we have not satisfied the customer's expectations because they, not we, had it all wrong. Classic in this genre was the Irishman who brought his family for a week's holiday. He was in his mid-seventies at least, brown and knurled as a shillelagh, with a brogue and belt; each of them thick enough to mark him both as a country-man and a martinet, and he carried a blackthorn stick. His children, all in their forties or early fifties were numerous, all very large, single and singular.

On their first evening with us, they came down early for dinner. Without a word, with the old man at the head, he marched them, in single file, straight into the restaurant; I suspected the file was in the pecking order of age, except for mother, who brought up the rear. This tyrant rebuked me when I tried to hand out the menus. "What are you doing man? Give me one menu, I will make the order," and so he did. "Bridget will have the fish, Declan the lamb, Seamus the lamb also, Maeve the boiled chicken, no fancy sauce." and so on right round the table. All his subject family sat, heads bowed, hands clasped in their laps, not a word, or even a grace, spoken. He finished "My wife Mary will have the salad and I the steak, well-done, no sauce." I just knew he would have the most expensive dish for himself.

As soon as they finished the meal, he packed them all off to bed. He followed behind, with his blackthorn stick, the very image of a stockman with a cattle probe. It was summer

# It Could be a Little Gold Mine

and the bar was very busy. At ten-thirty, down the stairs he came, in his dressing gown and slippers. "What are all these people doing here? Send them away at once, I came here for a quiet rest." Of course, I did nothing of the sort.

The following morning having made up his bill for the one night stay and their dinner, I was waiting for him. Down he came, this time in his dark brown Donegal tweeds, thin as a snake and full of venom, clearly one that St Patrick missed. "Now my man," he said, "I will be having a word with you. I ..." I cut him off short, with the sweetest smile I could muster, and said, "No sir, you will not, but I will have a word with you. Here is your bill; I require that you leave our inn, as soon as you and your family have had breakfast." This I followed by a further and even bigger smile. "But I have booked here for a week," he started. "But I have booked you out after breakfast; good day to you sir," I countered. I left him and went to hide in the kitchen. To my relief he paid Jeanne in full, for the one night stay and dinner, and left straight after breakfast. Again his family was in single file, this time his wife leading, with him bringing up the rear, waving his blackthorn stick.

His expectation had been of a secluded country house hotel. Our brochure clearly states, in contrast, that the Bentley Brook is a busy inn in the country, undeniably a far different experience. We lost a good booking that we could ill afford to lose, but to try to please him would have been a fruitless and costly exercise.

Some customers leave us speechless with their meanness. As with all restaurants, we receive many requests to donate vouchers entitling the winners of charity raffles, tombolas and lucky dips to free Sunday lunches, à la carte dinners, or

# To Serve Them all My Days

weekend breaks. We try to help as many as we can, not simply for philanthropic reasons, but because it often pays a valuable dividend. All restaurants suffer from what is known in the business as the *threshold barrier*. Many people are very nervous when entering a restaurant for the first time, for the good reason that they do not know what to expect. Encouraged by their good fortune in a raffle, or lucky dip, to cross our threshold, some find the confidence to come again as regular, if not always frequent, customers. Thus, both the charity funds and our funds benefit.

However, one man who won a voucher for dinner for four in our restaurant left us without words. This thin-boned Uriah Heap of a man came twisting and writhing up to me, wringing his bony hands around his winning voucher, "Mr Allingham, sir, as the voucher is for four people to have dinner, would it be too much trouble if my wife and I use it twice?" I do not think that my dropped jaw enabled me to deal with the request very well, but come twice they did, and though they passed over our threshold twice, we never saw them again, well not as paying customers.

Other customers have been incredibly generous to Jeanne and to me. None more so than a couple who booked to have a three-night break that included dinner as well as bed and breakfast. We noticed from the register that they owned and operated a famous highly rated hotel in the West Country. On their second night, they told me that they had just had a three-night break at Sharrow Bay in the Lake District and were on their way to Hambleton Hall for a three-night break there. "What on earth are you doing here?" was my astonished response. I knew that Sharrow Bay was top of all the review lists of this country's luxury country house hotels and

# It Could be a Little Gold Mine

that Hambleton Hall was, at the time, the fashion leader in nouvelle cuisine. "Oh that's easy to explain," they said, "We go to Sharrow Bay to rest, to enjoy the Lake District views and their antique furniture. We go to Hambleton Hall to see where food fashion is going, but we come here for your proper food and excellent beer." On their last night they ordered a bottle of Tokai Assencia, to be served as a dessert wine after their dinner. This unique half-litre bottle was on our list at seven times the cost of an average dinner, so we were excited. When Jeanne took it to their table for confirmation it was what they had ordered, they asked her to uncork it, for the lady to try. As soon as Jeanne uncorked the bottle, they both said, "No, don't pour, it is for you and David to enjoy, as we have enjoyed our stay with you." We have had big money tips, all of which have faded from memory, but their magnificent gesture was priceless, never to be forgotten.

It was seldom that I was able to respond to rude customers with a riposte of which I could be truly proud, but just occasionally I got it right. One was an occasion when it was barely mid-morning and I happened to be in the bar. Two rather arch ladies, clearly conscious of coordinated fashion, with severe lacquered hair, much make-up, perfume and nail polish, made an entrance. "Good morning" I sang out, "Welcome; would you like a tray of tea and biscuits or coffee perhaps?" in what I hoped was the genial style expected of a landlord. "Oh no!" was the reply, as brittle as their lacquered hair. "Two schooners of sherry, Tio Pepe should you have any, that would be nearer the mark." "Of course ladies," I replied, now a little wary. I had two very elegant copita glasses, left out of a set of six, that had been a wedding present. These beautiful thin short-stemmed tulip shaped glasses were rather special. I poured out the sherry into the copitas and took them to the table where the rather arch trouser wearing ladies had perched on the end of their chairs, rather than sitting in them. "Oh dear" said one to the other as they exchanged exaggerated supercilious glances, and then to me, "At our golf club we get a decent sized schooner." "Oh I am so sorry," said I, "Let me change them for you," Their smiles were as thin as rice vermicelli, when once again they exchanged glances. Quickly, I brought two empty Elgin schooners to their table, each shaped like the trumpet head of a daffodil, but set on a short stump of a stem. As I placed them on the table, they both said together, "That's much more like it, they are just like the ones we have at the golf club." "Good" said I, merry as a cricket. I took up the two copitas and poured the thin dry Tio Pepe from them into the replacement Elgin glasses, until the Elgins were brimful. I then took the good half-inch of sherry left in each copita away to the kitchen. I lost a couple of customers, but the look on their faces made it worthwhile. Their crushed thin lipped look reminded me of the *Tom and Jerry* cartoon cat, when he has been hit in the mouth by a baseball bat.

Sherry has gone a bit out of fashion of late and I am not sorry to see its passing. It did seem to gather to it a snob appeal that was difficult to understand. The people who insist that all beef must be cooked rare, forgetting brisket, shin and chuck, are the same as those who insisted that dry Manzanillas are the only sherries fit to drink. They forget the influence of the time of day and type of meal insisting that Tio Pepe is barely dry enough for their sophisticated palates.

One party who used to come for Sunday lunch always

# It Could be a Little Gold Mine

caused me to cringe as they marched, at double step, eyes front, straight into the restaurant, avoiding the bar. Every time they came, their senior member cut off any approach from a member of staff to enquire if they would like a drink before lunch. He would call out, in a loud high-pitched voice that carried the whole ground floor and half the garden, "No drinks thank you; we have had our sherry at home." "Cheapskates," I would murmur to myself, "Plus fours and no breakfast."

Some customers endeared themselves to me by their candour when caught out, having tried to impress or put me one down. One such occasion happened after a very pleasant atmosphere had prevailed in the restaurant and things had gone well. Finished in the kitchen I had come though to the bar for what I thought would be a well-earned, undisturbed, pint. A party of four, wishing to smoke after dinner, had come into the bar to have their coffee or tea by the log fire. One of the four was a particularly attractive woman, of an age when women have lost the first flush of youth and reached the full bloom of femininity. Although a member of staff was already taking their order, she spoke past him, directly to me, in what my mother used to call a 'cut-glass' voice. "Chef, do you possibly, or by any chance, have such a thing as China tea?" "Why yes, of course," I replied, pretty sure of my ground and seeing a chance to flirt with this stunning creature. "Would my lady prefer Yunan, Lapsang Souchong, or Heung Peen?" The bar went quiet, all sensing that I had called her bluff. Blushing, mighty prettily, all she could say, in what was now a little girl voice was, "Sorry, I was being a bitch. Could I just have a nice cup of tea – please?" Here was one customer we would not lose because she understood the art of flirting, an art now sadly lost. All is now competition to win at all cost. Flirting was not about winning or losing, just about playing the game.

Sometimes it has been unconscious or hidden humour that has made my day. Lunchtime had been quiet and I was happily preparing some special sweets to be ready for the busy evening ahead. I went behind the bar to get a measure of some liqueur or other and noticed a man sitting up to the bar with his chin cupped in his hand, as still as Rodin's *The Thinker*. Ten minutes later, I went back to the bar to get something else I remembered, as a vital ingredient, for one of my posh puddings. The man had not moved. He seemed as though he had seen something spellbinding, deep beneath the surface of the bar. A good quarter of an hour later, I went back for a third raid on the liqueur shelf. This time I felt obliged to speak, because he had not moved, he was exactly as before. "You're very pensive," I said, quite gently, not wanting to shock him out of his reverie. Slowly raising his head from his cupped hand and looking straight at me, but not fully comprehending, he simply said, "I never gave it a thought." This reply went straight into my memory bank, he had made my day, all was well with the world. He, unaware, drank the last of his long neglected beer, stepped down from his stool, and wandered off.

Another exchange, one more of body language than word play, gave me great pleasure. It was with a man I had not seen before, but who was clearly acutely aware of both his station and situation. It was mid-summer and the doors to the terrace were wide-open. I was standing behind the bar, dressed in dark blue blazer, formal tie, and clean white shirt. With shoulders back, hands, with thumbs crossed, behind my back, I was at

# It Could be a Little Gold Mine

ease. In through the open doors came a colonel type with his even grander lady wife and their debutante daughter. Father was all Norfolk jacket, military tie, cavalry twill trousers and highly polished brogues. Both mother and daughter were dressed in classic Pringle twinsets, tweed pleated skirts, pearls, sheer nylons and court shoes. Clearly, they were from the very best of quiet money county families. A young man followed them, who I guessed the daughter had chosen for herself, not for the family. He was in the archetypal, 'guess who's coming to dinner?' secret. Huge and bulky, he was well over six feet tall, with a shock of unruly red hair linked by mutton-chop sideburns to an unkempt full set of beard and rambling moustache. Most prominent was his pair of thick horn-rimmed spectacles. His attire was also out of keeping with that of his beloved and her family. His thick-knit dun coloured loose-fitting round neck sweater cascaded down to midcalf where it met with worn brown corduroy trousers. To complete his outfit, he wore open-toed leather sandals, without socks. The whole effect was more a statement than apparel. This young man made my week, let alone day, with his verbal response to my silent inspection. All that he said, and without question he said it directly to me, although I had neither moved nor spoken, was, "And I read the Guardian." What a man, what a delight. It was his use of the word 'and' that made it all so wonderful.

I did recognise and have fun with David Jacobs when he brought the Radio Four *Any Questions* team to Ashbourne. That was when the programme was both interesting and a pleasure to listen to, before Dumbleby and Co hijacked it and made it vulgar. Mr Jacobs, with great charm, called to me, "Mr Allingham, I have never been to Ashbourne and wonder if you could suggest something that I might use to introduce the programme?" "Well, why not use the Byron quote?" I replied, "It was in a letter he wrote to a friend: 'Was you ever in Dovedale? I assure you there are things in Derbyshire as noble as in Greece and Switzerland'." I continued, "You could say 'Tonight we are in Ashbourne, the gateway to Dovedale' and get into it that way." "Mmm it's a bit posh for my programme," he replied, but I was delighted that he opened the programme with just those words.

My mother made my delight the merrier when, five minutes after the programme finished, she rang from her home in Halifax. She told me she had just been listening to *Any Questions* on the radio and that nice Mr Jacobs had said something about Dovedale, something Lord Byron had said. "I've copied it down and will send it to you; I know you will like it."

# CHAPTER FOURTEEN

# Travellers' Tales

One way or another, I have learned a great deal from salesmen who came to the inn to sell their company products. We used to call them commercial travellers, that was before the 'unwashed' debased the word 'traveller'. Several of their honourable calling, when calling, revealed that they were expert in their field and freely passed on their knowledge and experience. The best of them also brightened our days with their travellers' tales.

Some salesmen were not good at their job. One was so dreadful that his sales technique stuck firmly in my memory and his sales aid very nearly lodged in my brain. This poor chap came to see me, by appointment, having told me over the phone that he had a device that would save me twenty per cent of my electricity bill. He arrived late and I could see that he was having a little difficulty trying to carry something quite hefty under his arm. He was painfully thin, not much more than twenty years old and dressed in a cheap grey tweed jacket under which he wore a Fair Isle jumper. This was tucked into his grey flannel unpressed trousers. As he came through the door, he gave a passing fair impersonation of Michael Crawford acting the part of Frank Spencer having a bad day in the TV comedy series *Some Mothers do 'ave 'em*.

# Travellers' Tales

The inconvenience under his arm was his sales aid, a thick wooden board measuring about three feet long by two feet six inches wide. On one side, there was a painted mimic diagram and many small torchlight bulbs and switches. On the other side, neatly clipped wires connected the bulbs and switches to a series of batteries. "Good morning," I said, "Come, sit you down, put that silly game away, then tell me in your own words, how this wonderful device of yours can save me money." It completely threw the young man when I made this unexpected suggestion. "But sir, this interactive board will convince you how it all works. The company have trained me to use it." It was clear to me that the only way to progress was to let him demonstrate the device. As he reached each of the key selling points in his parrot learned patter, it was obvious that he did not understand how his gadget worked. It was simple enough; all it could do was to use thermostats and timers, to limit the current to devices using electricity providing heat and light. I asked a few questions, none of which he had been trained to understand or answer. "You don't want one then?" he said, finally losing his temper. "No." I said, "it's a waste of money, if I wanted to do what your device does, I would just turn down all heater thermostats and change my light bulbs from sixty to forty watts. That would save me money without costing me a penny."

By this time, he had reached the door and was on his way out, but before leaving, he paused for a moment, head down, obviously deep in thought. Then, coming to a decision, he turned like a discus thrower of Olympian class and flung the three foot long by two feet six inches wide sales aid, complete with switches, bulbs and batteries, a full ten paces, directly at me. "You can keep the bloody thing," he shouted. "Do I take

# It Could be a Little Gold Mine

it you will be resigning your position?" was all I could get out before he was off into his car and gone. The board had knocked a lump of plaster from the wall, close enough to my head to cause me no little concern.

Another occasion when a salesman threw his wares at me was more fun. It was a June morning many years ago. I had finished cooking breakfast for our guests, when I heard a cautious knock on the kitchen door. When the knock came for a second time, a little louder, I was curious and opened the door to a tall rangy sort of chap, in his late fifties, with a two-day growth on his chin. He was dressed overall in drab green. Green wellies, without straps, green waterproof trousers and a green waxed-coat, all finished off with a green waterproof wide-brimmed hat. His was not the outfit of the wealthy sport out for a day's shooting. It was far too well-worn for that, being more characteristic of a Lincolnshire poacher and his gruff way of speech would not have passed muster at the *Officers' Club*. "Hello - what do you want?" I said in a friendly enough sort of way. "Are you the governor here?" he asked. "Yes, why?" was my response, now a little guarded wondering whether the bailiffs or health inspectors had gone underground. "I've got something you'll want, I'll get it from t'car," and he was off. Again, the knock on the door and this time it was obvious what he was about.

Hanging by the ears from his great fist, at the end of his outstretched arm, was the biggest brown hare I had ever seen. "I was just passing your place, it ran right in front o' t'car, and I just clipped it. It's not much damaged and it's a shame not to use it. I would myself but I won't get home for a few days." "Oh yes," I said, "Poor old boy must have given himself up, it's ancient." I could see the bars of age across most of its back and all fat had gone from it, showing its muscle structure like the plates of a rhinoceros. "What do you mean?" he says, "It's a beautiful young leveret, look how easily I can tear its ears." The scene was reducing to farce as he tugged and pulled at the ears that were as tough as a lorry tyre. "How much do you want for this cold cadaver that you just clipped with your car then?" I asked. "I'll tell you what, I'll do you a favour, a fiver will do it." "Ney lad, I'll do thee a favour," I replied in my best Yorkshire dialect, "I'll give you fifty pence and I'll promise not to tell the police your car registration number." It was then that he threw it at me, saying, "You can keep the damn thing," and he was off, quick as one of his Jack Russells after a rabbit. The hare had not been long dead so I took it in and dealt with it straight away. While I was gutting it and slipping off its almost threadbare fur coat, the lead shot I expected fell out into the kitchen sink. It was too old for jugging but it helped to make a savoury game terrine.

The worst of all the salesmen who came by appointment was a man intent on getting us to accept the credit cards issued by his company. He introduced himself, repeatedly assuring me that he was a very senior manager who would not normally be 'on the road' as he put it. He was at pains to inform me that he had taken the opportunity to give one of their new intake of university graduates some high level 'on the job' training.

I let this sharp suited unctuous self-appointed 'senior manager' go through his total spiel. It was full of management speak, and jargon. He started with the textbook sales technique by flattering our excellent and well-respected *hotel*, and going on to explain that it was because of the esteem in which it was held, that we had been specially selected to join

# It Could be a Little Gold Mine

in a partnership with his company. He went on at length to extol the wonders that this would bring. He pointed out that the privilege of using his company's card was only granted to carefully vetted, social class double As and ABs, all big spenders, who he assured me were all anxious to visit our inn. His self-aggrandising glances to the young man, each time he completed one of the compulsory plus points from the sales manual, I found profoundly irritating. His assumption that I was a bumpkin was even more irksome. I was so cross that I said not a word during his presentation. He followed his script, word perfectly, without prompt or reference to paperwork. When at last he was quiet, I begged, "Excuse me for moment, I must go to get a pen." I was sure that he was confident that his spiel had worked the charm and that this bumpkin wanted a pen to sign along the dotted line in the sheaf of agreement papers that he had spread out before me.

He was wrong. I brought both pen and paper and set them before his young graduate pupil. During the presentation, the young man had said not a word. He just sat with glazed-over eyes, whether listening or not to his master's voice I could not tell. "Now," I said to the young man, "pay attention most carefully. When you have heard and considered the issues, I hope that you will, with this pen and on this paper, write out your resignation and hand it to this fellow here who has told me, repeatedly, that he is a most senior manager of the company you have joined." I then continued, "I hope that you will then go out and get yourself a proper job." At this point, I was into my full stride. "Now listen and learn," I said this directly to the young graduate who by now was looking very worried. "Only a few days ago I had occasion to cut up one of your company's credit cards, one that had a two thousand pound credit limit. Your so carefully managed company had sent it, by post, to a young girl who works here. She has no living relatives, no home other than a very small room here at the inn. She would have to work night and day for six months to earn two thousand pounds, let alone save two thousand. She has no qualifications and has only been with us a few weeks. By the way, she came to us having been on the dole for months." To the very important unctuous representative with the sharp suit I simply said, "You too should also consider your position. Good day."

Sadly as time and the world has spun round a few times since then, cash is no longer king, cheques are rare and we now accept that hated card, but only as a last option against all other methods of payment and all other cards.

Those three dreary tales are not typical of our experience with those who call to sell and socialise. As we came to know them, the usual greeting we gave was, "Right then, shall we have a pot of tea?" One man, who we later learned had played soccer for England, came calling, not representing England, but a foreign brand of lager. Although a great raconteur, he never once mentioned soccer or his former achievements. I only learned of them when a customer recognised him and asked for his autograph, which he gave, graciously. His honesty and integrity impressed me mightily, as did his understanding of my attitude to business.

When we took over the inn, we inherited two brands of lager, both of which had about the same level of alcohol. Christopher, our eldest son, suggested that we would do better if we changed one lager, to a premium brand, with higher alcohol content. He was then fourteen, and as he was at Uppingham Public School, we bowed to his greater knowl-

# It Could be a Little Gold Mine

edge, if not experience, of what beers and lagers were popular.

The next time the unassuming lager representative called, I asked him if he could arrange the change. "Of course, it shall be done," he said. He made all the necessary arrangements for the changeover that took place without fuss. He continued to call each month, but never talked business, just family stuff. It was twelve months later when he asked if he might speak to me about the premium lager he had arranged to supply. "Is it - is everything alright?" I asked, a little surprised. "Well yes," he said, "It's been in for twelve months now and the company is well satisfied with how much you sell, but I have a problem." "Oh what?" "Well, when you asked me to arrange the change, the brewery had a special offer running. They offered to give a gold wristwatch to everyone who changed to our brand from another. I knew you wouldn't like it, thinking it a bribe, so I didn't tell you for fear that you might throw me out on my ear. The watch is still in my manager's safe. Please, will you let me give it to Christopher?" "Yes of course you may, you're a sound sort of chap you are," I replied. I was disgusted to learn that his company made him redundant a few months later; he was just too old-fashioned for them. Unusually, as well as having been a star footballer, he was a gentleman.

Mr Smith, like the swallows, returned to visit us in the spring of each year, having never been near us, all our long winter long. He was a master tactician and consummate practitioner of the soft sell. I liked him because he came from Halifax, my home town. I understood him, and he me. He also understood our enthusiasm to do well and the constraints of our cash flow. His product was catering equipment and the firm he represented one of the biggest in the country. His firm did not make anything but they had printed for them, beautifully bound catalogues, printed on heavy gloss paper. They were thicker than a London telephone directory. These heavy tomes were full of photographs of items essential to the caterer. Smith never once mentioned business; it was exchanges of photographs of the children and local gossip, and a great deal of banter and leg pulling. However, unseen, every spring Smith would discreetly leave one of his siren catalogues somewhere where he knew I would find it, after he had left.

On a day soon after the Easter bank holiday, I was in the garden, dressed as usual in blue overalls and digging a trench, when, on the cue of spring, all smiles and greetings Smith came walking down the car park. The garden was full of folk, so for a bit of fun I shouted at him, "Go away, you know you can't come in here, I banned you for life." To add to the drama I threw a few handy clods of earth at him. His response was immediate and marvellous. "But sir, I've given up the drink, I'm teetotal now, I've been off the booze for months, give me another chance sir, please. I've only come to pay for the damage I done." It was a great spontaneous performance. I was sure all the onlookers would remember the inn and tell their friends of the fracas. There was a good chance too that their friends would then come to see the eccentric landlord, hoping for more drama.

Filled with hundreds of photographs of kitchen wear; high tech combi-ovens, pots, pans, boilers and steamers, mixers, mincers, blenders; and gadgets, lots of desirable but useless gadgets, the catalogues that Smith left behind were my undoing. They also had sections showing beautiful napery, ceramic tableware, glassware, and cutlery both silver and stainless steel

# It Could be a Little Gold Mine

to tempt Jeanne and the housekeeper. These catalogues held us fascinated, in thrall, determined that one day we would have a kitchen and restaurant to equal the best. However, the lightweight poor quality paper, stapled together price lists he left with the catalogues dashed our hopes. But Smith, as I have told you, was a Yorkshireman; astute and cunning. Having spotted my weakness, he left a Trojan Horse in the restaurant.

It was less than half an hour after he had gone that I found it. There it stood, the answer to our needs, proud and gleaming with a warm copper glow, a very high quality, very expensive chafing dish. Attached to it Smith had left a handwritten note detailing a special discount, valid for one month only, bringing the price down to a little over three hundred pounds, excluding VAT. Smith had shrewdly added to the bait, by informing us that payment was not due until after the next bank holiday. Over three hundred pounds each, and that in 1978. We needed three at least, which would cost us nearly a thousand pounds; more than my beloved father ever earned in a year.

Smith knew that we served a carvery lunch each Sunday, but did not have the necessary equipment to keep the vegetables hot. He also knew that if our carvery was to meet the general customer expectation we must have good quality chafing dishes. His cunning trick worked, we found the money, despite being cash strapped, and he got the sale.

It turned out that the man from Halifax was indeed a good friend as well as a great salesman. More than a quarter of a century on, we still use those same high quality burnished copper chafing dishes at least once a week. We have now served well over seventy five thousand meals from them, taking over half a million pounds. I am at last content that the thousand pounds was money well spent.

One salesman who called at the inn worked for Bass Brewery. He never once sold us anything, but he brought us much news and knowledge of the business in which were innocents. He was a superb raconteur and kept us enthralled with his traveller's tales. Because of him, to this day, I have a nervous reaction every time I pay to clean our car using one of those automatic drive-through glass and concrete boxes, filled with huge multicoloured revolving brushes and forceful jets of water, both hot and cold, gales of hot air and streams of hot wax.

The man was accident-prone. One day he came to tell us about his latest accident. His top brass Bass Director had called him into head office to explain why it was that the cost of repairs to the company car he had given him was so much more than the repair costs of the cars used by other member of the sales team. When the day of the interview came, he explained to us that, understandably, he was a bit nervous. Seeking to make a good impression, he dressed in his best suit, put on a clean white shirt with starched collar, a new company tie, and a pair of smart leather shoes. He set off for his appointment with time to spare and that was his undoing. Nearing the company head office, with half an hour in hand, he spotted one of these automatic drive-through glass and concrete boxes filled with huge multicoloured revolving brushes and forceful jets of water, both hot and cold, gales of hot air and streams of hot wax. Thinking it would be a good idea if he turned up in a clean car, as well as a clean shirt, he stopped and purchased a token for *the works*, a full programme to clean and wax polish the car. He started the

# It Could be a Little Gold Mine

engine, engaged first gear, then let in the clutch to take the car onto the tracks where fate was patiently waiting. Having used the machine before, he did not bother to read the instructions. He selected neutral, turned off the engine and sat back to relax as he felt the car being pulled forward by the automatic rollers into the heaving maw of the steaming, pulsating beast. It was only then that he read the notice, 'Please ensure that your car aerial is retracted'. A quick glance in the mirror and horror! The aerial was full out. Fearing more damage to the company car, he leapt out and successfully pushed the thin protruding wand firmly into place.

Unfortunately for him, fate was bored and arranged for the advancing brushes to push the open door tight shut as he struggled, tried and failed to get himself back inside the car. To add to the fun, fate also ensured that the new company tie was inside the door and the clean white shirt and starched collar outside the door. The fate-driven machine had thereby trapped and pinned him to the outside of the car as it progressed on its two-pound fifty pence journey. Although fate had arranged for him to be pressed, bruised, and battered by the brushes, soaked through to the skin by both the hot and cold-water rinses, part dried only, by the blasts of hot and cold air, our hero of a thousand and one tales had a plan. He drove straight to the head office intending to call the director, by phone, hoping to rearrange the meeting with some contrived excuse. Of course, it was not to be. Bursting through the main doors into the marble and mahogany reception hall the first person he saw was the Director he was to meet. Worse, the Director saw him. As we cried laughing at his story he finished, "Well it was not all that bad, at least I had paid extra for the hot wax and had my shoes polished."

Sadly, most such wonderful salesmen men are now gone. In this electronic twenty-first century, the best we get is the telephone sales girl's cold call, "Oh! hi! - I'm Tracy, or Samantha, Tiggy, or Davina, is that Dave?" We never get such calls from a Nellie, Margaret, Joan, or Winnie asking for Mr or Mrs Allingham. I have the greatest difficulty in not just replying with a curt "No" and putting the phone down. Far worse are the spam e-mails trying to sell me diets, potency pills, mortgages, or the equivalent of the filthy postcards hawked years ago by the gully gully peddlers on the banks of the Suez Canal.

Where are the bagmen of years ago?

# CHAPTER FIFTEEN

# Charivari

Our life as innkeepers has not gone according to plan, nor has it been a steady progression or ordered existence. Like many couples seeking their 'Little gold mine', Jeanne and I hoped, that in time, the inn would keep us and our family. However, despite our best efforts, and those of our three children, throughout our many years as proprietors, we have remained its keepers. It has been a life of unorganised but instinctive reaction to events. All who work in the hospitality industry know this to be true. How could it be otherwise? Climatic events, infrastructure failure, mechanical, electric, electronic breakdowns, structural failures, the burden of ever changing ill-considered legislation and regulation and the charivari of incongruous individual and group behaviour of both staff and guests, drive our days and nights.

Our memories of events and our reaction to them are personal, coming as they do, unbidden, unorganised, and in no chronological order. Neither Jeanne nor I have kept a diary. I use this as my excuse when caught talking, out of turn, at customers. Our regulars are used to my rambling unconnected stories, tales and reminiscences that have no theme, sequence, logic, or plot. Jeanne worries when I hold customers with my innkeeper's tales. She tells me I am no Chaucer or Scheherazade, but more like Coleridge's glassy eyed Ancient Mariner, when she dryly points out that I merely detain, rather than entertain.

Agnostics, atheists and modern modelling mathematicians try to resolve problems of event management with random theory, proposing that butterflies in Bangladesh cause typhoons in Tottenham. I have a different, more perfect understanding that is not a theory, but theology. I know it is my god in his heaven who ravels my life, and that no method devised by mortals will ever solve my problems. I believe my god is not only my creator and forgiving father but also that he is a god with a genuine sense of fun, like my own progenitor father. When my heavenly Father gets a little bored, he brings interest to his day by tossing a pebble into my pond then watches to see how the ripples will run. I like to think my late father, who has been with him in heaven these forty years, gives him ideas and eggs him on.

How could it have been otherwise, when one recent busy spring Saturday, while we were at ease and confident that all arrangements were well in hand, he flipped a series of rather larger pebbles than usual into my small pond, to remind me that 'owt can 'appen'. Head Chef was to start his shift at noon. He did not arrive. Using the (then) modern miracle of the mobile phone, we rang to enquire when we might expect him. "Sorry, the person you have called is not available, if you wish to leave a message please speak after the tone," was the soulless synthesized response from the remarkable hand-held gadget. We coped. Second Chef was due in at three in the afternoon. He did not arrive. We rang his modern miracle mobile phone only to receive the same response from the same soulless synthesized voice. "Sorry, the person you have called is not available..." with the same invitation to leave a message. We coped. Also due to come to work at three was

# It Could be a Little Gold Mine

Edna, our Head Housekeeper. She did not arrive. We rang Edna, and heard again that same soulless synthesized voice "Sorry, the person you have called is not available..." with the same invitation to leave a message. We coped, just.

The first to call in answer to our anxious enquiries was dear Edna and her message was seriously worrying. "Sorry Mr A, I've just come outside to ring you, I'm at the hospital, my husband Paul has had a heart attack. I couldn't ring earlier because the hospital doesn't allow mobile phones." We coped, barely, but events were stretching our resources.

Well used to crisis management, Jeanne made a quick call to Chef Anton who comes to our aid when we are desperate. "Anton, can you come in? We are two chefs down," Anton, always helpful, replied "Oh! Hello! Er, wait a minute, I can't come in right now, but I can get to you about half past five." Then at about four o'clock, came the anxiously awaited call from Head Chef. "I'm sorry Mr A; I've had an accident on the way to work. Hit a tractor, I'm in hospital with a suspected punctured lung, I couldn't ring you earlier, mobile phones are not allowed in here and I've only just been given a bed."

Ten minutes later, Second Chef rang. "Hello Mr A, it's Dean here, I'm in hospital. I am sorry I couldn't ring you; they don't allow mobile telephones here. I was coming down the stairs with a glass in my hand when I trod on the cat. Now I really have got the glass in my hand." The next call, at ten to five, proved my point about the uselessness of modern management methods and theory. It was from Anton, "Hello Mr A, it's Anton, I did set off, twenty minutes ago, but my steering link broke. The car took off with a mind of its own and drove straight into a brick wall. The police are here and I'm waiting for the AA recovery. So sorry I can't be with you." Despite all, we coped, but only just. I believe these four pebbles were plopped into my pond during our twenty-sixth year at the inn, when experience had inured us to most happenstance, just to remind us of the frailty of human resources.

I have long held the opinion that personnel managers, who have screwed a nice little pay rise out of their companies by elevating themselves to the status of human resource managers, are just grit in the grease of industry. There are only two, tried, tested and proven techniques for the operation of small business: one, by the seat of the pants, the other by crisis management. It is no different in multinational corporate affairs; line managers cannot delegate their responsibility to

# It Could be a Little Gold Mine

manage the immediate condition, nor should they abrogate their responsibility to their workforce. No worker is responsible to a personnel or human resource manager, only to his or her line manager.

Given half an opportunity, I cannot resist teasing our customers. An early tease that I am sure did no harm but probably had lasting effect was one I practiced during our first winter at the inn. I was in my usual working gear, blue overalls and wellies, busily knocking out a wall and cutting up a two hundred year old pitch pine frame that had once been part of an outside door, but was now redundant, being half way down our main corridor. It was bitter cold and on the ground lay two inches of 'posh'. Posh is the Peak District onomatopoeic word meaning slush or wet melting snow.

Around the fire huddled an American family, Ma, Pa, and their American-beauty daughter. He was smartly dressed, dark blue suit, spotted bow tie, crew cut hair and thin-rimmed glasses; the very image of an Ivy League professor. Mother, elegant and very Long Island; the girl, perhaps twenty or twenty-one years old, a clone of a young Grace Kelly. As I cut each piece of the door frame free, I took it into the bar and used it to stoke the fire. It was aged pitch pine at least two hundred years old, rich in resin, so it burned beautifully. The blond golden skinned, blue-eyed California peach, asked me what I was doing. It was during the winter of discontent when the coal miners were on strike, miners fought picket line battles with the police, rubbish filled our city streets, and the dead lay unburied. Keeping a grim straight face and reverting to my Yorkshire dialect I intoned, "Well lass, tha sees, times are reet bad in this old country of ours, we can't afford any coal, so I'm having to burn skirting boards and t'door frames. It's cruel hard, but we've got to keep on." I am sure that father, mother, and daughter were completely taken in. I still have the happy thought that, back home in upstate New York or sunny California, they will have dined out, for many years, on the story of that run-down old inn where they burnt the furniture just to keep warm. Stingy devils never sent us a food parcel though.

Being a small business requires hands-on management. Never was it more so than when Mr and Mrs Rhodes-Otley came to stay. The Rhodes-Otleys were a charming couple. Forgetting my Yorkshire upbringing, for a long time I thought that their name was double-barrelled, hyphenated. Not so, it was just that Mr Rhodes, who came from the little Yorkshire town of Otley, as is the custom in the Dales when ringing to make their first reservation with us, naturally announced himself, as "Rhodes-Otley." Both were in their middle to late eighties. He was small but broad; his shoulders still straight back and he had a twinkle in his light blue eyes that immediately suggested a man of great happiness. His wife was clearly the reason for this. She was a classic English beauty, serene with natural grace and charm. We had only been at the inn for a few months when first they came to stay, he driving a beautiful highly polished shiny light brown and chrome old Rover car. "Could you please help with the luggage?" he asked, and specifically, "Would you mind bringing in my wife's bed board and slipping it under her mattress, you see she has trouble with her spine?" This was no problem but alerted us to her difficulty.

Their visit went well and they explained that they found the drive from Otley to Shrewsbury, where their son was a housemaster at the public school, a bit far. "At our age," said

# It Could be a Little Gold Mine

Mr Rhodes-Otley, "we like to break the journey halfway. Can we stop with you when we are on our way back home?" "Of course," Jeanne and I replied together. "We will look forward to seeing you again," and we meant it, they were our sort of folk.

A couple or three weeks had gone by and I had thought no more about the Rhodes-Otleys' return visit because we were very busy completely rewiring the whole building. To facilitate the work the electricians removed every carpet, underfelt and floorboard from all of the first floor landings, corridors, and most of the bedrooms. All was exposed wooden joists, beams, wires, cables, junction boxes, tools and workman's clutter. The disruption was so great that it forced us to close our accommodation business until we could relay the floorboards and put back the old carpets. New carpets were not in the budget possibilities.

It was late in the afternoon when I walked out of my kitchen onto the car park to be startled out of thoughts of plugs, sockets and light fittings by the sight of a car parked on the yard. It was a beautiful, highly polished shiny light brown and chrome old Rover car and surely, that was Mr Rhodes–Otley supporting his lovely wife along the path. "Hello," he chirped, very merry, "we promised we would be back, well here we are, could you please get our bags and you will remember the bed board won't you." All I could mutter was, "ah! er, well, er ... Oh Hell! Lo! Of course, how good to see you again."

Once they were in the bar, and sitting by the fire with a tray of tea, Jeanne came to them admitting, "We have a little problem, your room is just as you had it before, but it might be a bit difficult for Mrs Rhodes to get to it. You see the carpets, the underfelt and, er, well to be honest, the floorboards are, well, well they are not there; not there on the landing and they are not there along the length of the corridor." "Oh don't worry," sang out Mrs Rhodes-Otley, "I am sure David won't mind carrying me." And carry her I did. Up to their room so she could dress for dinner, down again for dinner, back to the room to sleep, then down again in the morning for breakfast. Never did I carry anything as carefully, measuring each step to match the pitch of the beams. That was hands-on management.

Rock groups have never been a success when staying at the inn but one remembered incident cheers my day. A group of young men turned up in a rather tired looking bus that had passed its prime. It could no longer be recognised by any livery of a coach company, and clearly, no City or Borough Council would own to it. However, to the manager and the band it was their home, recording studio and transport. They were over here from New Zealand, determined to break into the big time. They were good fun and enjoyed themselves playing the piano, singing and trying our, strange to them, warm beer, but they did not eat well.

Jeanne was determined that they should have something substantial and before they went to bed, she told them that a full English breakfast was compulsory. "What's that when it's at home then?" was the general question. "Well," said Jeanne, "Eggs, bacon, tomato, sausage, mushrooms, fried bread, beans and black pudding." "What's black pudding then?" was the next question. Jeanne, having some difficulty in giving a precise definition brought out a black pudding from the kitchen, and held aloft a classic folded link of the traditional North Country delicacy. The leader of this band

# It Could be a Little Gold Mine

of hopefuls took a hard look and then reduced us all to helpless laughter. All he said was, "I'm not up for that; it looks like a Jamaican's bum."

Food critics who write in the Sunday supplements, foodie magazines and good food guides often miss the point about a good meal. A meal, to be successful, must meet several criteria. It must be esculent, that is, fit to eat, it must be ready when wanted, at the right temperature, pleasing to the eye, easy to eat, and most importantly, of sufficient quantity to satisfy the appetite. In all restaurants, any novel concoction of ingredients or innovative presentation is only of secondary consideration. With the lingering influence of that foolish French fashion *nouvelle cuisine*, all too often, chefs dictate what the customer can eat, not may eat. They commit this fascist act by presenting their created dish, all of a piece, on one plate.

Restaurant chefs should never allow their conceit in their presentation of a dish to leave a customer hungry. Encouraged by glossy photographs in Sunday supplements and catering magazines still they do it, tarting up a single plate with slivers of syrup, a dusting of cocoa, and a couple of crossed chives balanced on all that you are going to get. They forget that appearance is only one of the necessary criteria for a satisfying meal. As they stay in their kitchens, they do not see that the towered delight they send out, balanced on a bed of mashed potato, or swede, falls at the first touch of a fork, and becomes nothing more than a stodgy stew.

By my criteria, one of the best meals I ever served was a double bacon butty, buttered and dipped, with a side order of a pint mug of strong hot sweet tea. Winter in Derbyshire's Peak District can be severe. On one particularly bad Novem-

# Charivari

ber day, with fog, snow, and ice making the roads treacherous, we had the log fire blazing in the hearth. Gathered round the fire a group of brave souls, who had ventured forth, seeking sustenance, sat warming their toes. Working in my kitchen I heard the sharp hiss and slam of air brakes from what was, obviously, a large wagon parking up at the top of our yard. Peering through the gloom, I saw that it was a huge articulated beast of a tanker, one of a fleet used to carry limestone powder out of Derbyshire. I have often said that with the rate that we quarry and send limestone afar, the Peak District will be as flat as the fens before long.

It was not long before the driver of the behemoth came into the bar where I had gone to wait for him. He was small, balding, and pushing sixty, dressed in blue overalls and big black boots befitting the driver of an articulated lorry. With the strain of driving over ice, in fog, his eyes were bloodshot and standing out, as they say, 'like chapel hat-pegs'. He was hesitant, nervously searching for an opening. "Er, can I have half a bitter please," he finally got out, still most uncomfortable and clearly wishing he was in a transport café. "Good Lord no," I replied, "Indeed you can't." His face fell because he did not immediately pick up the tease. "How about I fry up a couple of bacon butties for you, buttered and dipped, brew a pint of sweet strong tea, and serve it front of the fire instead?" I said this, staring hard at the group clustered round the fire. Immediately they pulled away, brought him a chair, and set it in the very middle of their group. It did not take long for me to serve the meal of the century. His look of absolute content was worth more than the little we charged.

Another memorable meal was of *five fast fried fish fingers*. It was the most difficult meal that I have ever prepared, but one

# It Could be a Little Gold Mine

with the most fun. We had a reservation for a double room with a request that we provide, in the room, a put-you- up bed so that an eight-year old boy could share the room. When they arrived, during the late afternoon, it was obvious by their clothes that the couple had come straight from their wedding reception, her second I presumed. "Now then," I ventured, "about dinner, shall we feed junior at about seven o'clock, he can then watch television in your room, and you two can come down about eight, have a drink and then dinner." The bride, who was obviously a protective mother, was clearly worried and said, "No, he must eat with us, you see today has been very stressful for him." I could see that the new husband was all for my idea. "No, no, that won't do at all," I prevailed. "I tell you what;" I went on, speaking directly to the boy, "Why don't you come with me into my kitchen, where we can make your supper together, would you like that?" He was clearly a bright lad and understood more than his mother could imagine. "Yes please," was his immediate response. "Right then, take your case upstairs, take off that posh suit of yours, then come down changed when you are ready." He did not take long, then hand in hand we went into the kitchen. I found him a clean apron that, when I doubled it and tied at the back, sort of fitted him. "What shall we cook for your supper?" "May I have fish fingers and chips please?" "Of course, dead easy" I replied, but before I knew it, there was a pebble in my pond again and the ripples were running.

When I opened the deep chest freezer where we kept all the fish, to get a packet of frozen fish fingers from the slot where we kept the fish fingers, the slot was empty. There were no fish fingers where the fish fingers should be. A frantic scrabble about from top to bottom of the deep chest fish freezer proved there were no fish fingers where the fish fingers should not have been. So too, after a lot of under-breath cursing and swearing I proved the same for the meat freezer, the ice-cream freezer and all the other freezers. There were no fish fingers. "Ah!" I said, buoyantly to the little lad, "Yes ... we have no fish fingers; is there something else you would like?" "No, not really, you see my Mum won't let me have them at home and I do like them." His crestfallen look and bottom lip pout did it. "Right then," I said, remembering to say it long and drawn out, "We'll have to make some, won't we?" I supposed that his over-anxious mother was worried about the E102 Tartrazine; the yellow colour in the crumb covering of some mass-produced supermarket fish fingers. First, I had to find the frozen cod fillets in the jumbled up fish finger free zone of the fish freezer.

Having at last found what I was looking for, I had to defrost and chop the fillets, and then find a way to get the chopped fish flakes to stick together in neat six-inch long bars of rectangular section. I tried flour, tried egg white; tried a mixture of the two; and threw away the first two or three failed attempts. I defrosted more cod fillets and finally got a sort of satisfactory mix to form half a dozen, just about oblong, fish bricks, but they lacked straw. These precious few I put in the refrigerator to firm up. This was the job only half done. I then had to make the golden crumb. I grated half a loaf of bread, dyed the crumbs with orange food colour but it was a failure, the crumb turned to paste. I tried and tried again. Two loaves later, I had the secret. Dye and dry the bread in the oven before grating it. Then, with my flour, egg and breadcrumb coating covering the chilled fish bricks

# It Could be a Little Gold Mine

I had a set of six real, but lumpy and irregular homemade fish fingers. Flour and fish bits covered us, orange crumbs decorated our hair, and the kitchen looked as though Mr Pastry had had a fight with the Marks Brothers.

I was happy, and the little boy supremely so, when I took off his apron and sat him down at about seven o'clock to his supper of five fast fried fish fingers. Why did he only have five fish fingers? Was it for alliteration? No I ate one, I had to, didn't I?

# CHAPTER SIXTEEN

# Thieves, Con Men and a Vagabond Vicar

On our first day as owners of the renamed Bentley Brook Inn, thieves made it clear to us that pubs, inns, restaurants and hotels are rich pickings for those of their calling. Jeanne and I had long held that ladies judged such places by the décor and cleanliness of the *ladies*, the *loo*, the *toilet, convenience, lavatory* or whatever euphemism they chose to describe the water closets reserved for their use. Indeed, some years later, I had the signal honour of presenting to the winners of the Midlands 'Loo of the Year' their well-deserved awards.

Jeanne decided that because our ladies toilet was in a parlous state of repair,* we would provide a range of fine scented soaps, hand creams, hair spray, and good quality terry towels to compensate for the poor state of the basic facilities. She also set in place a large double-sided mahogany framed antique mirror. We thought these additions would show that we cared. We were determined that our guests would immediately recognise that we were trying, no cheap paper towels or part used blocks of soap would do for our establishment. Although we only had a few curious customers who had only come to see what these new folk were like, our investment in

*In 2002 the whole modern brick-built structure parted from the 200 year old stone building and had to be demolished and rebuilt.*

# It Could be a Little Gold Mine

fine scented soaps, hand creams, hair spray and good quality terry towels were an immediate deduction from any hoped for bottom line profit. They lasted no more than forty-eight hours. Thieves stole them all, even the large double-sided mahogany framed antique mirror.

It was not long after, that some thieves from a nearby home or campsite must have organised a cheese and wine party and found themselves short of glasses. Joyce, the first barmaid we employed, was highly numerate. Each evening she would check that everything was back in its proper place by counting every bottle, ashtray, menu, and glass. As Joyce was clearing up after closing time, she called for Jeanne to tell her that nineteen wine glasses had gone missing that evening. A quick till check showed that our thieving customers had paid for exactly nineteen glasses of wine, either dry or medium white during the early evening. We just hoped that it was a cheese and wine for charity, but it grieved us that their charity began in our home.

We soon learned that all public houses, inns, restaurants and hotels are not only a target for thieves, but also a mark for confidence tricksters. Based on his years of experience in the police force, my Dad gave me a few tips on how to spot the most obvious con men, tips that have usually stood me in good stead. His often-repeated lesson was, "If a man looks you straight in the eye, leans towards you to show the open palms of his hands and says, 'Trust me, do I look like a confidence trickster?', don't; most likely he is a con man." (This was the pose and the favoured expression of Tony Blair, long serving Prime Minister of the UK, when appearing on television).

We had a classic encounter with one of their kind, 'The

# Thieves, Con Men and a Vagabond Vicar

Queen's Ranger'. He came to reception at about five in the evening. He was tall, raw-boned, bronzed and weather-beaten, a lookalike of Sir Edmund Hillary, of Everest fame. On his back he carried a commando style framed rucksack. He wore boots, laced up to just below the knee, into which were tucked his camouflage trousers. Over his trousers, he sported a many pocketed camouflage bush jacket. To complete his outfit, on his head was a hat, as good as any worn by Baden-Powell when he was the Chief Scout.

"Good evening; I shall require a couple of pints of your best bitter before a good dinner, a glass or two of wine, port, then a bed for the night; tomorrow an early and hearty English breakfast," was his opening remark. This was a warning signal, no enquiry about cost or availability. The apparent lack of concern about money is the first part of the scam leading the mark to think that the con man is well provided for. "Yes sir, we have a room available, at... (I forget what), including VAT and full English breakfast, will that be alright?" I asked. "Yes, that will do very well," he replied. "You see, I am the Queen's Ranger, I'm here to inspect the Peak District National Park as her personal representative." "Oh how interesting," was my reply. I alerted Jeanne to my conviction that he was a con and asked her to make sure that we only accepted cash for his account.

The following morning I made sure that I was in the hall, close to the reception desk, when Jeanne presented him with his bill and was pleased that he paid, in full, with cash. "Thank you for your hospitality, it will be included in my report to HRH." That sealed it for me, as soon as he was out of the door I ran to the phone and called the local police. "Hello, it's Allingham at the Bentley Brook, a man has just

# It Could be a Little Gold Mine

booked out and I am sure that he is a con; he called himself 'The Queens Ranger'. The reply was instant. "Good man, follow him if you can, we want to talk to him." I think that my loitering around reception and insistence on cash had alerted him to my suspicions because he had gone to ground, without trace. The police turned up in strength, and in no time, but their longer and more thorough search was as unsuccessful as was mine. "Thanks Mr A," said one of the policeman ruefully, "we really did want that fellow, he's notorious, he's even done our sergeant out of fifty quid."

It was not long after, that we were subject to another attempted swindle, one that was common at the time. The trade journals had reported this fashionable fiddle so we were alert to it. It was a simple enough fraud. A party would eat all that was set before them, save one, who would leave his or her chosen dish hardly touched. After all the others in the party had eaten their fill, the one who had not eaten would complain, making as much fuss as possible. The protest would be about the quality, description, freshness, or size or some other such made-up complaint. The lead in the drama would add that under no circumstances was he, or she, going to pay, because the made-up complaint, had ruined their unique and special joint celebration, not just for him or her, but for them all. The lead would go on to declare an intention to report the matter to the Environmental Health Department, the Trading Standards Office, the AA, the RAC and the local Tourist Board. This charade was usually successful, as most restaurant managers, not being the owner of the business, would ask them to leave immediately without taking any payment, this being the option that would cause least disturbance.

# Thieves, Con Men and a Vagabond Vicar

I thought something might be wrong when, early one lunchtime, a party of eight arrived without a reservation. One man, obviously the host, was in his mid-forties with all the trappings of the pseudo rich. He engaged people in the bar, those who would listen to him, with stories of how the country was going to the dogs. He told them that he was a successful businessman and financier, forced by the government to live overseas as a tax exile. I was sure he was a fraud because his cheap shoes gave him away as a fake, despite his camel coloured coat, ostentatious Rolex, the chunky bracelet and regimental tie. I had a quick word with Jeanne and said, "If he is not a con, I'm Auguste Escoffier; keep a careful eye on them all and remember, take only cash in payment."

This particular trick requires that the party should be early into the restaurant so that when the fraud is pulled, the restaurant is full of people and the embarrassment most effective. Sure enough this cove, claiming to be time pressed because of urgent business, asked to eat as soon as possible. I was now certain for sure that he was up to no good. All went well with the starter course with my suspect fellow polishing off a great bowl of sustaining soup and more than one of our home-baked bread rolls. It came as expected, a call to me in the kitchen from one of our waiters, "The chap you told us to watch out for has asked to see you, and by the way, he has not touched his steak." "Right then - I'll see to it."

I put on a clean apron and went to meet him. He opened with a tirade of abuse, "Now look here Chef, if that is what you call yourself, this is not fillet steak and you know it. You are passing off inferior meat, you are a fraud. I eat in famous restaurants all over Europe and America. You have ruined a very special occasion for all of us." "Oh!" I replied, "Is that

# It Could be a Little Gold Mine

not fillet steak? Just one moment and I will go and check for you sir." That day luck was most definitely on my side. The steak that I had cooked for him was the first cut from a prime fully trimmed fillet of beef. The rest of the joint was perfect, still in one piece and longer than my forearm. Swinging the fillet steak, held firmly at the thin end in my great fist, I came back to his table, my arm raised as though the raw steak were a caveman's club.

"Here we are sir, the very fillet from which I cut that prime piece that lies untouched on the plate before you." All chatter had stopped, there was absolute silence, I had the attention of all the other diners, as well as his party. "Now," I went on, "If you don't stand up and apologise to me, and to all my guests and friends here, I will wrap this prime piece of fillet steak round your neck and use it to detain you until the police arrive." He did as instructed, in a thin wavering voice that was unrecognisable from the flash financier who had held court in the bar. "Now you will ask your friends to wait for you outside while you pay for all the meals, in full, in cash." They did, he did, and I blew a great sigh of relief. When he had gone, I took the fillet back to hang it in the cold room. Jeanne quickly brought me down to earth. "You might well hang it, one day, someone will call your bluff and you will be good for a hanging."

We were not always successful in spotting villains, rogues and confidence tricksters. In our twentieth year we were completely taken in by an ex-army major type who we appointed as a manager, with tenure of the flat we had created in the restored coach house. He was in his early fifties, of ultra smart appearance, good posture, excellent voice and vocabulary and a quiet mature personality. Deliverance, we thought, a relief, someone to take some, if not most, of the workload and so it seemed, for the first two or three weeks that he worked for us. However, the first stocktake after his appointment showed a significant and unexpected variation in the gross profit margin of our wine sales. I put it down to an inaccurate count, but was a little worried. Nothing in his behaviour caused me to suspect him of any default. Nevertheless, we were becoming concerned. Although we had agreed that his day off should be Monday each week, he seemed to get in a complete panic if we asked him to change the day. He always had a different, but plausible, reason why it was, that although he would normally and any other week, be very happy to oblige, unfortunately, that particular Monday was quite out of the question.

By the time of the next monthly stocktake, some peculiarities in his behaviour had become noticeable, and he had taken money from the till, albeit with a plausible note of explanation. This stocktake happened to be on a Monday, his day off. It revealed an even bigger loss of profit on wine sales. On the same day, Jeanne took a telephone call that finally blew the cover of our crook manager. I was in the office with Jeanne and listened to the comical conversation. "Good morning, could I speak to the owner please," was the request made by a pleasant voiced but unrecognised lady. "Yes, can I help you?" replied Jeanne. "No I'm sorry," said the lady "this is a confidential call; I need to speak to the owner direct. I'm sorry, I will ring later." "But you are speaking to me, I am the owner, proprietor, manager, gofer and dogsbody," Jeanne said quickly, to prevent the call being terminated. "Oh! Er..." came the puzzled reply, "I must have dialled the wrong number, I wanted the Bentley Brook Inn, I'm so sorry to have bothered

# It Could be a Little Gold Mine

you." Jeanne again "But, just a minute, this *is* the Bentley Brook Inn and I am the owner." The lady "Oh dear ..." then after a long pause, "Do you happen to know of a Major ...?" (and she gave the name of our new manager). The voice of Jeanne's interlocutor was now very shaky. "Yes," said Jeanne "he is our new manager, why?" "Oh dear, this is the regional office of..." and she mentioned the name of a national agent dealing exclusively in the sale of hotels, inns, and public houses. She continued, "I'm afraid he has told us he is to use the Bentley Brook Inn as security against another hotel he is buying to build up his chain of small but exclusive hotels."

A quick search of his flat solved the wine stock discrepancy. We found many dozen empty wine bottles that he had stashed in cupboards, under his bed, along the kitchen shelves, anywhere where we could not have seen them from outside. He remained the con man to the very end with his head against my chest, sobbing and swearing that he would go straight from now on, and whining, "please, do not tell the regiment." The following Monday morning we found out why the first day of the week was so important for him to have as his day off. His probation officer rang to ask why he had not turned up to comply with his community-service order.

Bank Holidays are a mixed blessing for the pub trade. We can hardly cope with, let alone look after, the customers who seem to come from a different planet from our usual cross section of gentle well-mannered folk who we are pleased to meet and greet as friends. "Down't yer do crocodile and cucumber crisps mate? yow, they do ever such a lot down our wai." "Down't yer sell mild me duck? oo I dooo fancy a drop, do yer do Mackeson's then?" We smile and carry on, as the

# Thieves, Con Men and a Vagabond Vicar

healthy cash flow injection builds up a store against the coming winter famine, and, hopefully, gets the VAT paid.

One August Bank Holiday Saturday evening, at about ten o'clock, I had finished cooking and came behind the bar intent upon a pint or even three, or perhaps, because it was a bank holiday a well-deserved shed full. The first pint, straight down in one draught, simply to restore the fluid balance you understand, the others that would follow were to enjoy. Unashamedly content that I had done my bit, I stared blankly at the mob without a thought of serving any one of them. I ignored them. I feigned not to notice the sweaty faces, outstretched arms and sticky hands that were waving mugs, jugs, tankards, glasses, bottles and trays, together with notes and coin of the realm. I ignored their shouted orders as they clamoured against the bar, like a boarding party of drunken pirates.

Above all this uproar and against my determination not to become involved, one small grey haired man did catch my eye and hold my attention. It was not his saintly smile or twinkling eye that held me, or that he was leaning right over the bar, both feet off the ground, while nursing a glass of beer in one hand and a whisky chaser in the other, it was that he was wearing the cloth and collar of a vicar of the Church of England. He seemed content in his own company but it was obvious that he was very drunk, at least seven over the eight. After closing time the mob slowly drifted away until the vicar was alone at the bar, still drinking, still leaning right over the bar, and now kicking his left leg up behind him in a steady recognizable involuntary drunken upward left leg lift.

"Hello Vicar," I said hoping to get a sensible reply. "Good evening my son," he replied, "Will you have a drink with me

# It Could be a Little Gold Mine

now that I am a famous man?" "I think that we have both had about enough already," I replied noticing he had a bunch of keys in his hand. "Where do you think you are off to?" "Well," he said "they tell me there is no room here at the inn and so, like Joseph and Mary I will have to look elsewhere. Do you have a stable by any chance?" "You are not fit to drive anywhere at all," I said, taking the keys from him and putting them secure in the till. "I'm not fit to be anywhere at all," he replied and went on "Tomorrow when you read the papers, you will know why."

All our letting rooms were full, but I made up a bed on a huge settee we had in the residents' lounge and set him to rest there for the night. The following morning, early, I took him a cup of hot sweet tea and told him to come down for breakfast. I had already read the Sunday papers about the vicar who had gone missing and the appeal by his Bishop asking for news of his whereabouts and calling him to return. When he came down, the first thing he asked for was a pint of lager and a small whisky chaser. "Not for you vicar, you will have a full English breakfast, like the condemned man you are," I said, laughing at him. "Oh! You've read the papers then," he said. "Only some, just what have you done?" I asked.

"Well," he told me, "I had a funeral service to do last Friday afternoon and I admit, I had had a drink, but he was a very bad man who I was to bury. When I gave the eulogy, my memories of the man rather carried me away. I told the congregation just what a terrible man he had been and what a blessing it was, that he was now before his maker, required to answer for his many sins and great wickedness. After the service, I realised that I might have overdone it a tad, so I thought it best to make myself scarce for a bit." "Right then," I told him, "you will stay here until you have had a good breakfast and rest awhile, only then will I let you have your car keys, but you must promise me you will drive straight home." "Right oh! Boyo, agreed, I suppose I shall have to own up sooner or later."

We waved him off at about half past eleven, after he had read all the papers that chronicled his fall from grace. The rest of the day was very busy and I had thought no more about our reverend visitor until I came late into the bar. Immediately I recognised the involuntary drunken upward left leg lift. He was there again, leaning over the bar, both feet off the ground, a glass in each hand, and gloriously, but quietly, drunk. "Oh Vicar, you promised to go straight home." "Well so I did dear boy, but you were both so kind to me I just had to come back to thank you and your lovely wife, for your Christian kindness."

I took his keys again, locked them in the safe, and soon had him tucked up in bed. I then got the number from telephone enquiries and rang his Bishop in a far away see. After insisting that I speak to the Bishop, and to no-one else, he came on the line. "Bishop, I believe that you are missing a vicar." "Yes," was his reply, "we are most worried, do you know anything of his whereabouts?" "Indeed I do, I keep the Bentley Brook Inn, in Derbyshire, but have him tucked up in bed, and somewhat the worse for wear I'm afraid." The Bishop's voice indicated his relief: "Thank the Lord that he has not done anything to harm himself. I will get my chaplain to come for him tomorrow and an aide to drive his car back. Please keep him with you until they collect him." This we did, but I did not get a blessing, a thank you, or even thirty pence. Who was it that said, "I am not my brother's keeper.

# CHAPTER SEVENTEEN

# Brief Encounters

The briefest of encounters was that of my elbow with the Yankee kid's ear. An American family had booked in for a two-night stay. Ma, Pa and their somewhere about twelve-year old kid, not a word I would normally use for a child, but apposite in his case. He was all that we dread when dealing with a spoilt brat of an overindulgent mother. His behaviour was extremely unpleasant and I sensed that Pa was getting close to doing something about it. It came to a head during dinner on the second evening of their stay, when the three of them were in the restaurant, occupying a corner table. The kid snapped his fingers and clearly addressing me, called out, very loud, in a Cagney-like voice, "Waiter, get me a Coke and make it snappy." Pa was the typical mid-west American dad; bald, short, fat-bellied, narrow-belted, open-necked short-sleeved shirt wearing sort of a guy, a pleasant, patient man. Ma was an as yet an untamed screechy-voiced shrew. I pretended that I had not heard the kid's call for a Coke, but went directly to their table to silver serve their vegetables. Leaning to the left of the boy, I hit him hard with my right elbow, smack on his ear, a blow accurate to a millimetre. When he squealed and started to bawl, not cry, the shrew, now a tigress, was out of her chair and coming across the table intent on tearing my heart out, but for once ... I had read the runes correctly.

# Brief Encounters

"Blanche, shut up and sit down; he got what he deserved and if he don't stop bawling he will get more from me," (Pa said this in a voice not to be challenged,) "and you Junior, you apologise, right now." Then to me, "Thanks pal, it has been a long time coming, too long, it's about time for me to take over now." We enjoyed a long chat late into the night, me with a pint or two, he with rye whiskey and water. I was sure that I had understood and acted correctly and that a better order would prevail in their house from that day forward.

Innkeeping is undoubtedly hard work and few who take it on make a fortune, but the rewards are great for those who have a consuming interest in people and their behaviour. This particular reward may not be enough to wholly satisfy one's total ambition, but the brief encounters made during the daily challenge of keeping a lid on things, stimulates an adrenaline rush that nine to five, key in the door drones, only find in costly entertainment; hobbies, theatre, sport, sex or drugs. As innkeepers, we get our entertainment free, because man and his mate beat a path to our door.

Our visitors present all the theatre required, often comedy, both black and light, sometimes farce, occasionally even slapstick, and certainly drama. For my taste, they introduce far too much sport, albeit vicarious, with their endless late commentary, banal analysis, and argument. They exhibit enough overt sexual behaviour to fill a soft porn magazine, but praise be, we have had no hard drug problems. The soft alcohol we serve, seems to serve our customers' needs.

The people we daily encounter run the full gamut of the human condition. They are not only our customers, those we serve, but also those who come to serve us. Then there are those who come to tax not only our income but also our

# It Could be a Little Gold Mine

patience. Amongst these are inspectors from the Inland Revenue, VAT and Her Majesty's Customs and Excise, officials from the National Park, the County, District and Parish Councils, all with authority over us. Worst of those who taxed our patience were the visiting Licensing Magistrates.

On one occasion, their improper behaviour so angered me that I rang our legal aid line to ask for their advice. I was angered because they talked to us as though we were lesser mortals. They assumed that we were in the employ of a brewery, supposed we were members of the Licensed Victuallers Association, a trade union, not an employers' association, and arrogantly probed into matters that had nothing to do with them. At the same time, they displayed an ignorance of the law that left me speechless. "Oh! Ignore it," was the brief's brief response to my telephone call. He was laughing as he said, "You've had a visit from *Condescending Cow* haven't you." He went on to add, "We get two or three calls a week, from all over the country, all from irate licensees rightly complaining, as you have. My advice is, forget it, they are a waste of time."

Best of all those who have authority over us have always been the police. When on duty they have always been supportive, never failing to be reasonable and helpful. When staying as guests they have been the best of raconteurs and good company.

We were content with our decision to become innkeepers but we did have some family opposition. Jeanne's mother, a lady of great character and determination, was not best pleased to learn that her daughter and I had bought a hotel and intended to run it as a family business. Her displeasure tuned to horror when she learned that on the first day we changed the name from the Bentley Brook Hotel to the Bentley Brook Inn. That her daughter should become a publican, rather than hotelier, was too much for her to endure. Many times she reminded Jeanne that she had opposed my courting her daughter saying, "Nothing good will come of you marrying a northerner, particularly him, a Yorkshireman, who is only interested in beer and sex."

Things hardly change, even to this day. Jeanne has made a good friend with Sarah who is the other half of the Gourmet Grannies who make marmalades, jams and biscuits for sale at the inn. When Sarah told her dowager mother that she was working at the inn she replied, in a shaky voice, but without hesitation, "Oh my dear, how awful for you, whatever will you do if someone we know should come in?" Her mother was only a little better pleased when told by Sarah that she was to go with Jeanne to run a stall at the local farmers' market. "Oh well, if you have to dear, I suppose that at the market, you will at least be meeting a better class of people."

Not all the gentry, those whom my mother-in-law and Sarah's mother were so anxious for their daughters to socialise with, come up to the mark. Soon after our taking over the inn, the local branch of the Conservative Party reserved our small dining room for an evening meeting. They were none too friendly and none too profitable, but they seemed to be happy enough with the arrangements that we had made and the simple buffet we served. As they drifted away, in small talkative groups, I noticed the chairman, our local squire, leaving alone. He was weaving a bit as he crossed the yard in the direction of our home that had once been the gardener's cottage. I do not know what previous owners of the inn, or

# It Could be a Little Gold Mine

Mr Sheard the gardener who had lived in the cottage, had done to him, but I was astonished to see him, quite purposefully and deliberately, urinate against our cottage front door. I was furious and gave him a dressing down the like of which I suspect he had not received since leaving prep school. I warned him that should he ever come onto our property again I would forcibly eject him and tell everyone present the reason why. He never did cross our threshold again, although he remained chairman of the local Conservative Party branch for many years after and they had many meetings with us at the inn. I often wondered how he excused his absence and how it was that he kept on accepting re-election.

A more senior and deserving knight of the realm restored my faith in the orders of chivalry. It happened during a Sunday lunch session when we were fully booked for our popular carvery. As I was crossing the hall from the restaurant to the kitchen, I saw Jeanne talking to an elderly couple who were wonderfully dressed in matching tweed cloaks and tweed deerstalker hats. They were the very image of the highland laird and his consort, he with his staff she with her stick.

"I am so sorry, but every table is taken at the moment," said Jeanne, "But if you would care to take a seat and wait in the bar I am sure that we can reset a table for you just as soon as one comes free." "Ah, there is a bar then?" said the man with the staff, the tweed cloak and deerstalker hat. Jeanne took them through to the bar. "By Jove," he said, "you do indeed have a bar and what a wonderful bar it is." "What name shall I use?" asked Jeanne. "Sir John and Lady Harvey-Watt" the lady replied. Jeanne quickly reset a table and they enjoyed what we had to offer. As I passed their table, he caught my sleeve to detain me and called to Jeanne, "You should hang on to this chap, he's alright." Being a late arrival and because in those days our licence finished at three in the afternoon, they were the last couple to leave the restaurant. When he gave me his card, his visiting card, not credit card, he noticed my raised eyebrow for it showed he had an order in the gift of the Queen. "You're bright." He said - "you see I was Parliamentary Private Secretary to Sir Winston Churchill for all but the first six weeks of his Premiership." "Oh you're the chap who took over from Brendan Bracken then," I replied without thinking. "How did you know that?" he queried. "Well I have just finished reading Churchill's *History of the Second World War*," was my response. "Good gracious, all six volumes?" – "Yes, I have read nearly all his works, including *Savrola*, the novel," I went on. "Mmm ... I spent hundreds of hours on the work, correcting dates and names etc" he added, looking a little glum.

At that time we were at the very lowest ebb in our fortunes, our financial state was desperate with the bank pressing us to sell the business. In fact, bankruptcy was once again staring us in the face. As we talked I knew our decision to take on the inn was right. It had given me the opportunity to meet and talk with dukes and dustmen, the good and the great, and the downright dangerous. Talking, on easy terms, with a man who had served Churchill and our country so well, gave me new heart and the will to stare back at bankruptcy. When, a week later, a signed copy of his autobiography *Most of my Life* arrived by post, with an enclosed letter of encouragement, it redoubled my determination to succeed.

That an innkeeper encounters overt sexual behaviour is inevitable. It is a normal part of the job as we go about our regular innkeeping business. It is so, because the average cus-

# It Could be a Little Gold Mine

tomer does not notice us.

We enjoy the times when we take a group booking taking all rooms at the inn and the group come determined to enjoy themselves. This happened on an occasion when a group, all members of a Round Table, came with their wives for a week-end break. It was long ago in those simple days when I could confidently call their lady partners, their wives. Their visit had gone very well, and as I had been in the Round Table in Hong Kong, we had much in common. I was content as I sat watching the last four young men, still playing cards, a little after two o'clock in the morning. The fire was still glowing brightly, the lights had been dimmed and all was serene when the bar door opened.

# Brief Encounters

One of the wives, who had retired hours earlier, glided in as though on a cloud. I thought there might be a bit of a row but no, not at all. None of the young men moved or seemed to notice her as they concentrated on their hand of cards. The cloud was of perfume and powder that floated around her; she looked wide-awake and quite stunning. The lady said only one word as she took a firm hold of the right ear of what I took to be her husband. The word was bell like, resonant and clear, "Bed." They left happily together, she still holding his ear, he with an arm around her slender waist. "Does she often do that?" I asked. "Oh yes, you mean walk around naked, yes, she's lovely isn't she. Will you play out his hand for him Mr A, and then we had all better go to bed."

Before I had to give up the practical side of innkeeping, because of injury, most nights I did the rounds of the strict locking up procedure, turning out the lights, checking all was secure and no-one loitering, or worse collapsed, in either toilet. One evening, after all the customers had left or gone to bed, I heard the sound of running water where no running water ought to be. I unlocked the door to the smaller of our two restaurants to see water cascading through the ceiling. I realised, because of its expensive perfume, that it was most certainly bath water. I could hear muffled laughter and giggling and the sloshing of water as two people frolicked in the bath upstairs. Two people, in room eight, our only single room!

I raced up the stairs and knocked firmly on the door of room eight, the single room. Now that I was upstairs, the laughter and giggling were clear to hear, so I knocked loud on the door, then louder, and again louder, until at last I got a response. The door swung back, open-wide, to reveal a young

# It Could be a Little Gold Mine

woman, framed like the living image of one of my favourite paintings, *La Source* by Ingres. She did not have a ewer on her left shoulder but her right arm raised so that her hand could hold back her shiny wet hair, gave her about the same pose. This nubile creature had, in the very best sense of the word, no shame. No head only peeping round a part open door, no hastily flung on towel for her.

'Beauties self she is when all her robes are gone' from the old unattributed poem, long a favourite of adolescent boys, flashed into my mind as this nymphet, still glowing pink from the hot bath, said, all wide-eyed and innocent. "Yes, is there a problem?" "Will you please stop spilling the bath water, you are flooding the restaurant downstairs," was all I could garble, not knowing where to look. "Oh dear, I'm so sorry; John, we must get out and dried, we are causing a flood," she called. Then, giving me a winning smile, she turned and wandered back into the room, now the very image of a Velásquez Venus. She left me to close the door.

Etiquette, modes of behaviour and address have changed out of all recognition over the years since we bought the inn. No longer do unmarried couples pretend to be married when they register at reception. These days it is Mr Smith and Miss Jones, Mr Jones and Mrs Smith or Mr Smith and Ms Jones or even Ms Smith and Ms Jones. This has taken away one of our simple pleasures, taking imaginary bets on whether couples staying with us were, or were not, legally bound in wedlock and not just lustfully bound in bed-lock. "You know that Mr and Mrs Smith in Room 4 who are having breakfast, he has just said to her 'Oh do you have coffee with breakfast?' as he ordered tea."

Couples come to the inn, confident that they can have a

liaison without risk of their personal affairs becoming part of the public domain, as the courts and press now have it. Not long ago a middle-aged married man, thinking to play away, brought his much younger secretary for an assignation. He drove the full two miles, from his house in Ashbourne, confident that being out of town, none of his acquaintances would discover his indiscretion. His smart about-turn, done with military precision, was immediate. Our young barmaid was his next-door neighbour and his young lady companion greeted her excitedly as they had been best of friends at school.

Recently, a handsome well-dressed couple were so infatuated that they could not keep their hands off each other. They risked the most intimate fondling. Neither did they whisper their libidinous exchanges, assuming that I was just part of the pub furniture. Finally, they left to go to their separate cars where they had parked them, hidden from the road, but not before both had used our lavatories. She went in wearing stockings and came out bare legged, he followed a discreet minute or two later.

When he passed me, I put on a silly spiv voice and pulling my mouth right down at one side, whispered, "We do short lets," and he laughed. A few days later, while I was eating a late breakfast Jeanne clipped my ear. "What have I done now?" I said, unaware of any present shortcoming. Jeanne explained, "I've just had a man on the phone saying that he was here for lunch last week, with a lady friend. He told me that a great big fellow, who he thought might be something to do with the place, had whispered to him, 'We do short lets.'" Jeanne went on, "he then asked me whether it was true." "Oh heck, I was only joking." I said, taking a defensive

# It Could be a Little Gold Mine

position. "Well I'm not," replied Jeanne. I ducked, anticipating another cuff on the ear, but it did not come as expected. Jeanne was now laughing as she announced, "I've just let room three for the next three Thursday afternoons, at full price too."

Not all those who practise infidelity get away with it. One Christmas, in an attempt to boost trade, I followed the recommendation of the marketing gurus by sending a mailshot to all those people who, during the year, had stayed at the inn. Countless articles in trade journals had assured me that this would be a winner. Painstakingly I copied out all the addresses from the register and sent to each and every one, a Christmas card with a line drawing of the inn. In the card, my message wished them well and thanked them for their business. I added a postscript, 'We hope we might have the opportunity of serving you again in the coming year'.

The phone rang several times with angry men telling me that they had never stayed at my lousy hotel and instructing me never to write to them again. One irate man went so far as to insist that I speak to his wife and tell her that he had never stayed at the crummy Bentley Brook Inn. I simply told her that our computer must have sent the card in error; a little white lie I thought to be appropriate, but happy that his wife would not swallow that one as the card was handwritten. I did wonder though, as they all so emphatically denied having stayed with us, how they were able to rate us between lousy and crummy and, if they had stayed with us, why the cheating cheapskates had not taken their mistresses to a better class of hotel.

There is a downside to my delight in meeting people by chance or brief encounter. We genuinely worry when it dawns on us that we have not seen or heard, for some time, from a well-liked regular customer or couple. We wonder if we have done something to upset them, or if they have fallen on hard times, or worse. With the increase in failed marriages, separations, and divorce, we inevitably lose some regular no longer married couples. Neither party will come again to the inn after a divorce, for fear of meeting the other. I firmly believe that there should be a compulsory part of any divorce settlement detailing who has the rights to visit which of their favourite inns or restaurants.

The worst of the downside is a parting that leaves one with a feeling of uncertainty. One such still bothers me, even after many years have passed. I do not know whether it was because she was beautiful, or whether I valued their friendship more than usual, because it crossed a generation. They were young and not long married, full of optimism and plans for the future and we would talk late into the night of those plans. When they were leaving, after a happy weekend, I made a point of coming to the front door to wave them off. Having said her goodbyes and walked to the car where her young husband sat waiting with the engine running, the girl turned and came back down the front steps to me. Quietly she said, "I could not go without a proper goodbye," then gave me a soft kiss on the cheek, turned, ran to the car and they sped away, neither looking back; and we never saw or heard of them again.

Each time I read Robert Burns' poem *Ae fond kiss*, written about his parting with Mrs McLehose when he left Edinburgh, that brief encounter on the steps comes back to mind.

> *Ae fond kiss and then we sever;*
> *Ae fareweel, and then forever!*

# CHAPTER EIGHTEEN

# Pure Theatre

To be 'a little gold mine', any inn, restaurant or simple pub must have a touch of the theatre about it, a unique feature to set it apart, something special to bring it to mind when thoughts turn to entertainment and celebration. Some succeed by inheriting or creating a set with historic, unique, or curious trappings. Some rely on the cast, the lead usually taken by an over the top eccentric host or restaurant manager, with his staff acting as supporting actors. After twenty years wandering worldwide, at about the time I gave up my first profession of engineer and found my true vocation as a cook, it began to dawn on me that the meals that I had enjoyed the most were those that had a sense of occasion and theatre.

Sense became certainty in La Parolaccia, a small trattoria somewhere in Trastevere, the unmapped slum on the other side of the Vatican from St Peter's Piazza, in the ancient city of Rome. I was the guest of the chief economist of I.R.I, Italy's industrial conglomerate. He was a charming aesthete and gourmet, younger than me, who had previously taken me to several wonderful restaurants for dinners of unsurpassed quality. Surely, I thought, there must be something very special about this restaurant to risk venturing, even with his two well-armed bodyguards, into an area noted for robbery and kidnap. The something special became immediately apparent when we entered the small noisy colourful bistro style restaurant. On the walls were recent copies of all the leading Italian newspapers. These reported, in headlines and with photographs, that one of their waiters had 'goosed'* Queen Soraya, then wife of Pahlavi, the Shah of Persia.

The food was good, but the evening entertainment was pure pantomime for grown-ups. The diners accepted the badinage and teasing of the high-camp waiters with unrestrained good humour and called for more. All was slapstick and innuendo. The presentation of their sweets and desserts was nothing short of pornography on a plate. The method and mime acting of the waiters, as they opened bottle after bottle of champagne, was pure hardcore. However, they acted with such speed and panache that it left us all exhausted with laughter. When we took our leave, I made sure to get a sight of the bill. It was sheer extortion. The cost charged per head being the same as charged for a Gala Night at La Scala, Milan.

At the inn, we are more demure. The brass ceiling of our overdraft limit determined that we must personally do almost all of the work required to run the inn. It came naturally to me to both cook and serve the meals, while Jeanne looked after taking orders and making out the bills. No restaurant manager or head waiter for us, ours was to be genuine personal service. It followed that I would carve when, within the first week or two, we introduced a carvery as our regular Sunday Lunch. This brought me face to face with the public for the first time, with an opportunity to introduce a touch of theatre. I had cooked three prime roasts, a seventeen-pound

* MAD: - 'Goosed' a pinch on the bottom - an Italian mark of respect for a beautiful woman. A sort of hands-on assertive gesture, more positive than the feeble remote English 'wolf whistle'.

# It Could be a Little Gold Mine

hen turkey, a boned out leg of pork and a majestic topside of beef. Standing behind the glowing golden roasts, dressed in a spotless new white coat and blue and white striped butcher's apron, I was as pleased as could be. The turkey I had basted to golden perfection. The well-scored leg of pork, its crackling crisp as a cinnamon stick, was just as I wanted it to be. The topside of beef, looking like the Rock of Gibraltar, was set firm and steady on its salver. Thinking of that trattoria in Trastevere I knew that I was the principal actor and the customers my audience. My brand new carving knives were razor sharp but, to add a little *business*, as the thespians say, I did pretend to whet the blade with a few showy strokes across my brand new sharpening steel.

First up to the carvery was a red-faced local farmer, built like a grainstore with hands like excavator buckets. Round his waist he wore a black leather belt, long enough and wide enough to drive a mill. "Beef" was all he said. In his hands, the eleven-inch dinner plate he held looked like part of a doll's tea set. "Yes sir, of course," I said, slicing through the joint. I had cooked the beef rare because that was the fashion in *smart* restaurants. I was proud when I lay a huge slice of blushing pink beef across his plate, but soon fallen. Sounding like a blurting bull, he bellowed for all to hear, "What's matter lad, did thy oven go out?" The restaurant was full and they all roared with laughter, signalling their agreement with his assessment of my efforts. From that broadside, I learned to leave the beef in the oven until it was cooked through to the middle, to suit the Derbyshire folk who came to the inn for their Sunday Lunch. No blood should follow the knife for my customers. I was so embarrassed that I went as pink as the beef, but I did not worry, because I was sure it was all good theatre. I did not care that he had reduced me to playing the stooge while he took the lead. I knew we were both playing to a full house and my first audience had enjoyed the play.

Not all culinary disasters were my fault. The Women's Institute from a nearby village had chosen our inn to celebrate Christmas with a traditional dinner. It was to be cream of winter vegetable soup, followed by roast turkey with the traditional trimmings, then Christmas pudding and mince pies. All was going well with the soup when I decided to show the ladies that their turkey was a genuine bird. A turkey, roasted whole, just for them. I wanted them to know that it was not some preprepared turkey roll, or other reheated catering wheeze. To introduce a bit of drama, I carried the golden whole roast bird, set on a stainless steel tray, high over my head, all the way around their table. With the turkey set around with roast potatoes, baked onion and carrots for colour, and its legs furnished with white cutlet frills, it made a grand sight. My display drew a gratifying round of applause and I shot back to the kitchen, to carve as quickly as I could. It was then that the first ripple from a new unforeseen pebble that my god had tossed into my pond reached and rocked me. The first slice I cut into the breast of the bird released the unforgettable, overpowering reek of vitamin B. It was obvious that, just before its judgment day, this particular turkey had filled her crop full of the neat vitamin that a mixing machine had failed to spread evenly throughout tons of feed delivered to the farm. A second slice at the bird and a quick chew on the meat confirmed that it was good for nothing. I dropped it, whole, into the rubbish bin and calmed myself with an expletive 'bother and blow', or perhaps it was a 'damn and drat it', or maybe something a little stronger. I

# It Could be a Little Gold Mine

had no choice but to go back to the restaurant to explain that, for 'technical reasons' the main course would now be Sirloin Steak Chasseur. "Please talk amongst yourselves for a while," I ventured.

I did it in twenty-five hectic minutes. Made the sauce, trimmed and grilled twenty-five sirloins and fried off lots of chips. I did not ask for call orders of rare, medium or well-done. All went well with the Christmas pudding and brandy sauce, the tea, coffee, and mince pies. I positively glowed with pride when Madam Chairman sent for me, so I thought, to receive the plaudits of her members, the equivalent of a curtain call. She was an imposing woman, wearing a high-necked black bombasine dress over a tightly corseted ample bosom. As expected, her voice was that of strong contralto and it rang out like Edith Evans's rendition of 'A handbag?', in *The Importance of Being Earnest.* What she said was unexpected. "Chef, we do not wish to know of the technical difficulty that denied us our Christmas turkey. In fact, we commend you for your honesty. Also, we congratulate you for presenting such an excellent alternative meal." My reply was all false modesty "Er-oh; thank you: it was, er, the, well er the least ..." "However," she cut me off sharp, but with a wry twinkle in her eye. It was then that the second ripple from the pebble tossed into my pond hit me like a tidal wave. "Pray, do tell us what happened to the turkey's traditional Christmas trimmings." Ungentlemanly and unusually for me, this time I gave a spontaneous real oath, "Oh! Bugger!" I followed this with a mad dash back into the kitchen. When I opened the oven door, a thick black cloud of smoke shrouded me, as I choked and peered into the gloom. I saw roast potatoes that looked like lump-wood charcoal. I could just make out the lovingly prepared bacon-wrapped chipolata sausages, now reduced to the size and appearance of roast witchetty grubs. The crossed Brussels sprouts were now little brown *Malteser* lookalikes. Worse, were the strange blackened lumps that once were the bread sauce and sage and onion stuffing. All had taken hours to make. Once again, I was a fallen man. All profit gone, I could have wept.

Sometimes real drama came unbidden into the restaurant. One evening I had to remove, forcibly, two homicidal homosexuals. They started quietly enough with a lovers' tiff. In their passion, they let it fulminate and explode into a full-blown stand up cat fight. They gave a performance worthy of any West End production or even *EastEnders* on a violent night. Their hissed exchanges used language in a way that was unfamiliar to me. It seemed to be gender inaccurate. You cow, bitch, whore, tart, old queen and other terms unfamiliar, but all full of jealous spite and hate. The surprising thing was that throwing them out was not physically difficult, because both men were small, slightly built and in their late seventies. When they had gone, the relief amongst those remaining in the restaurant was palpable.

# It Could be a Little Gold Mine

On another night, we had a courtroom drama. This time there were four principals. They arrived punctually for dinner, all well-dressed, both men in suits, one woman in a severe black trouser suit, the other in a rather spectacular tailored red dress, all cutaway and cleavage. They seemed well-heeled and certainly, the lady in the red dress very highly heeled. They behaved normally at first, except that the lady in red hurried through two or three gins and one of the suits kept pace in whiskies. As they made their choice from the menu, Jeanne called into the kitchen to warn me, "All is not *quite as it should be* with the four on table 12."

It was not too long before Jeanne was back in the kitchen to ask, "Just go and have a wander in the restaurant will you?" I was busy, but something was worrying Jeanne who has a way of sensing when, all is not *quite as it should be*. Two of the four had cleared their plates of the first course I had sent out, but my creations lay untouched on the other two plates. One was in front of the lady wearing the rather spectacular tailored red dress, all cutaway, and cleavage, the other in front the man who had been keeping pace with whisky. "Is everything alright?" I asked. The frigid reply from both people with the untouched food "Yes; I'm just not hungry." I had no choice but to clear their plates and return to the kitchen to send out their main courses. Jeanne was soon back. The two who had not eaten were now up and at each other across the table, shouting and screaming for all to hear, even those in the bar. Tennessee Williams could not have done better with the fully scripted torrid detail about their infidelities and dysfunctional relationship. My response was immediate, just one word of dialogue: "Out." All four made a quick exit, followed by me, mad as a bee-stung bear. The man who had eaten his meal was waiting for me at reception. He was most apologetic. "I told them it was not possible, I begged them not to try, but they insisted. I am acting for the soak and the bird in black is acting for the bitch in red. They wanted to agree a settlement in their divorce, like civilised people, over a quiet dinner. Look, I am awfully sorry old chap, here is my card, please send me the account and add a hefty tip. I will pay you and charge them both, doubled, in spades." I got many a kind smile when I went back to see how our other guests had taken to the real life drama. "Better than *Coronation Street* and those murder mysteries," said one old lady who clearly had enjoyed it all. We did get the money, later.

I have to be careful not to allow, too often, my caustic tongue and acerbic turn of phrase out in public. From time to time, I fall from grace, they do get loose, and we lose another few customers. When this happens, Jeanne admonishes me something dreadful, knowing that the parlous state of our finances requires that we keep all the customers we can get. Occasionally I would stick to my guns and say, "Eh Jeanne, it was worth it, we don't need their sort anyway."

On one such occasion, I felt some justification. I had been reading from one of my favourite cookbooks, *Ma Cuisine* by the great chef Auguste Escoffier. This had inspired me to cook a casserole of pigeon breasts. His recipe was rich in wine, with many different root vegetables, onions, and peas. The great man had stipulated the addition of button mushrooms, stem cut off and discarded, the cap peeled and quartered. Following the recipe, I peeled and quartered the mushroom caps and added them to the dish at the point specified. It was a busy Saturday night when I offered this old-fashioned dish and it proved to be popular.

# It Could be a Little Gold Mine

When the restaurant staff had taken out the last of the main courses, following my customary habit, I threw down my oven cloth, put on a clean apron, and went through to the restaurant to talk to the customers. Jeanne denies that I have conversations; she tells me I harass the customers rather than converse with them.

On this occasion, I admit that she was half-right. I was engaged in conversation with four regular customers when a voice rang out clear across the restaurant, "Oh Chef, the pigeon was divine, but it could have been improved if you had used cèpe instead of mushroom." All conversation stopped, not a knife or fork scraped on a plate, not a chair squeaked, no one coughed. At every table, I saw unmistakable looks of alarm from our regular customers, as they wondered, "What is he going to say and do now?" At first, I said nothing. I then slowly turned to look at the woman. She was dressed like a nineteenth-century Romany fortune-teller. A dress of flowing multicoloured thin pleated crepe de Chine, ginger strands of hair escaping from under a white turban, highly rouged cheekbones, long dangling earrings, at least twelve necklaces of coloured stones and two rings on each finger, supported my idea of her origins.

I do not know where the lines and stage direction came from, but to this day, I remember them well. Still not speaking, I took the long, yellow painted pencil from the headband of my toque, that tall starch stiff pleated white hat worn by chefs as a badge of rank, not as a head cover. I paused to look at the pencil for a long time. I became conscious that all eyes were upon me, waiting. I then spoke in the high language. "Madam," and I paused again, "the dish I cooked for you this evening is so rich in many flavours and so varied in textures that you would not have known if I had used the rubber off the end of this, my pencil." Not content with that, I went to the kitchen and brought forth my well-worn and battered copy of the best of food dictionaries *Larousse Gastronomique*, the world famous encyclopaedia of food, wine and cooking. The young Prosper Montagné compiled the book and the elderly Escoffier wrote the preface, just before he died. With a great show, I set the great book before the lady, open at the page with the entry for 'cèpe'. I asked her, in a voice loud enough for all to hear, if she would accept Larousse as authoritative on the matter of cèpe. Answer came there none, as her many-ringed finger found the entry. I did not expect one. After a suitable dramatic pause, I took up the book and read aloud "'Cèpe, an inferior sort of mushroom'."

I should not have done it, I was rude and arrogant, but it did me a power of good. I hope that on some future occasions, my bad behaviour might save other chefs, in other restaurants, from pretentious arrogance. A few of the diners did tell me that the exchange had made their evening and that I was quite right. Jeanne was of a different opinion. On reflection, I just hope that we did not have any American guests that night.

Customers provided comedy, both light and black, they also provided drama, but it seemed that I had to do the slapstick scenes. I was on red alert as Jeanne's elder sister and her husband were dining in our restaurant for the first time. I was desperately anxious to give a good impression, knowing that Sister-in-Law would report every detail back to Mother-in-Law. I knew that with Jeanne's mother, I had made no progress since our first meeting. She still could not understand how her nice well brought up daughter had let the

# It Could be a Little Gold Mine

family name down by conjoining with a vulgar northerner in trade.

For once, I thought that I was in luck. The host of a party of ten had challenged me to cook, dress and serve a ten-pound salmon he had caught while on his annual visit to a reach on the Tweed. It was a prime example of fresh run, wild salmon, not a spent fish, those that look more like barracuda than good Scottish salmon. Too often, proud rapists of the river bring such skeletal cadavers to me, asking that I "Do something with it."

To cook and dress a whole salmon was hardly a challenge except for the unusual request that he wanted it garnished as though it would be for a formal cold buffet, but silver served while still hot. Now that was a challenge. I worked like a whirling dervish; the court bouillon to poach it had been prepared during the afternoon, as had an array of garnish. I had ready thinly sliced cucumber, glacé cherries for the eyes, roast capsicum, a hard-boiled egg and a tomato cut ready as a crown. From the garden, I brought in three large smooth pebbles and some iris leaves. To fill the spaces on the huge silver mirrored salver, from which I planned to serve it, I had ready watercress and chopped aspic. As soon as the first course went out, I lifted the still very hot fish from the court bouillon and, as we Dales folk say, I *set to*. I had arranged the pebbles on the salver to support the head, with the iris leaves trapped in the pebbles for effect.

Before the very delicate move to its position on the salver, I had to remove not just the fins and skin from the body but also the dark fatty tissue along the spine, while leaving the head and tail skin in place. That was difficult enough at speed, but once done it was critical to transfer it to the silver mirrored salver without breaking it. Three of us, each using two spatulas, completed the transfer without a hitch.

I was safe, or so I thought, but other factors were at work, another pebble of different origin was poised ready. I quickly dressed the whole of the pink flesh with shrimp sauce, cucumber scales, fitted the tomato crown, cucumber fins, glacé cherry eyes and popped the hard-boiled egg in its mouth. Finally, I strewed the mirror with chopped aspic and the watercress to represent the sparkling stream and its bank. It took me, with help, no more than ten minutes.

It looked fantastic. It was still hot; we had met the challenge and won the bet. As soon as Jeanne called "Mains away," I swept through to the restaurant to show my triumph to the table of ten. Such was the excitement that diners from other tables came to look at the dish and I was thrilled to hear the 'oohs' and 'aahs', but of course, disaster was inevitable. The mirrored silver salver held on my outstretched arm concealed at least eight feet of the floor in front of me. I was like the captain navigator of a supertanker, but without radar or a forward lookout. When I turned to acknowledge the appreciation, I could not see the rocks and icebergs that lay before me on my uncharted course. The hazards were in the form of two large ice buckets on stands, each one full of ice cubes, water and a bottle of champagne. The collision, although not of Titanic proportion, was spectacular. The corks popped, a tidal wave of ice-cold foam broke on the carpet and swept over the shoes of my sister-in-law. Once again, the pebble in my pond turned triumph into tragedy and our profit had gone out with the tide.

# CHAPTER NINETEEN

# Dysphrasia

My first recollection that I had been born with the dread syndrome of dysphrasia* occurred when I was still at infant school. I was standing with my mother at a bus stop outside school when the driver of a bus went by without stopping, even though my mother had clearly signalled for him to pick us up. "Why did he not stop for us?" I piped up. "Because he was going to the terminus," mother replied. I thought for a moment, then felt sick with embarrassment. Until that moment, I had thought, with a deal of logic, that the single word 'terminus' was in fact three words *turn he must*, and I had had a scrap in the school yard to prove my understanding.

Some years later, when to everyone's relief and surprise, I passed the intelligence test, and was at Heath Grammar School, the disease had developed through incubation stages of malapropism and spoonerism to full-blown dysphrasia. This infection forced my tongue to frequently get in first, before what little intellect I had could restrain it. It was during the third year when I was struggling with Latin grammar and syntax. One cannot remember a lesson that one had not attended and Latin was all Greek to me. I missed classes because I was often ill with one thing or another, and my reports showed actual attendances hovering around seventy

*MAD: Dysphrasia - (dis-fraizier) the unerring ability to say the wrong thing, to the wrong person, at the wrong time.

# Dysphrasia

percent of possible. My form master, Larry Gain, was also my Latin teacher. He was just wonderful and inspirational. Of tubby stature he looked, in his black gown, like a rook in winter, with its feathers fluffed out against the cold. He never blasphemed or swore, but would explode at my incompetence with original and bold expletives, "Bust a frog" and "Bindlesticks" being two of his favourites. I was sitting at the back of class, trying not to look inane or stupid, when, recognising like for like, he commanded that I construe the word *inanise*. This was a word in the second chapter of the second book of Caesar. Well, I had not got past the first chapter of the first book and in desperation offered, "That's what the horses were in sir." Here ended my classics lessons. Larry took me firmly by the ear and putting me out of the classroom door, into the corridor, kindly said, "Go and do woodwork." Even now, as I walk on three legs, the condition still affects me.

It was only recently that it happened, it wasn't my fault; I wasn't there; well I should not have been there. I had only come across from our cottage, to collect some bits and bobs for breakfast. With a jug of milk in one hand and a loaf of bread and some eggs in the other, I was about to leave the inn when I bumped into a young couple at the main entrance. Christopher, our eldest son, was on duty at the reception desk waiting to greet them. However for some unexplained reason she seemed compelled to disregard him and to speak to me, didn't she. I did not then and do not yet understand why she should choose to do so, but do so she did. She ignored the obvious reception desk with its bell and register, and Christopher, who can pull birds like a young polo player driving a Ferrari. She taxed me, an old grey hulk, even though I was not dressed, as one would expect an innkeeper to be

# It Could be a Little Gold Mine

dressed, and was obviously intent on leaving the building with my clutch of eggs and staples.

I should have known better than to listen, because when injury forced me out of the kitchen, I took a job working for local government that lasted for three and a half years. That chilling experience led me to understand that it is just the sort of thing that the assertive thoroughly modern Ms's* do these days. Television adverts have told them, so often, *that they are worth it*, they believe it. She who spoke to me was a young woman. Understandably, women of her ilk do not like men to address them with the courtesy title of ladies anymore. For many of them it is understandable, because their behaviour and demeanour do not warrant it. Dressed overall in a dull square shoulder padded brown trouser suit with pockets, I guessed that she would be in her late twenties. This woman who had arrested me at the door would never admit to a husband, but her male companion was a well enough dressed youth. He knew his place though and stood, dutifully, well behind her, and did not even manage a grunt.

"Excuse me," she said, assertively, only just missing out the *My man* bit, "I would like to book into our room early; you see we are going to a wedding." Ignoring her strange conjunction of I, our and we, acting the genial elderly innkeeper, I foolishly responded. "Why of course my dear, I am sure that something can be arranged. Christopher here will look after you," as I indicated his obvious presence at the reception desk.

I realised, because I was withered by her now colder than frosty look, that I was dealing with the truly modern Ms. In her gender deficient worlds the, *my dear* bit had been a bad

*MAD - Ms. - 1963 abbreviation -introduced by feminists. (Miserable sisters.)

mistake on my part. I know, I should have left them to it, but no, I ploughed on, regardless that years of experience urged me to cut and run. "Where is the wedding?" I asked, digging a deeper furrow. "St Oswald's church in Ashbourne" was the tart if not tart's reply. "Oh how lovely, it is a beautiful church and a grand place for a wedding. What a good idea you have had to book in early, to change into a pretty dress." The words were out, irretrievable, irreversible, irrevocable; the damage done. Her face was now as sharp and twisted as a broken bedspring, and said it all. I should have known; she was already wearing her chosen outfit, that drab brown trouser suit. She gave a few short instructions to her consort and they turned heel and left without a further word.

I was left to face Christopher who had witnessed and heard everything. He stood with his arm raised and fist clenched in a victory salute. He was jubilant, "Good old Dad, you can still do it." Suitably abashed, I said, "Don't tell Mum for God's sake." Christopher, unusually solicitous, just smiled and said, "I won't mention it, you were quite right, it was an awful outfit." I was not so cheerful, more profit gone and I knew that Jeanne would ask questions about the *no show*.

This was only one of the all too many times that my tongue has tripped me up. I have always matched my dysfunctional coordination of arms, legs, body, and balance with equally chronic dysphrasia.

About fashion, my dysphrasia has no equal. The girl came into the bar with her father and mother; it was as though Cecil Beaton had designed their outfits for an outing to Royal Ascot. I recognised the daughter because she was attractive and had been several times before with her boyfriend. She looked positively radiant in a sleeveless heavy linen buttoned at the

# It Could be a Little Gold Mine

back summer dress which had brightly coloured broad stripes, running from shoulder to hem. As they left I called after the girl, "Taking it back t'deck chair attendant then?" hoping for a smile from her father at least. Smile there was none, no reaction at all, so I thought no more about it. It was some months later that her father and mother came again, this time without their daughter. The mother was wearing a spectacular broad-brimmed hat suitable for a society wedding. "Not a word from you," pointing at me, was her opening greeting. "Who me, what have I done?" I questioned, sensing that something more was to come. "Yes you; you horrid man, you cost me a lot of money last year." "I did?" "Yes you did, do you remember asking my daughter if she was taking her dress back to the deck chair attendant?" "Oh yes, of course," I owned, laughing. "Well, as soon as we got home she took it off and burnt it on the middle of our back lawn, and she jumped up and down on the ashes, ruining her shoes." 'Dad' then got in his two pennyworth, "And there's still a bald patch where the grass won't grow." However, we remained friends.

Some of my opening gambits to start a conversation have left me with nowhere to go. During a wedding reception, I noticed the Best Man, standing alone, and as he did not look as though he was enjoying himself, I went to him intent to give him a cheery greeting. "Hello, where have you come from today?" "Oh!" he replied, "I'm local really, from Cubley," "Oh yes," I pressed on, "It's a nice little village, except for the crossroads, they are so deadly dangerous, aren't they?" "Yes, that's why I am here," he replied quietly. "My brother, who was to be the Best Man today, was killed there a week ago today." Double dysphrasia. These are only a few of the

# Dysphrasia

many times dysphrasia has caused me grief. My kindly publisher has struck out the two worst stories. For a time I took a vow not to talk to customers, whatever the reason. However, time heals and eventually the thought of reducing our inn to the stultified banality of the chain hotels bore me up and I gave up my Trappist vow. I find irritating beyond endurance the overused phrases used by staff working in franchised food outlets, group hotels, and restaurant chains. Their statement *there you go*, as they place a meal before you when you are determined to stay, is just stupid. Worse is the waiter's arrogant command, *enjoy* that denies any comment, request, or answer. Given the opportunity, I would strike from the lexicon that American import of insincerity *have a nice day now*. Dysphrasia or not, despite the risk, I determined to continue to engage with our customers. Even if my genuine enquiry, "Have you something good planned for today?" risks the answer, "No, we are going to our son's funeral."

Sometimes my remarks have been rewarding, though extremely rude and to say the least undiplomatic. The sun was shining and the summer garden looking beautiful. Edward, our second son, thought a little light music would be a good idea, so he took one of the big black speakers onto the terrace and played a middle of the road non-vocal musical tape. First into the garden and onto the terrace came a party of four Germans, two herren, and two frauen. They settled themselves at a table and began to talk loudly, in German, pointing to various features and generally establishing a beachhead, albeit this time without tanks or towels. Just as I came onto the terrace one of the herren, tall, Arian blond, rose from the table, walked to the big black speaker and yanked at the cable, disconnecting the jack plug, to shut off

# It Could be a Little Gold Mine

the music.

It was his exaggerated swagger and the arrogant smile he gave when he turned to his companions that made me do it. In a quiet but steady voice, but not so quiet that his companions could not hear, I said, "If you do that again, I shall restart the Second World War." I could not have had a better reaction if I had dropped on him a stonk from my battery of twenty-five pounder field guns, the guns I commanded during my service days with the Royal Artillery. I said no more. He was in real fear, they left immediately, his hands covering his private parts like a footballer in a defensive wall facing a free kick from just outside the penalty area. He backed away, spluttering, and muttering in a high-pitched whine, "There is no need, there is no need, we are all friends now." As their car left the yard, them coffeeless, and me profitless, I wondered, are we?

Although sometimes it has been a problem, being built like a bear with a voice like a bullhorn is useful. The expression is not mine but one used by the *Daily Express* to describe me in a two-page spread they had about me, 'The real Mr Grumpy'. Jeanne had taken a booking for a coach party of fifty retired head teachers for a lunchtime reunion. It soon became obvious that this lot had all been into education politics, because the noise of their chatter was decibels above the Black Dyke Mills brass band playing the *Overture to William Tell*. All was ready in the kitchen, and time was going on, so I rang the big brass bell that hangs behind the bar and shouted, "Lunch is served." The general hullabaloo now developed into full-blown pandemonium. At the chime of the bell, each and every ex-headmaster or headmistress reverted to type. Unilaterally, each one tried to organise who should sit

# Dysphrasia

where and with whom. There was only one thing to do; I strode into the middle of the melee and roared, "Sit down, shut up and behave." It had worked before and it worked again, like magic. Instantly, they fell silent, then there was shuffling of feet and scraping of chairs, followed by happy laughter as they saw themselves as others see them. The lunch went well.

Dysphrasia struck again on St Valentine's Day. As usual, we had advertised and arranged a special Valentine Dinner. I noticed a young couple coming shyly into the bar, and I was sure that all of our other more mature customers took notice of them too. They were obviously a little nervous and it did not take a psychic to see that it was the big day for both of them. I think everyone in the bar would have bet very short odds that the young man was going to propose marriage and that the young lady was determined to accept.

He was wearing a sober suit, a white shirt with a collar too big, and a very formal tie. She was demure in a little black cocktail dress that must have set her back a couple of months' wages. I took the menus to them and said in very formal terms, "Good evening sir, good evening madam, here are our menus for tonight's special St Valentine's Dinner," and then thinking to break the ice, I lapsed into my Yorkshire brogue. "By gum lad, she's a big improvement on that one thee brought in here last neet." As I returned to the kitchen I heard many a chuckle from the other guests. When, some minutes latter, I came to take their order, the table was bare, they were not there, they had not stayed, they had not moved, they had gone. My other guests were laughing. "Eh Mr A, you've blown it this time," said one old friend. "She believed you and left in a flood of tears with him chasing after." "Oh

# It Could be a Little Gold Mine

damn, surely not" I said, as I ran for the door. Of course, I was too late; the rear lights of the car were already out of the car park and onto the road going north, back into the hills.

When I came back into the bar, I was crestfallen and sad that once again dysphrasia had caused hurt feelings and lost us customers. However, another old friend soon bore me up. He was a regular customer, a local hill farmer, and country gentleman. "Dunna thee worry master, you've done a good lad a right good turn. I knows them both, him and the lass. She's right mardy, allus has been, she'll never turn to wi' him. Anyone could reckon they wunna suited."

Not all of my chat has been disastrous, one particular voice that I have used, ever since we came to the inn, has been an unfailing success. I use it when talking to children, if they are at least three or four years old. At first sight of me, younger children usually cry and cling to dad or mum for reassurance. The voice I use is 'duck talk'. To make myself clear I do not mean the decoy duck noise of the duck hunter in his canoe, but a passing fair imitation of Walt Disney's Donald Duck.

I must be getting old, as young parents have started to bring their children to the inn and ask me to say something to their offspring in 'duck talk'. "Just like I remember you used to do for me when I was young." A generation gone by and it still works, but never better than an occasion just recently. The mother of a six or something year-old boy and his younger sister came and asked, "Mr A, will you please, please come and do Donald Duck for my little boy?" Always glad of an audience, I went with his mother and quacked and squawked in good form. I was happy to see his face light up as he looked, first at his Dad and then his Mum, with a sort of, *I told you so* look in his eye. It was then that his Dad spoke for the first time, "I've just wasted two thousand pounds because of you." "Oh! Take no notice of him," said the boy's young mother, taking over, "It's just that we have been on holiday to Florida and to Disney World. When we were watching Snow White's procession, the one they do everyday down *Main Street* their Donald Duck broke out of the procession and gave our son a hug. I asked him if he liked meeting Donald Duck and honestly, this is what he said: 'That's not Donald Duck, the real Donald Duck lives at the Bentley Brook'."

The few examples of the downside of my dysphrasia pale into insignificance when put alongside my most heinous error. My late mother, long a widow, but always ever-loving of her family, used to visit our inn just once each year to mark our progress. She had kind neighbours who visited relatives in Derby and passed us en route. Each year, on the appointed day, mother would be dropped off just before lunch and picked up again just after tea. This particular year Mother rang me to tell us of the chosen day and I forgot to write it in the diary; worse, I forgot to tell Jeanne.

It was a glorious July day with the sun blazing from a clear blue sky; I was busy in the kitchen, while Jeanne was out shopping. Just before lunch, someone rang the reception bell. I continued with my work thinking that the bar staff would attend to it. The bell rang again, a longer burst, then again for longer still. "Damn, where is everybody," I was chuntering to myself, washing my hands and putting on a clean apron ready to answer the bell's now pressing call.

Composed, I went into the hall only to see against the blinding light of the entrance, the silhouette of someone

# It Could be a Little Gold Mine

standing at the reception desk, someone about to ring the bell again. "Good morning, can I help you?" I enquired in my most ingrate voice. "I'm your Mother," was the reply, in a voice that indicated I was out of her will, for ever. If only I had just said "Hello."

Dysphrasia.

# CHAPTER TWENTY

# Many Weddings and a Few Funerals

Despite being involved in the arrangements made for a couple of hundred or more wedding receptions that we have catered for at the inn, as a mere male, I am unable to understand the hysteria that these occasions generate.

Negotiations usually start with the bride, or her mother, writing, ringing or e-mailing, asking us to send our wedding brochure. About a third respond and come, to interview us about how we could possibly cope with their very special and unique requirements for *Her Special Day*. This is the cue for me to leave the scene and let Jeanne make all the arrangements. If I stay, I usually lose the business by upsetting both the bride and her mother by pointing out that it is an equally special day for the groom. I normally go on to make matters worse by telling them that there are only two things that can go wrong on the day; either, Chef could oversleep and not get the roast into the oven on time, or the vicar would have the wrong date in his diary and be on holiday in Australia. My well-intended reassurances only add two more eventualities to the disaster catalogue that the bride's mother had previously not thought of. If the bride's father is present I detect some sympathy with my ideas, but these are usually unspoken. That is, until I try to steer the day chosen for the recep-

# It Could be a Little Gold Mine

tion away from Saturdays. Saturdays are always busy at our inn; a wedding reception needs exclusivity of our facilities, and we lose our regular trade. Unless the realisable income from a reception is much more than we would expect from our normal weekend take, exclusive receptions are just not viable. I try to suggest a midweek wedding and tell them that there are at least three great advantages with such a novel arrangement. "First; true friends will come to see you wed, whatever the day of the week. Second; those who make excuses, and don't come, will save you hundreds of pounds on the reception, because we charge per head. Third; those who send their excuses will give you much better presents because they will feel guilty." I have said this to over a hundred brides and have always seen hope shining in the eyes of both the bride's father and the groom, but this fades as the ladies' shoulders stiffen and the bride's mother's eyes freeze me into silence. Only once did I persuade the bride that a midweek wedding would make sense.

Difficulties have occurred with wedding arrangements at our inn, but none so great as those for the sole bride who did take my advice. She was a charming young veterinary surgeon, an expert on animal nutrition in general, but pigs in particular. A local youth, who lived in one of the hill villages, only a few miles from the inn, had wooed and won her. At first, all was well, the bride's mother arrived to stay with us the night before the wedding, and brought with her two simply gorgeous girls who were to be bridesmaids. The church was booked, I had all the food prepared ready for cooking the following day. All three of the boys were home from school and together with the bridesmaids, we had a wonderful evening, with the bride's mother playing the piano. All of us joined in the singing and playing party games. The two elder boys thought that Christmas had come twice in that year, as they flirted, and more, with the bridesmaids. The log fire was blazing, the curtains were drawn and I was happy because I had my own way for once, but of course, my god sought to bring me down a peg or three and dropped another pebble in my pond.

We did not notice the silent snow as it fell and drifted over both hill and dale. We did not hear the crash as it brought down telephone and power lines, only in the morning did the problem reveal itself. The bride had gone home to her village the day before and could easily walk the short distance to the church to meet her groom, but the snow had cut off the high country parish where the vicar had his manse. He could not get to the church. After a counsel with the bride's mother and discussion with the vicar, who had trudged miles to find a phone that worked, he agreed to delay the wedding for twenty-four hours. The party at the inn went on.

In the evening, the vicar rang to tell us that all was well. Using a horse-drawn sledge that a friendly farmer had offered, he would be able to get to the church on time, to conduct the marriage service, at noon on the following day. I had everything ready for the reception meal and first thing next morning I tried to get the bride's mother to the church in my car, but failed. The vicar agreed to delay the service for four hours. A second attempt to get the bride's mother to the church in a borrowed Range Rover also failed. Ma politely declined the offer by one of our neighbouring farmers to take her to the church in a tractor. As we did not have a troika or sledge of any kind, the bride, quite rightly, when all is said and done, put her foot down and said she was not getting

# It Could be a Little Gold Mine

married without her mother being present at the church. The vicar said he would try to postpone the ceremony for another day but warned that, as it would then be Sunday, he would have to get the Bishop's special agreement. The boys and the bridesmaids did not seem at all fussed by the delay. I was now getting worried about the state of the food, but we did not need artificial refrigeration, it was everywhere available.

During the night, the thaw set in, the Bishop gave his dispensation and the bride's mother and the two bridesmaids went to church. The vicar was there, the bride and the groom were there and the knot was tied with due ceremony. I went to the door hoping to greet the modest blushing bride when she finally arrived for the reception, only to see that I had it all wrong. As she came to the top of the steps, in her beautiful long white bridal gown she called out, "Look Mr A," and bending, she picked up the front hem of the dress with both hands, and raised it high above her head to show off a pair of thick grey woollen long johns tucked into Wellington boots. She was obviously an upper class girl; her boots were green and had straps.

Some brides' mothers are most felicitous and anxious that we should feel at ease. One such came to see Jeanne and me, without appointment and without her daughter. She came to ask that we show no surprise when her daughter arrived at the reception straight from the church. "You see," she said, she will be wearing black, all black." Clearly mother did not approve but the bride did look stunning in a three quarter length, very full, black taffeta strapless creation. Her jet-black hair, plaited in dreadlocks contrasted with her flawless very white skin. She carried it off beautifully, she was confident and radiant, but I was pleased her mother had forewarned us.

# Many Weddings and a Few Funerals

FOR GOD'S SAKE, DON'T SHOUT 'MORE! MORE!'

At most wedding receptions that I cooked for, by the time the Best Man was on his feet to start the formalities and speeches, I was able to vacate the kitchen and listen to the toast to the bride and groom and to the bridesmaids. Some are just dreadful and it disappoints me when nervous fathers, and the best man, make a bad job of it. If only they would understand that everyone in the room is willing them to do well and would laugh and cheer, even if they trotted out the oldest jokes and aphorisms. However, not all fail. One groom gave the best speech I have heard at a wedding or club dinner. He spoke for almost two hours, holding the guests entertained, instructed and at times helpless with laughter. The reception had been arranged for one hundred and thirty guests in a marquee attached to the inn. I had asked him what he wanted to happen between the formal reception, that we had planned to complete around five, and the evening celebration that was not due to start until seven, a hiatus that usually leads to people making excuses and leaving before the

# It Could be a Little Gold Mine

party begins. "Leave it to me," he said, "you just get on with clearing and setting up, I will talk to them." Talk to them he did. He took as his subject, each section of the guests in turn. First he talked about his parents, then her parents, followed by the best man, the ushers, the bridesmaids, his friends from school and work, then finally her friends the same. He spoke for a few minutes about each group, complimentary only to the parents, then wickedly witty about the rest. The two hours passed with few leaving their seats, even for a comfort break.

This fear of speaking to an audience is very real, if not understandable. At one wedding, when I knew the father of the bride, and the father of the groom, I was surprised to see the groom's father stand up to deliver the formal speech of welcome to the guests and propose the toast to the happy couple. Of the bride's father, whose duty it was, there was no sign. His seat was empty, although moments before he had been at the table with his speech all written out on cards before him. He had panicked and done a bunk when he saw the best man rise to start the formal proceedings. I think that I was the only one present, apart from the forgiving bride, who noticed the switch. Totally unprepared, the groom's father even got all the names right and had everyone laughing at his recycled jokes. "It was dead easy," he told me later, "I just remembered what I did and said, when I had the job at my daughter's wedding."

A function, celebration, or ritual, whatever it may be, that has developed during the time we have catered for weddings is the away day, or weekend stag or hen night. Jeanne took a particular interest with one bride and her friends who booked all the rooms we had available, for a hen party they planned to hold a week before the wedding. They were a grand set of girls and the bride was very anxious that the weekend should be a great success. She called to see Jeanne, on more than one occasion, to make minor requests and alterations. She also told Jeanne of several surprises and practical jokes she planned to play on her friends, fearing that they would be planning mayhem for her. This inspired Jeanne to play one on her. We had a very pleasant couple who were regular customers. They worked in Birmingham during the week, staying in rented accommodation, but owned a cottage in a nearby village. They often came to have their supper with us on Friday evenings, before going to their weekend retreat. Jeanne talked them into a bit of play-acting. We knew the bride-to-be was due to arrive with her friends, in a fourteen-seat minicoach, at about 7pm on a Friday night. Jeanne had fully scripted our two Friday evening regulars how to play the scene.

At the appointed time, they took up position behind our reception desk, he formally suited and peering through borrowed pince-nez spectacles. When the girls tumbled through the door, giggling and squealing, he gravely intoned, "Good evening, how may I help you ladies?" giving them all a disapproving look. "I am Wendy and these are my friends, we've booked all your rooms for the weekend," the bride chirped. "May I enquire in what name the reservation was made?" our straight-faced interlocutor asked. When the bride gave her full name, he replied in a graver tone, "I am afraid I know nothing of such a booking, there is nothing here in the diary, in fact we are fully booked already, are you sure you are in the right hotel?" The now anxious Wendy, "But I booked it myself, with Mrs Allingham, the proprietor, weeks ago." "Oh dear, oh dear, I don't know quite what to say, you see we

# It Could be a Little Gold Mine

bought the inn a fortnight ago from the Allingham's and they never mentioned anything about this." Our friend was a natural actor and became all felicitous, offering to do all that he could to find them a few rooms here and there in local bed and breakfasts. Only when Jeanne could hear that it had gone far enough did we appear from our hiding place. It was slightly cruel, but no one was hurt, and it set their weekend off to a wonderful start. The several practical jokes that the bride-to-be had planned to play on her friends were forgotten.

Stag nights tend to be boisterous, but usually good-natured, only occasionally getting out of hand. One summer night, a slightly merry stag party of rugby players laid out the groom on the lawn, just as nature made him. I had forgotten to put away the croquet set and they used the iron hoops, driven in with mallets, to pin down his wrists and ankles. Less unkind, but following stag night convention, a group of likely lads, all RAF officers or ex-RAF, decided to debag the groom, as was customary in their mess. The spry groom-to-be, took a huge risk trying to avoid the inevitable. He crawled right through the central fireplace from one side to the other, clambering over the foot high dog grate, while the fire was burning merrily.

Not all were so brave. I caught one guest at a stag night crawling through a window into the locked Traveller's Room. The sound of the Tiffany style light on the window ledge crashing to the floor drew my attention to his out of order behaviour. I was livid, and using my most commanding voice sent him to bed, although it was only just after nine. An hour later I was in the bar with the other young men, who were doing what young men do on such occasions, arm wrestling, surfing on bar stools, bottle-pushing, drinking games et cetera, when the miscreant gently pushed open the door and while still outside the room, asked in a schoolboy voice, "Please sir, may I watch television?"

Funerals have also had their funny side, and in one case almost caused a problem. The funny side is the fact that, as I have mentioned before, the barman is invisible to the conscious perception of the average frequenter of public bars. The first funeral tea that we catered for taught me a great deal about the ritual of such events and human nature. However, I had to keep looking around to make sure that the cameras were not rolling, filming a scripted domestic comedy. The old lady who had passed away came from a large well-respected family. She had kept a nearby pub for many years and had had a very good reputation as a cook. In her last will and testament, she not only specified that after her funeral the

# It Could be a Little Gold Mine

mourners must gather at the Bentley Brook, for a funeral tea, she had specified exactly what the tea should be. It was to include most of the usual things, pies, sausage rolls, filled sandwiches and finger rolls, but at the top of the list, I was required to serve 'barm bread'. It was a thing I had never come across in my travels but my collection of cookbooks soon had me on the right track. It requires the cook to use brewer's not baker's yeast, to make the barm bread or cake.

The mourners arrived in force, not long after the usual lunchtime trade had melted away. It was soon apparent that it was not barm bread and cups of tea that they were after. It was the busiest bar we had had since we bought the inn and their demand for service made it hard for us to keep up. Soon we started to hear the lines one could only expect from an Alan Ayckbourn, or Alan Bennett play. "You see that fur coat she's wearing, that was to come to me." "That's nowt; she promised me that she would leave me that brooch, the diamanté, the one that that one over there is flaunting. She said I deserved it for all I've done for her; just look at her, she hasn't put foot inside the old love's door since she took badly, and that were two years ago." The last of the mourners only left around midnight with many cries of, "Good night lad. It's been grand," and "You've put on a right good bit of a do, you have, you did her proud." They had celebrated her life straight through the then afternoon closing time of 3pm to 6pm. Jeanne and I were very late to bed, because we sat in front of the dying embers of the log fire and told each other about the many bits of real life drama we had overheard and the laughter we had had to hide.

There is a fear that lies deep in the subconscious mind of all chefs, hotel managers and innkeepers, occasionally waking

# Many Weddings and a Few Funerals

them in a cold nightmare sweat from their fitful well-earned sleep. It is the *Mother Hubbard syndrome*, that dread prospect of a large number of people arriving for a formal function, or event, properly arranged by them but missed by all at the venue. I call it *Mother Hubbard syndrome*, because of the many mouths to feed, and nothing in the cupboard. When this happens at a small country inn it also means that there is no-one available to help to recover the situation.

With my luck, it was inevitable that such a dread scenario would happen to me. It occurred at about ten to one, on a fine summer Friday. Jeanne called me from the kitchen, where I was happily cooking lunch for a few customers, to answer the phone. I did not get chance to get past the "Hello" part of my usual "Bentley Brook Inn, how can I help you?" routine when a dark voice cut in, "We will be there in ten minutes," There was a short pause before I replied "Pardon?" Again the dark voice said clearly, "We will be there in ten minutes." "Excuse me, who is this?" I asked. A long pause followed. "Is that the owner of the Bentley Brook Inn I am speaking to?" "Why yes," I replied, by now a bit impatient. After a further and longer pause, there came a tired sort of expletive that had almost lost its will to explete. "Oh damn, I knew I should have made the arrangements myself. Look here, I am the undertaker, we have just buried a chap at Tissington, and the hundred or so mourners are coming to you for the funeral tea; we will be there in ten minutes, I can't stop them now, the vicar announced it from the pulpit." 'Click' and the phone went dead. I did not know if it was a practical joke, or whether it was for real, so I could not even begin to think about what to give the multitude until I knew for certain if it was for real. Anyway, I knew that ten minutes either way would not make much difference, I did not have the knack with the loaves and fishes.

I ran to a window overlooking the road that the cars would have to take from Tissington and within less than ten minutes, a stream of cars turned at the end of our garden and filled the car park. The funeral director was not a happy chap. He told me that the deceased was a young television producer and that his company had assured him that they themselves would make all arrangements for the wake. They had forgotten their promise and he asked me, "What can you do? It's a right mess." "Well you and I are both lucky men today," I was delighted to tell him. "If you can keep them drinking for three quarters of an hour, I think we can cope. You see, I have a buffet wedding reception booked for tomorrow, and I can use a lot of the stuff I have prepared for that." I did and it all went well and for once, we were in a position of being able to charge a good fee for our trouble. However, by the time the luvvies had drifted away, the kitchen looked as though there had been an explosion in a bakery. It was late afternoon, and I had to get special deliveries that evening to replace the food used for the funeral, to be ready for the wedding reception the next day. Once again, it meant working late into the night.

Christening receptions are no different from weddings and funerals. The guests behave much the same whatever the feast. This is good for the innkeeper, as the same menus are suitable for hatch, match and despatch; they just need a different cover.

Weddings are usually good fun, often bringing unexpected joy, but occasionally they cause anxiety and concern. One such happenstance occurred after a particularly jolly wedding

# Many Weddings and a Few Funerals

party. The bride's father had arranged for the guests to travel to and from the reception in three luxury coaches; one from Manchester, one from Derby and a third for the immediate family who lived in Belper. I was in a good mood because all had gone well throughout the day, but unknown to me a pebble was already causing ripples in my pond.

At about two in the morning, I had waved the Manchester and Derby coaches away, and was happily shaking hands with the bride's father, as he boarded the Belper bound bus, when, from within the bus a sweet small voice asked, "Where's Granddad?" This gentle enquiry came from the youngest bridesmaid, a girl of about eight. "Pardon?" we both asked before she asked again, "Where's Granddad?" I panicked, the bride's father panicked, and pandemonium broke out. A general search failed to find Granddad. He was not on the Belper coach, he was not in the bar or the restaurant, or the toilets, he was not in the marquee, or the garden, he was nowhere to be found. Granddad was missing.

A quick call to the police and they responded magnificently. They stopped the Derby coach as it entered the city and reported - "No Granddad." The local police, failing to catch the Manchester bound coach on the A515 alerted colleagues further north, the Greater Manchester force. They stopped the coach on the A6 in Stockport and found Granddad, fast asleep, on the back seat. They drove him to the county border where the Derbyshire police waited in one of their fast patrol cars. They took Granddad into their safe custody and brought him back to the bosom of his family at about 4am, full of tales of his exciting ride. And so finally to bed I went, a happy though very tired man. I had breakfasts to do, for a full house, in just three hours time.

# CHAPTER TWENTY-ONE

# Food, Fashion
# and other Frailties

*It's true we are what we eat,*
*You know it stands to reason.*
*Vegans may just find a pulse*
*While sipping a herb tisane,*
*Left outside society*
*To wonder where life has gone.*
*Vegetarians' diet*
*Reduces them to complain*
*Of coughs and colds and migraine,*
*Enough to drive them insane.*
*But the healthy omnivore,*
*Devouring fish and meat,*
*Loves life, good food and friendship,*
*It's true we are what we eat.*

The events told in chapter 6, 'Accidents will Happen,' prove it was no fault of mine, that at precisely 7.30am on Sunday 18 October 1987, just six days short of my completing ten years as chef at the inn, I stopped cooking for a living. A defective Derbyshire County Council manhole cover forced this change in my circumstances when I fell, unbidden, into the manhole. The caring County Council, eventually owned up to owning the thing, but of course referred to it as a personal access opening, not a manhole, because they were anxious to be both politically and gender correct. They were not a bit anxious about the damage they caused me, a white Caucasian self-employed male, who was not represented by a trade union or a trade association. When we realised that I was not going to be able to do any physical work again, we instructed a law firm to write to both the County Council and District Council, because we did not know which of the two were responsible for the defective cover. It did not surprise me that the first surveyor to turn up to inspect the site of the accident came from Severn Trent Water Board. Both councils had naturally said "Not ours." The so-called caring county council end played me, just as my learned counsel told me they would. After ten years, when court fees would have bankrupted the business, had my claim not been allowed, they paid into court a sum, imposing just sufficient risk on me, that I had to accept it.

The injury proved permanent and I joined the bad back club; the biggest club in the world even though the membership is costly. This forced change in my circumstance did not affect my love of food, but meant that I must find a different way of expressing my feelings. No longer capable of working in the kitchen and not being capable of much else, I turned part of our bedroom into a day room, by bringing in a desk and computer, and started to write. I arranged matters so that I could look out of the window to watch sheep and cattle graze and keep an eye on the gardeners who happily do a proper job of work in their kitchen garden and nursery.

Of course, I first wrote about my love of cooking. I set down recipes, including detailed lists of ingredients, comprehensive instructions about methods, measurements and the

# It Could be a Little Gold Mine

temperatures and times required to make ingredients come together, to taste and feel good. I also included suggestions of how to present each dish in ways that I knew that our customers had enjoyed, always taking care that my ideas would ensure that the food would be easy to eat as well as being pleasing to the eye. Experience on both sides of the kitchen counter taught me the importance in civilised society, that food presented in restaurants should be easy to eat. Too many chefs, seeking for eye appeal, forget that once handed over to the diner, disaster occurs and their beautifully decorated towers topple and tumble into the deep bowls in which they are served becoming no more than a mess of potage. Branded skin left uppermost on a fillet of fish, just for effect, is inedible and unless the restaurant staff provide a side plate for the debris, it spoils the dish because it forces the diner to push it round the plate. In Conran's fashionable Quaglino's Restaurant they do not provide side plates with any dish. An abomination.

In seeking to provide a pleasing presentation the French lose all sense and reason when serving snails, their trademark escargot. After taking the snails out of their shells to clean and poach them, they return the little cooked cadavers, like squatters, to special shells reserved for that purpose. The best part of the garlic and parsley butter in which they are poached usually splashes down the tie, shirtfront, or blouse as the customer wrestles with a winkle picker to lever out the now unrecognisable morsel.

My, as yet unpublished cookbook, a tome of more than a quarter of a million words, rests heavily, but secure, on the shelves by my desk, waiting for its time. That time will only come when people cease to follow the frivolities of fashion that favours flash-in-the-pan mixtures of too many incongruous and irreconcilable ingredients. The television celebrity chefs assiduously promote this current vogue, as do magazine and Sunday supplement food critics, whose jaded palates seek only novelty. In trying to be unusual, to produce new effects, or to introduce new ingredients, some modern celebrity chefs have achieved theatre, but it is theatre of the absurd. A very well- respected and publicised chef, with Michelin Red Star accolades for his restaurant, is on record as saying he produces food to suit the guides, not to suit his customers, nor sadly, dishes that he would himself enjoy. I am confident that the foolish fashion for innovation and trickery will pass. Without a driving force, even the largest pendulum will eventually come to rest in its true state of equilibrium. I hold to this belief, because I remember when I played rugby at school, and even after leaving school, when I turned out for the occasional game with the old boys' team, I was never able to keep up with play. I was so weedy that the selectors only allowed me on the coach to away matches, so that they could offer me to the other side if they were a man short. But, if I did get a game, I realised that if I feigned concussion, and lay for a rest, as the twenty-nine other chaps played on, exhausting themselves, the game would eventually come back my way and I could make a remarkable recovery. Refreshed and renewed I would rejoin the fray. It will be thus with food; fashion will no longer dictate, good sense will return and the manuscript resting on my bookshelf will be dusted down and published, God willing.

I have two aphorisms and two famous authorities to back my belief that the only way to cook well is to use first-class ingredients and not to spoil them;

# It Could be a Little Gold Mine

*God gave the earth good food;*
*The Devil sent chefs.*

*The problem with cooks is not what they know,*
*But what they know, that ain't so.*

Curiously, both my authorities are Frenchmen. More than two hundred years before we were subject to the media and PR hype about current food fashion, Voltaire, the French sage of rationalism, wrote a friend,

*"I cannot tolerate nouvelle cuisine .... used to disguise*
*ingredients which are perfectly good in themselves."*

I am sure that he would have had the same to say about cuisine minceur, fusion cooking, new classic cuisine and the ridiculous molecular gastronomy. Voltaire, and the supremely perceptive Prosper Montagné, writing one hundred and seventy odd years later, were of the same mind. In his great encyclopaedia, *Larousse Gastronomique*, previously mentioned, the young Frenchman defined English cooking as follows:

*'The essence of English cookery lies in choosing ingredients of the finest quality and cooking them so that their flavour and texture are fully developed. This is done with the minimum addition of ingredients so as not to mask the fine natural taste of the food.'*

He goes on to say -

*'England has long been the producer of beef, mutton, lamb, pork, pheasant, grouse, partridge, duck, salmon, sole, plaice, turbot, halibut, butter and cheese etc of a quality unsurpassed, anywhere in the world.'*

He extolled the virtues of Lancashire Hotpot, Cornish Pasties, bacon and egg, Welsh Rarebit, Manx Kippers and of course Yorkshire Pudding.

I came to the inn and took up cooking with no catering qualifications but with firm convictions about formal dining,

# Food, Fashion and other Frailties

sensible diet and keeping things simple. Although I had no training as a cook, I did have a head start and good reason to feel confident that my experience gave me a solid grounding for my new vocation. For twenty years, in more than sixty countries worldwide, and in all but two of the counties of Britain, my palate was educated in classic, regional, and exotic cuisine. This was by courtesy of my company expense account. Using this open cheque book, I enjoyed fabulous and costly meals and wines in world famous ships, hotels and restaurants. In England, the yard-long flaming kebabs, cooked on gold-hilted swords at the Epée d'Or, in the tatty Marble Arch Hotel, made me laugh. It was well over the top, but it was fun and I enjoyed it. Simpson's on the Strand was famous for its laconic staff, as well as for its roast beef and Yorkshire pudding. The carver, when he brought to our table the silver trolley on which was a huge joint of beef, asked me in a flat voice whether I was a Yorkshireman. When I responded with an enthusiastic "Yes," he simply said "Dunna have t'pudding then," and gave me another slice of beef instead. The bill for one memorable dinner I organised, to celebrate a huge contract won by the English Electric Company, came to more than my yearly salary. Thankfully, when I had to survive on my own account, I tempered the high life with simple local food. On such occasions, the companionship and generosity of cooks in cafés, canteens and roadside food stalls, from whom I learned, about not only their local dishes, but also some of their secrets, stimulated my ambitions to cook.

All this experience had the added advantage that there were no tuition fees. The meals served on formal mess nights, when I dined with the regiment were just superb. They gave me, a bobby's lad from Halifax, an insight into another

# It Could be a Little Gold Mine

world. The English Electric and Hong Kong Electric Companies graciously allowed my colleagues and me to stay at the finest of hotels and to eat in the very best restaurants as we entertained clients and as others entertained us. My basic studies, in addition to regimental dinners, the Epée d'Or and Simpson, has included the formality of meals at the Savoy Hotel, L'Ecu de France, Ketners, and the pre Conran Quaglino's in London. Quaglino's had tablecloths and side plates in those better days. During this period of my early training in food appreciation the *Three Horseshoes in Rugby*, when it was under the stewardship of Mr Spencer, a great restaurateur, was unquestionably the finest.

In Europe, further studies included the grandeur of the Vierjahreszeiten in Munich, the Imperial and Tri Hussaran in Vienna, and the glorious Terrace Restaurant in the Tivoli Gardens of Copenhagen. Here the practiced banter of the head waiter entertained me. This was while he cooked flambé, on a trolley by our table, for the thousand and many more times, his version of *Steak Diane*. He had made the mistake of cooking it on Danish television. He had performed so well that he and his dish became a tourist attraction. Danish businessmen thought it a necessity to take their foreign visitors first to see the little mermaid on her boulder by the sea and then to witness this special ceremony in the Tivoli.

The general manager of the main research centre of *Siemens*, the mighty German engineering firm, invited me to a formal dinner at a three Michelin Star restaurant, in Nuremburg. On the way there, we spotted a busy sausage house and we chose to eat, drink and sing there instead. He sent the rest of his staff on to the ultra-posh and far more expensive restaurant, but I am sure we two had had the best of it.

In Asia, I enjoyed the best of food. Hong Kong's cosmopolitan Mandarin, Hilton and Peninsula Hotels, and restaurants such as Jimmies Kitchen and the unequalled Red Room and Jackson's at the Hong Kong Club provided European food and service second to none. The strangely named Amer-

# It Could be a Little Gold Mine

ican Restaurant in Happy Valley was a favourite of mine, but only one of hundreds of restaurants serving wonderful Cantonese food and specialities from all of China's many regions. I was thrilled as I watched the swearing, sweat-shirted cooks in roadside night markets, as they prepared, in minutes, quite fantastic dishes. They used flattened ducks, and squid with which one could repair your shoes, foot long crayfish, crabs the size of dinner plates, nests of noodles, soups of snake, clutches of chitterlings and other diverse delicacies. These call-order chefs used huge iron woks, heated over roaring kerosine flames, to cook at speed. The best of them were real showmen. To attract customers to their stall, they tossed the sizzling ingredients six feet or more in the air, caught then in the wok before scooping them into a bowl and selling them for little money. In mainland China, I ate bear's paw, swan, civet and snake soup. The most expensive dish of all, freshwater clams, handfed on goose liver, satisfied me, but I declined the offers of both dog and live monkey brain.

In Japan, the quiet art of the tempura masters and the knife skills of the sushi chef enthralled me. I did eat the sometimes deadly blowfish, but only to call my host's bluff. Most of all I enjoyed the more simple fare of *Tapan Yaki*, tender cubes of finest *Matsusaka* or *Kobi* steak cooked with a lot of garlic on a hot iron plate.

In India, I learned the best curries are not those that are so hot that they bring you out in a sweat, but those cooked with freshly prepared spices that keep their flavour to savour.

In Africa, an elegant English style afternoon tea completely charmed me. Hundreds of pink crooked legged flamingos, the flamboyant shrimp catchers of Lake Naivasha, in the Rift Valley, looked on, as we sheltered under great parasols to take

# Food, Fashion and other Frailties

tea on an immaculately kept lawn. The table was laid up with tea trays, teapots and water jugs, knives and forks, all of solid silver, down to the little silver tongs for the sugar cubes. Cups, saucers and plates made of the finest porcelain and napery of pure white linen completed the perfect setting. Our gracious hostess was a lookalike of Scarlett's housekeeper in the film *Gone with the Wind*. She fussed over us, poured the tea, passed round thinly-cut cucumber sandwiches and toasted muffins, all food fit for Lady Bracknell. It was simple but superb, truly a wonderful meal that reinforced my opinion that British colonisation was not all bad. In Ghana, a feast of five beasts, roasted whole, each set on mounds of rice filled with fruit overawed me. In Nairobi, a tranche of grilled swordfish was so big and rich that it overfaced me.

Of the Americas, my meal memories are mixed. In Brazil, in a cantina that was crowded with cowboys, wearing high-heeled boots with spurs, the cook used an open fire to grill, just for me, a fillet steak. It was rare and succulent but almost defeated even my huge appetite. Truly, taken from a Brahma, their favourite breed for beef, it was as big as English supermarket topside. In the Unites States, during our two long journeys travelling from Hawaii to New York, with many stops along the way, except for a barbecue on the beach in Kauai, the northern Island of the Hawaiian chain, the best we could find was a pastrami on rye from a New York deli. It was so good it made up for the mediocre rest. On a later visit, it was only the *Blooming Onion*, recommended as an aperitif, that I remember. This amazing creation was not indigenous to the States, but a feature exclusive to a chain of restaurants called *The Outback* featuring Australian fare, one of the two continents I have yet to visit.

# It Could be a Little Gold Mine

The most consistently excellent meals I have ever enjoyed were not on any of the world's five continents, but on one of the five oceans. Mr Mitchell, then Executive Chef on the *Uruguay Star*, provided them to keep us from becoming bored, on board. For every one of sixteen days, of a voyage from London to South America, he set us up with a sumptuous breakfast of many courses. This he followed with elevenses, then a substantial lunch between noon and one. He served tiffin at four. After aperitifs at seven, he challenged us with a five-course à la carte dinner that foxed me for choice every day. On the four nights, when the crew arranged cinema shows after dinner, he showed his continuing concern for our welfare. When the films finished, he sent out a gaily-coloured canvas-covered pushcart with fish and chip suppers, all individually wrapped in the *Financial Times*, just to make sure we did not go to bed hungry. This total luxury rounded off my esculent education. Twenty years of eclectic dining and years of late night reading about food and the work of other chefs, gave me the theory; the practice of cooking professionally I was happy to learn as I went along.

When I first started to cook at the inn, I tried to change the menu every day. This idea quickly modified to a *three-fives* menu. We changed the five starters, five main courses and five sweets or puddings each Saturday, but still cooked everything to order, from fresh. We thought this to be the ideal way for a restaurant to operate, providing the finest foods, using only what was the best available in the market. We were still learning; soon the *five-five-five* menu became a *six-six-six* as more and more requests were made, finishing, after about a year, as a *seven-seven-seven* still met further customer demand. "Don't you do Pork Normandy any more?" or "Can't I have

# Food, Fashion and other Frailties

Beef Wellington? I had it last time, it's my favourite." This meant, that in addition to the seven special dishes offered, many other dishes had to be cooked, in amongst, causing difficulty with all. Change was often a disappointment to some of our regular customers who had decided favourites, the most popular, after a simple grilled steak, being our easiest dish to cook, Supreme of Chicken in a Cream and Mushroom Sauce.

To try to appease all appetites we introduced a fixed menu that we only changed with the changing seasons. Each had a choice of twelve first courses, five soups, four fish courses, and twelve main courses. It is less than thirty years ago that many of our guests, gourmet warriors, ate all five courses. Nowadays we have to put up with the two course only food worriers who witter on, "If I have a first course, I won't be able to have a dessert." I cannot remember when anyone had a fish course between starter, soup and mains, although in the early days, many of the wedding receptions we catered for included a fish course.

We cooked all the dishes in our kitchen, but by this time, Jeanne insisted that I had help, and Pasquale joined me. Together we learned how to batch cook dishes, ten at a time, and freeze some of the sauced dishes using hi tech materials. To allow for my flights of fantasy, and to stop me becoming bored, we introduced a Daily Special. This allowed me to take advantage of anything exceptional turning up in the market, at the butcher's, or even through the back door during the game season, when keen shots, fishermen and the occasional poacher, used to come to banter and barter.

The years that I have spent talking to customers in our restaurant have not only confirmed my food philosophy but

# It Could be a Little Gold Mine

they have served to reinforce my ideas, particularly about diet. I have already told you a little about my love of cooking, but I realise that I have not told you much about how my ideas differ from the current perceived wisdom about what and how food should be cooked and served, or what is good or not for you. I cannot let the opportunity pass, because I have strong opinions about all these important matters. Simply stated, I believe that food is good for you and good food is very good for you. For too long the press have given the neurotic, and hypochondriacs, disproportionate influence on our thinking about food. The media in general have published, as the new truth, unproven, untried and untested theories, postulated by disciples of organic and GM free food production, adding unproved credence to the vegetarian and vegan lobbies. "We eat too much, we are all too fat," they tell us. "For what?" I reply.

In England, during Queen Victoria's reign, our leaders ate breakfast of porridge, salted or with treacle or cream, followed by a huge grill of bacon, eggs, sausage, black pudding and fried bread. In case the men were hungry the host arranged dishes of kidneys, pies and cold meats on the sidetable. Lunch was of three courses, with a suet pudding and beer, dinner ran to five courses with a bottle of claret and a glass or two of port. Great Britain was great. We had an Empire, ruled the waves and bent our knee to no man. Then came *Weightwatchers* and we lost the lot!

Without trials and controlled group experiments, pressure groups call us back to nature and all that is natural and organic. However, in our garden here at the inn, the free-range hens scratch about eating worms, their own droppings and the occasional live mouse or shrew. There is enough nat-

# Food, Fashion and other Frailties

ural poison here to kill off the whole village of Fenny Bentley. Henbane, deadly nightshade, fly argaric, poison ivy, yew, foxgloves and the highly toxic early flowering aconite, they all grow here, unbidden. The seeds from the bracts of our flowering wysteria could provide sufficient poison to kill the whole population of the surrounding villages. All are natural, organic and free from genetically modified genes, yet deadly. Other natural products in daily use are just as lethal, such as alcohol, tobacco, cannabis, caffeine and tannin. Other well-meaning, but ill-advised groups, tell us that we all need more bran and roughage. Whenever I hear this argument, I can picture, so clearly, the pathologist at the postmortem saying to his colleague, "Pity this chap died of mineral deficiency, he had a perfect colon." *

The British Medical Association, backed by government, publish blanket statements about healthy eating, without qualification of gender, age, or working lifestyle. A bad example being their recent advice that we must all cut down drastically on the salt that we eat. We, the public, are not all adult office workers; the need for salt varies according to what one does to earn a daily crust. When I worked in the foundry, it was essential that I took salt tablets every working day. Hard working labourers sweating cobs in summer would do themselves real real harm if they reduced their salt intake. Even the

*High fibre diets: the Government COMA committee advising on health for several years recommended that we should all eat wholemeal bread and not white bread. This advice had to be withdrawn when epidemiological evidence showed that too much wholemeal, or ordinary brown bread in the diet inhibited the body's ability to absorb essential trace elements that are vital to good health and well-being, including zinc. (Who would have thought that we needed to be galvanised?)

# It Could be a Little Gold Mine

pet food manufacturers are ahead of the BMA and COMA using different formulations for puppy and kitten food than those for mature animals.

One cannot generalise about diet. Blanket general statements cannot be fact and are often downright dangerous. Doctors and dieticians are not the only ones who err in this regard. Regrettably, many arrogant chefs in the kitchen of up-market restaurants generalise about what is an appropriate portion to serve to their customers, by arranging the whole meal on a plate. They have no idea whether the customer is a young man who has spent the day hunting, or if she is a convalescent old lady. This is just café service, however delicate and imaginative the presentation. It suggest savings on staff wages, or the chef's lack of confidence in the restaurant staff. What makes such service completely unforgivable is that it dictates how much each customer can eat. This is hard on healthy appetites. I accept that it is reasonable for the nominated dish to be arranged and garnished on a plate, such as a steak, a trout, or half a roasted duck, but only if generous amounts of each supporting vegetable, pasta or rice, are offered separately. Customers must be able to choose to have as much of what they like, and of equal importance, the chef must give them the choice of missing out, without embarrassment, things that they do not like.

It took man several millions of years to develop from the living cells that nature first cast up from the primeval soup to become the highly developed animal we are today. For all that time our progenitors were obliged to be omnivorous. First, being legless, they could only eat what they banged and bumped into. Then, when at last erect on two legs, the hunter gatherers thrust down their hungry throats anything that

# Food, Fashion and other Frailties

came to hand, be it animal, vegetable or mineral. (They had not yet invented the knife and fork). Hence the human digestive organs work best on a selective system, taking in what is required and rejecting that, which for the time being, it does not need. Any concept of change to improve this system is fraught with danger particularly when the change is to a selective, rather than a quantitive diet. Eat well, eat varied and be fit. Let the ladies remember that when dieting they lose the most interesting bits first. Let the men remember that if others point to their bulging waistline with contempt, tell them to have a care and say, as I do, "Consider the beasts of the field, for like them man is gregarious. All pack animals of the wild - the lion with his pride, the bull elephant with his herd, the hart with his hinds, the wolf with his pack - observe the boss fella: all mature figures with bellies like a barrel and shoulders like stuffed settees. The lean rangy males are kept outside the family and are allowed nowhere near the female of the species." Take your choice - eat like a king and be a leader of men; diet and live long; but outside society. Do not forget about the Irishman's donkey. They had just got it used to not eating, when the damn thing died!

# CHAPTER TWENTY-TWO

# A Destination to Aim For

*Private old house at the fork in the road,*
*Half-timbered folly, decaying with age,*
*Surrounded by trees that nature bestowed,*
*As a winding shroud, its faults to assuage.*
*Wild winter weather had left it bereave*
*Reduced to ruin, in debt to its eave.*

*Restored as an inn, now customers come,*
*To chatter and eat, not gossip and dine.*
*For here people meet for friendship and fun,*
*Music and laughter, real ale and fine wine.*
*The winter welcome of open log fire,*
*Or summer garden is all they require.*

It was twenty-eight years ago that Jeanne and I bought the Bentley Brook Hotel, renamed it an Inn, and opened it to all who had a few shillings to spend. We hoped to make what was a semi-derelict half-timbered folly, shrouded by trees and brambles, into our 'Little gold mine'. I was so confident of success that Jeanne often reminds me, and she will go on to tell customers, friends and relations alike, that I duped her. I do not deny it. I assured her, "It will only take us five years to get this lot sorted out and all in order. The business will generate income, pay for the school fees and provide for the

# A Destination to Aim For

comfort and well-being of our family." Jeanne reminds me still, that I even told her I would go back to my profession to work as an engineer, leaving her to arrange the flowers, choose the décor, furnishings and such other light duties as would befit her status as chatelaine of a famous county inn. I did so, because I was sure our professional staff would manage all the routine operations under the light touch of our direction.

Well, I got it wrong. I did not predict the many coming failures in the British economy, particularly the run down of industry in general and farming in particular. I did not foretell the Callaghan - Healey years, when inflation and interest rates ran amok at more than twenty per cent. I did not foresee Chancellor of the Exchequer Lawson foisting on us Black Wednesday, the nadir of the United Kingdom's ill-conceived attempt to track a foreign currency. I did not envisage a matter of greater consequence, that English people would lose the will to work. How could I? I had been twelve years away in Hong Kong where people did work hard. During all my journeys in Asia, visiting India, China, Japan, Malaya, Singapore, and the Philippines, I never heard the mantra *Don't work too hard now*, nor did I hear it in the Americas, North or South. Here in the United Kingdom I hear this dright defeatist injunction almost daily. We have become the lotus-eaters of the twenty-first century, forgetful of our past industrial might and political glory. Inevitably, our wealth will drain away to India, China, and Brazil. I was not alone in failing to see the future. Twenty-eight years on, rural pubs, once little gold mines, the focus of country life and the magnet of our tourist industry, are closing, for good, at a rate of more than five each week.

# It Could be a Little Gold Mine

In Hong Kong, I had been used to working in a free society where there was a flat rate tax of 15% and minimum regulation and where entrepreneurial endeavour was prized. When we bought the inn and set out on our great new adventure, the obstacles of the future were obscured by my *can do* Hong Kong experience, natural enthusiasm and a rose-tinted view of our future. Alas, our little family business was not free of the economic and social pressures of the times and they bore down on us most cruelly. We realised that if we were ever to get our little gold mine then we must grow and develop the business so that the Bentley Brook Inn would become more than just a stopping off point for what, in days gone by, was called the carriage trade. We must become a destination to aim for, a place to be, and a memorable day out.

From the beginning, we tried to realise profit from all our assets but we were amateurs and finding our way. Our first effort to provide a little more interest for people coming to the inn, we coupled with an intention to reduce our food costs. We decided to grow our own vegetables in what we came to know as the *Quarter Acre*. This bit of land was included with our purchase of the inn, although separated from the main site by the road to Bakewell. I learned, some time later, that since 1805 this *Quarter Acre* had been the kitchen garden and nursery for our property, then a gentleman's residence, known as Bentley Cottage. This land lay derelict. It had not been touched since 1947 when Mr Sheard retired. He had been head gardener at Bentley Cottage for more than fifty years, only retiring at the time of the death of Mrs Howell, who had owned the property, all his working life. All was rank and overgrown with only a few very old, very dead, apple trees giving a clue to its former use. I was

# A Destination to Aim For

enthused. I was determined to restore the kitchen garden to its former glory. Answers to my enquiries from older residents of the village confirmed that Mr Sheard had been a master gardener. During the years between the two world wars Mrs Howell employed an undergardener, and many of the village women, to help Mr Sheard create a garden masterpiece. The talk was of espaliered peach, plum, and apricot trees, of grape vines black and green, exotic melons and pineapples forced in the cold frames, glasshouses and the hot pots of his domain.

Our greengrocer's father-in-law was retired and at a loose end. Seeing a possibility, he came on site with an excavator, a small tractor, and rotovator. He dug out the dead fruit trees and turned over the soil to a fine tilth. "Right then," he said as he finished, "That will give you a start, you should get some good greens out of that." We bought two thousand assorted brassica; cabbage; green, white and red, cauliflower, broccoli and Brussels sprouts, all sturdy little plants ready for pricking out and heeling in, just as soon as we were sure the last spring frost had gone. We spent two long days of back-breaking work with cord, line, and dibber. We also had to haul seemingly endless watering cans full of water across the road until we had pricked out, heeled, and watered in all two thousand seedlings. When I looked at the neat green evenly spaced rows of my little seedlings, I was pleased as a best in show winner at the Chelsea Flower Show. However, not being a true countryman, I failed to take up arms against unseen forces that were massing ready to strike. It had not occurred to me that when the last of the spring frosts are gone, the first of the bonny Easter bunnies bounce out from their burrows. They come out, not just to play, but also to eat. It took

# It Could be a Little Gold Mine

Peter Rabbit and his flopsy friends just two dawns and two dusks to devour all two thousand, carefully nurtured plants, every last one. All leaves had been eaten, and each stem chewed down to ground level, leaving the twin track of their front teeth as clear evidence for all to see *who dunnit*.

I took this defeat hard and put the grand scheme of restoration to the back of my mind, but I did not forget. Well, I thought, if I cannot grow cabbages, I will keep a few hens so that we can offer free-range eggs to our guests. As is my habit, I went in search of knowledge. I purchased the current copy, and a few back copies, of the magazine *Smallholder*.

I soon found a supplier of what they described as the perfect hens for smallholder free-range egg production. They called their hybrid birds Comet 40's and sold them to me at *point of lay*. The specification amazed me; how many days before they would come into lay, how many days before the eggs reached grade two size, what colour the shell would be, for how many days they would lay, and even that they could not fly over a four-foot fence. All went well, our first handyman, Mr Ford, built a suitable hen house and erected a four-foot wire fence. The Comet 40's did just what the specification said they would do. Each morning, from the twenty hens we had taken on to our staff, I had a yield of about seventeen lovely brown eggs. I am sure that every customer truly believed that our hens had laid every egg they ate during their stay with us. Their self-delusion was good for our image but my poor hens, just to keep the larder stocked, would have had to lay eggs at the speed of a rattling Gatling gun.

This second attempt to yield profit from our over the road asset also came to naught. By September, Peter, and all his flopsy little bunny friends, they who had eaten my precious

# A Destination to Aim For

brassicas, had in turn been eaten. It is what naturalists call the balance of nature. With all the easy pickings gone, the cunning fox, who had culled the conies, called again and killed all my lovely hens. He was so full of rabbit that he did not bother to eat them, he just bit off their heads. I took this defeat even harder.

Trying to grow vegetables and to keep egg producing hens had taught me a little of country ways. It also gave me pause for thought when *Guardian* readers, veggies and foodie guests would extol the wonders of our fresh free-range organic eggs. These townies did not know that I had often seen my Comet 40's scratting about eating worms and their own droppings or that I had witnessed two of them fighting, tug of war, over a live mouse. The victor celebrated the spoils of war, by swallowing the live mouse, whole.

I was still the optimist when Bill, our youngest son, asked if he could keep some pigs, over the road, on the Quarter Acre. As always, he was plausible. "Dad, we could buy in weaners from a farmer I know and then we could have our own pork, it will save you a fortune. For his enterprise, I paid for and he built a fine sty and fenced it off, with strong wire mesh, one third of the Quarter Acre. Four little piggies came to stay and I bought straw, feeding troughs and weaner nuts, all to save me lots of money. The four little piggies soon transformed into huge biomechanical excavators. They turned up the ground into troughs, trenches, and ridges that looked like the Somme battlefield after months of rain. Our four prize podgy porkers were incredibly clever and obviously thought their sty and exercise pen no better than Colditz. They were also house-proud. They kept the straw in their sty so clean that two young men, who had set up their tent nearby, when

# It Could be a Little Gold Mine

the night turned cold, wet and stormy, left their tent and moved in with the pigs. Early the next morning, I found the six pals fast asleep, two in their sleeping bags, four in the buff, all in their clean, dry, warm billet.

To this day, I swear that the four porcine pals had a formal escape committee and a plan. Acting the innocent random excavators, they made such a mess of the ground that I did not notice that they had dug a tunnel under the strong wire perimeter fence that limited their exercise area. Crafty and cunning, they waited for the first wild, wet, bog black, bible black, moonless, starless night to make their break-out. Their intelligence was good. They waited until the chosen moonless bog black, bible black night coincided with a Saturday night, a night when they were certain sure that our customers would keep us fully occupied, if not distracted. They would have got clean away, were it not for my good fortune and their bad luck.

Most unusually, I had to leave the kitchen to fetch something from our cottage. Through the driving rain, I saw four pig snouts pushing under the locked five bar gate to the quarter acre field. Using their cleverly concealed tunnel, they had escaped their pen and were now tackling the outer perimeter. It was evident that the break-out was coordinated and planned to the last detail. As soon as they had lifted the gate off its hinges, it fell away to the ground in front of them. Then they were out, running free, going for the elusive home run. What convinced me that it was all preplanned was the quiet nod they gave to each other as two turned to the north, making for Bakewell, and the other two turned south, heading towards Ashbourne.

I raced back to the inn and burst in to startle the drinkers

# A Destination to Aim For

and diners with my urgent cry, "Pigs are out, come on, all of you." Waiters, cooks, bar staff and cleaners; we all ran to head off and recapture the fugitive four. It took some time and soon all of us were wet through, cold and up to our knees in mud. John, a newly recruited restaurant waiter, who was on duty for the first time that night, was helping me to push on the rump of the last of the podgy porkers in a joint endeavour to get it back in the pen. Uncharacteristically this particular pig decided to be a bit difficult. It turned and bit him, hard, on the ankle. "Boss, is this in my job description?" he shouted, to be heard above the wind, rain and squealing. "Shut up John, keep pushing," was my exasperated reply.

Back in their pen, the four piggy prisoners became great pets. Christopher, our eldest son, has a knack of bonding with animals. When he took feed and water to them, they would roll over on their backs to have their bellies scratched.

# It Could be a Little Gold Mine

It was just too much for us when we issued them with a one-way ticket, to the abattoir. We wept and decided never to have pigs again. Three failures to make any profit from the old kitchen garden bothered me, but still it was in my mind that one day we would get it restored. I knew that I could not do it; I am no gardener, I can wither a mature oak at a glance.

One Sunday afternoon, early in spring, I was watching Prince Charles presenting a television programme from his home in Gloucestershire. Along the walls of the house were some beautiful creepers with huge soft blue hanging flowers. I learned later that gardeners call them bracts. "A creeper like those would look wonderful on the front of the inn," I said to Jeanne. "Well you had better go and buy one then," was her immediate reply. Astonished, I took the first opportunity to visit one of our customers who I knew had a small plant nursery business in the old walled garden on the nearby Osmaston Estate. The walled garden had survived the demolition of Osmaston Hall, the great house it had once served. "Hello," was his cheery greeting, "you're the chap who has the pub at Bentley aren't you?" "Well yes," I replied, "I'll tell you what I've come for, I was wondering if you have any of those creeper type things with blue flowers that I saw on the television yesterday? It was from Prince Charles' home." "Yes," was his knowing reply, "I saw the programme, they're called wisteria they are. Those at Highgrove must be a hundred years old." "Well have you got one to sell?" "Yes that's one," he said, pointing to a six-inch plastic pot with a single leafless whip waving in the wind, "and that's another." "Nay! them's just sticks." I replied. "No! No, they're good healthy plants they are, I'll guarantee them." "Well go on then," I said, "How much do you want for this stick of yours?" "Ten pounds," he said and we struck a deal. Back home, more in hope than expectation, I planted the stick according to his direction, against the south-facing wall, just to one side of the front entrance of the inn.

It was more than eighteen months later, in the autumn of the year, that the nurseryman came for Sunday lunch, bringing with him his wife and children. Again, the cheerful greeting, "Hello, how's the wisteria?" "I told you it was a stick," I replied laughing. "What? Let's have a look," and he abandoned his family diving through the door out into the garden. "Where is it?" "Well that's the stick there, but don't worry, I am sure it was me that killed it, I'm no good with plants." "Nay lad; now lets see," he bent and snapped the dead whip and then with his thumb nail scratched at its bark, down to the level of the soil. "You're right lad, it is dead, who'd have thought it." Straight away, he had a ten-pound note out of his wallet. "There you are Mr A; I told you I would guarantee it." He insisted that I keep it saying, "A bargain's a bargain" so I gave in, but with a guilty conscience, sure that its morbid state was really my fault.

On a spring day six months later, two years after I bought the plant, there it was, thrusting three and a half feet into the sunshine. The stick was complete with unmistakable new green leaves. It was the wisteria, vigorously alive, very healthy, and happy in the sun. I told Jeanne and said I was off to the nursery with ten pounds to pay for this remarkable Lazarus plant. As I drove into the walled garden, my heart sank. All that there was left was just a few broken pots and dead leaves scuttering in the breeze. It was obvious that he had gone out of business. I drove slowly home with many thoughts of kitchen gardens and the difficulty of making one pay and put that damned ten-pound note into *Sooty*, the charity box on the bar.

It was pure serendipity that the restoration of the kitchen garden and nursery finally got started. Aged ninety-two, my dear Mother, after almost thirty-eight years a widow, had gone gently on to join her beloved husband, where she knew he waited. Mother knew of Father's love of poetry and kept his copy of part of William Allingham's poem in her wallet.

> *Yours still, you mine, Remember all the best*
> *Of our past moments, And forget the rest;*
> *And so, to where I wait, come gently on'.*

It astonished me to learn from my brother that she had left us, her three children, equal parts of her estate. The equality was not unexpected; the surprise was that there was an estate at all. In his will, my father had left me his penknife and I lost that. The third part of Mother's estate was enough to make a start on the restoration of the kitchen garden that had failed me three times. I know that she would have approved of the venture as she loved flowers and had green fingers. Fortune also smiled as Sarah Stone, an experienced qualified horticulturalist, who lives in the village, had just come free to take up the post of Head Gardener. The restored kitchen garden and nursery, now sold to Sarah, is a new attraction at the inn. Alongside the progress of the kitchen garden, other activities are developing. Jeanne and her good friend Sarah Lacy cook luxury jams, pickles, preserves, biscuits and cakes and sell them using the brand name The Gourmet Grannies. Their traditional home-made products are very successful; guests buy them as they leave as presents for family and friends or the neighbour who looked after the pet canary. On their breakfast or tea table, the packaging advertises the inn and brings new customers.

Following my conviction that no man or woman should carry on with the same career for more than twenty years, at the end of October 2003 we took a decision to step aside from the day to day operation of the inn by letting Christopher run the inn and Edward the brewery. You may observe that I said earlier 'We have been at the inn for twenty-eight years and that simple arithmetic indicates that it is at least eight years longer than my prescribed limit. In my defence, I did have an almost five year long sabbatical after falling down the manhole, so I still think I am, in part, justified.

I still bother the kitchen brigade with my suggestions and corrections as I miss the excitement of cooking. They usually suggest that I go and bother the brewer. He tells me to go and hassle the gardeners. They in turn tell me that the Gourmet Grannies need my help. Jeanne and Sarah give me a cup of tea and then tell me to push off. They tell me, "We don't want your help or your suggestions. We are organised, thank you very much, don't interfere."

With no one else to bother and as I have told all my tales, many times, to our regular customers, I have joined forces with the computer in front of me. Starting, in my seventieth year, I hope my god will allow me one more twenty-year career, this time as an author. I pray that he will go a little steady with the size and frequency of the pebbles that he drops into my pond to test me, because I am not as agile as I was, but I am still as clumsy both physically and verbally as I ever was.

The inn still whispers to us "Perhaps". Enthusiasm remains undimmed, but my aspirations are now time-limited; I am running out of road. Nevertheless, like Mr Micawber in Dick-

# It Could be a Little Gold Mine

ens' novel *David Copperfield*, I still believe that 'something will turn up'. It may be that we shall never achieve our 'Little gold mine', but perhaps, at the end of our life's rainbow, we may find that our inn has turned into a conciliatory 'Crock of gold'.